Deacon Bill McK

Deacon Bill McKechnie

A Baseball Biography

MITCHELL CONRAD STINSON

McFarland & Company, Inc., Publishers

Jefferson, North Carolina, and London

ISBN 978-0-7864-6066-3
softcover : acid free paper ∞

LIBRARY OF CONGRESS CATALOGUING DATA ARE AVAILABLE

BRITISH LIBRARY CATALOGUING DATA ARE AVAILABLE

Front cover image: Bill McKechnie strikes a pose during his
tenure as manager of the Boston Braves (courtesy
Boston Public Library, Leslie Jones Collection); feather
background © 2012 Shutterstock.

Manufactured in the United States of America

*McFarland & Company, Inc., Publishers
Box 611, Jefferson, North Carolina 28640
www.mcfarlandpub.com*

To the Joyner 5 —
Alexia, Gabby, Adren, Savannah and Sofia.

Table of Contents

Preface

When your subject was born a few years after the shootout at the O.K. Corral, you cross your fingers and hope he has grandchildren willing and able to pass along a few family stories about him. In the case of Bill McKechnie, my wildest dreams were surpassed by the discovery that a daughter still lived and lived well. She's really not all that old either. McKechnie and his wife were in their mid–40s when Carol McKechnie Montgomery was born in December of 1931. She grew up around ballplayers and ballparks, and remembers every step of her life journey. Carol was a big help with this book, sharing family history and photographs that greatly enhanced the final product. She also provided a copy of her autobiography, *The Deacon's Daughter*, which became a valuable source of information.

Supplying personal and professional insights was former *Bradenton Herald* sports editor Kent Chetlain. A good friend to Hall of Famer Edd Roush, he also knew McKechnie and frequently interacted with him. I'll always be glad I met McKechnie's former neighbor Pamela Wilson, granddaughter of a well-known player and manager named Jimmie Wilson. I'll always feel sad that she died young, months after our sit-down interview at her Bradenton home. Her grandfather died prematurely, too, so she never met him, but Pam told a few family stories that she'd heard and, more important, painted a childhood picture of life in McKechnie's neighborhood. Looking younger than her 53 years, she was a friendly host who allowed me to look through memorabilia and scrapbooks. Since Jimmie coached under Bill and became his friend, I wanted to learn as much about him as possible.

Edd Roush and McKechnie went way back, all the way to their days as Federal League teammates in 1914. Insight on that long relationship came from Roush's granddaughter, Susan Dellinger, who wrote a magazine article about it for *108: Celebrating Baseball*. More information was gleaned from the Baseball Hall of Fame, which houses author Lawrence Ritter's tape-recorded interview with Roush and his wife.

Libraries were invaluable resources and not just for the obvious reasons. For the author/researcher, human resources are just as important as history books. In Bradenton, Florida, I was pleased to discover that the public library had a thick file on McKechnie and even more pleased when the staff passed along phone numbers of people who knew him and his family. It was a similar situation in his hometown of Wilkinsburg, Pennsylvania, where the library mailed me photocopies from a McKechnie file and connected me with experts on local history. Many thanks are due James B. Richard, Anne Elise Morris and the Wilkinsburg Historical Society.

Among the tips I received from them was the phone number of a childhood friend of McKechnie's oldest daughter. I did not use any quotes from the ensuing interview with 91-year-old Betty Cummings, nor did I make any reference to her in the text. But we actually had a long, productive talk that educated me on everyday life in a Pittsburgh suburb during the 1920s and 1930s. She confirmed some things I'd read and added interesting anecdotes; Cummings remembered Wilkinsburg as a fine community of churches, no bars, and a high-class high school. Lunch cost a quarter and Klondike ice cream bars went for a nickel. If your Klondike had a pink center, you got the next one free. Her father worked for Westinghouse and had his hours cut back during the Depression. Sometimes dinner would consist of apple dumplings and nothing else, or eggplant and nothing else. It's a shame there was no place for those stories in this book.

Through interlibrary loan, I obtained newspaper microfilm that chronicled McKechnie's early minor league stops in Washington (PA), Canton (OH) and Wheeling (WV). I followed his entire career and most of his life in the combined pages of *Sporting Life*, *The Sporting News*, the *Chicago Tribune* and the *New York Times*. For specific stops along his playing, managing and coaching journey, it was the *Newark Evening News*, *Indianapolis Star*, *St. Louis Post-Dispatch*, *Boston Globe*, *Cincinnati Enquirer* and *Cleveland Plain Dealer*.

Spicing up the storytelling were tales gleaned from vintage franchise biographies — Lee Allen's *The Cincinnati Reds* and Fred Lieb's *The Pittsburgh Pirates*. Also falling into that category was Ed Fitzgerald's 1952 chronicle of the National League. The photographs come from various sources. McKechnie's daughter loaned some of her family pictures and his great-nephew — Thomas Shontz — provided some others. I stumbled across the Boston Public Library's online postings of the wonderful Leslie Jones Collection that shows, among other things, shots of McKechnie with Babe Ruth. The National Baseball Hall of Fame and Library of Congress collections filled most remaining needs.

Prologue

On the night of July 11, 1962, a month shy of his 76th birthday, Bill Mc-
Kechnie sat all alone with his memories. His wife had been dead five years and
his four children had lives of their own. Such was the story of so many Florid-
ians who had moved to the picturesque Sunshine State for their golden years.

But McKechnie was no typical retiree; he was a walking monument to
national pastime history. In a career that spanned nine presidents and nearly
five decades, he'd rubbed shoulders with baseball's greatest figures; as player,
coach and manager, he became part of the game's fabric. If anybody wanted
to learn the meaning of baseball life, it wasn't necessary to climb a mountain
in search of some guru; the task required only a knock on the door at 3504
Riverview Boulevard in Bradenton.

After buying property on the banks of the beautiful Manatee River,
McKechnie built a charming home there around 1950. Its living room featured four large picture windows that provided a peaceful view of the water.
The home was still charming in 1962, though missing something without the
lady of the house. McKechnie adjusted gracefully to life as a widower but,
outside those walls, the world changed so fast that it was hard to keep up. In
the early days of McKechnie's career, some fans still arrived by horse and
buggy. Now men were flying into space. And not terribly far from Bradenton,
two superpowers would soon point nuclear bombs at each other in a dispute
over Cuba.

Though famous for its glacial rate of change, dependable old baseball
looked different, too. Dodger Stadium opened in Los Angeles in 1962, four
years after the Brooklyn Dodgers and New York Giants franchises moved to
California. The National League added two teams (the Houston Colt .45s
and the New York Mets) in 1962 and expanded its schedule from 154 to 162
games. The American League had done the same in 1961, adding two teams
and eight games. That was the year Roger Maris hit 61 home runs and toppled
Babe Ruth's unbeatable mark of 60, set in 1927. Now the Dodgers' Maury Wills

was challenging a 47-year-old record — 96 stolen bases by Ty Cobb. Wills would finish with 104.

Of course, nobody could ever beat Cobb's hit record or Ruth's career home run mark, but modern stars were still putting their own indelible stamp on the game. Did anyone ever do it better than San Francisco center fielder Willie Mays? He was in his prime in 1962, on his way to a 49-homer season and career highs in runs and RBI. In Milwaukee, Hank Aaron would post similar numbers. Stan Musial was winding down an epic career that ranked among the best ever, while Mickey Mantle did the same for the New York Yankees. On the pitching front, signs of greatness emanated from a couple of starlets named Bob Gibson and Sandy Koufax. The game was well stocked with exciting talent in the early 1960s.

Not one to wallow in the past, McKechnie kept up with modern baseball and its latest crop of stars. He saw some at spring training and lots more over the airways. He had a favorite chair from which he'd comfortably watch games on his television. Those eyes had seen so much. As a green minor leaguer in 1909, he played an exhibition game against pastime pioneer Cap Anson. When he joined the Pittsburgh Pirates a year later, Honus Wagner became his mentor. A switch-hitting infielder, McKechnie proved ordinary as a player, and that part of his life ended about the time Babe Ruth gave up pitching for swinging lumber. As a manager he was sublime — one of the greatest ever. In all of baseball history, only two men have led three different teams to the World Series, and McKechnie was the first. He's also the first of three to win it with two different teams. A coach in the inaugural All-Star Game, he later became manager of the National League's team.

Bill McKechnie wasn't there at the beginning but he could chronicle most of baseball's history by firsthand experience — from the dead ball to the lively ball and the accompanying change in batting styles, from place hitting to free swinging, from the days when a spitball seemed as natural as spring water to the time it was outlawed as dangerous and disgusting. He saw players leave to become soldiers in two world wars and one in Korea. He watched baseball struggle through the Great Depression and mentored the first black player in the American League. McKechnie could remember when society dismissed ball players as lowlifes, ranking slightly above tramps and hobos. He'd been there every step as reputations and salaries slowly rose, and probably helped change perceptions through his own strength of character. Everybody came to know him as a God-fearing, church-going, fatherly role model. His nickname was "Deacon."

In the twilight of life, Deacon Bill still wore the nickname and reputation quite well. He was a man of stature in this part of the state and especially so in his adopted hometown of Bradenton, which lay south of Tampa and St.

Petersburg. Along with other icons of the baseball retirement community, he appeared at spring games and related events. For those who didn't recognize him, they still sensed he was somebody. McKechnie had an air about him — a regal bearing without pretension or ego. Like his younger self, he kept a trim body and stood erect. People always thought him tall but it was deception through posture; the Deacon's playing height was officially listed at 5-foot-10.

Hastened by the sunshine of a half-century's worth of baseball summers, deep wrinkles marked his face; the furrowed brow represented the disappointments, the laugh lines the fun. He had a full head of white hair — one strand for every pupil or meddling executive who had caused him consternation. The hair never fell out, however, and maybe that signified that there were more good times than bad. He had tried black dye before but eventually let nature take its course and she rewarded him with a beautiful, silvery mane. In a long, distinguished career, McKechnie earned every skin fold and alabaster follicle. He earned his restful retirement with the river view. Living on a nearby bayou was his longtime pal, Edd Roush, the old Cincinnati Reds star. Just down the street from Roush was the family of the late Jimmie Wilson, former Philadelphia Phillies manager and unexpected star of the 1940 World Series. It was a nice neighborhood, maybe too nice for somebody living alone because the McKechnie home drew the attention of some people who weren't kind at all.

Around 9 P.M. on July 11, McKechnie was watching TV in his living room when he heard a noise from behind. He turned around to see two young men with paper bags over their heads. One held a three-foot piece of iron pipe, the other a pistol. They'd gained entry by cutting the kitchen screen door, then reaching in and unlocking it. Wearing dark pants and a dark shirt, the intruder with the pipe stood about six feet tall and weighed around 170 pounds. His gun-toting partner was much shorter and slight of frame. Both were white, and both talked with a northern accent.

"What's this, Halloween?" McKechnie said. He knew exactly what it was — a robbery. "Why, you're an old man," said the taller one. "I'm not so old," McKechnie replied. With the cool-headedness that defined his baseball career, the Deacon reacted fearlessly and immediately developed a game plan. He would joke with the robbers and exchange banter, lulling them into a false sense of security before grabbing his shotgun at first opportunity. It was under his bed. The tall one responded to his quips, while the little fellow never said a word. Eventually, McKechnie made his move. He told the bandits he wanted to get his slippers from his bedroom. "Ohhh, no," answered the six-footer. They weren't falling for the harmless old man routine.

At this point, the course of action should've been obvious — just give

them the money and any valuables they desired. McKechnie refused. His yesteryear reputation for a gentle guiding hand was well deserved but, when
pushed too far, he wasn't afraid to clinch that hand into a fist. In younger
days he'd occasionally lost his temper and taken a run at opponents or umpires.
Old-time baseball required that even the brainy guys needed to have some
barroom brawler in them. On this night in 1962, however, Deacon Bill had
no chance of winning. His younger self would've been hard pressed to survive
these odds: two men versus one, two weapons against none. He was also far
older than the bandits' combined age.

It was a no-brainer at any age — just give them what they want.
McKechnie couldn't. It was a matter of principle, pride, and manhood. Not
only did he refuse to comply but he would fight — however feebly and hopelessly. The robbers meant business, one gripping his weapon and poised to
swing at brittle bones, and the other with his finger wrapped around a trigger.

These should've been happy times, and they were before the break-in.
Twelve days later, McKechnie was to be inducted into the Baseball Hall of
Fame in Cooperstown, New York. He felt deeply honored and uncommonly
emotional about the whole thing. This frightening crime came on the eve of
a scheduled trip north, where McKechnie would visit a daughter in New
Jersey and make appearances at two games at the Polo Grounds in New York
City. On July 23, he was scheduled to join the immortals at baseball Valhalla.
Now it looked like none of it would happen.

Ironically, McKechnie had very little money in the house because he'd
spent most of it on transportation for the trip. So why not just give what's
left to the thugs? Maybe his wife could've convinced him to acquiesce if this
had happened several years ago. But only memories remained of the late Beryl
McKechnie, and these punks offended the home where she used to bake bread.
A battle broke out, and Deacon Bill was shown no mercy.

1

In the Beginning

The baseball bug got into him early, with the neighborhood sand-lots as the first proving ground. Pittsburgh, long one of the richest cradles of the diamond sport, even then had many fields, even if most of them were on hills or promontories. — Charles J. Doyle, *Pittsburgh Sun-Telegraph*[1]

The National League was ten years old when William Boyd McKechnie came into the world during the summer of 1886. The American League wasn't even a twinkle in Ban Johnson's eye, and professional baseball itself had been around less than two decades. Early chapters were still being written during his childhood, and it wasn't terribly long before he earned pages of honor for himself. He became a fresh addition to the game's Old Testament and lasted well into the New. He was new when Cy Young was old, old when Leo Durocher was new, and very old when Mays and Mantle were very young.

When it comes to managing, few did it as long or as well as Mr. McKechnie. Yet his name is rarely mentioned in the same breath with the game's greatest skippers. If baseball had a managerial Mount Rushmore, the rock carvings would probably depict John McGraw, Connie Mack, Joe McCarthy and Casey Stengel; all merit the honor but perhaps they should share that metaphorical mountain with the Deacon. His 25-year reign ended in 1946 with 1,896 wins. Throw in his six-plus seasons as a roving coach emeritus, and he tasted victory 2,446 times.

McKechnie's stat line can't compare to that of Mack, who won 3,731 games, but the "Tall Tactician" managed for 53 years and lost 3,948. In five decades at the Philadelphia Athletics' helm, he had some of the best and worst teams in history. McGraw went to nine Series with the New York Giants, McCarthy saw nine with the Yankees, and Stengel took the Yanks to another ten. Each became the face of a franchise while dipping from a deep well of talent. The Deacon drank from shallow puddles, yet somehow skippered three different ships to the Promised Land and had a different crew every time. His greatest work may have come during an eight-year stint with the Boston Braves, who never came close to contending. They usually played above their mediocre talent level, however, and that was a direct reflection on the manager.

In the garden of baseball, McKechnie displayed a green thumb at every stop. He was particularly skilled at growing pitchers — teaching young ones or breathing new life into veterans who'd lost their bloom. Pitching and defense were the Deacon's pillars of success, and his approach produced pennants in Pittsburgh, St. Louis and Cincinnati. When McKechnie had the material he could take his team a long way; even without an abundance of talent, he often produced winners. Managing would be easy if it were just a matter of plugging stars into positions but, in most cases, the stars are part of a larger team fabric that includes role players and reclamation projects.

Nobody orchestrated it any better than Bill McKechnie in the 1920s, 1930s and 1940s, and maybe nobody has since then either. His baseball IQ ran off the charts while his character ranked just as high. Deacon Bill was a calm, guiding hand in the storm of professional sports, and he taught players so much more than baseball. He showed them how to be men.

McKechnie became encased in time as a favorite teacher to generations of "students," and few could fathom that he was ever young. But he didn't come out of the womb wearing bifocals and holding a lineup card. He was a kid once, and a baby that didn't know a baseball from a beanbag. His story began in Western Pennsylvania, just 21 years after the Civil War's end.

The son of Scottish immigrants Archibald and Mary McKechnie, Bill came into the world on August 7, 1886 — the same summer that saw the surrender of Apache chief Geronimo. Also born that year were Ty Cobb and *The Sporting News*. Bill's parents hailed from Lanarkshire County in the central lowlands of Scotland. They lived in a small town not far from the metropolis Glasgow, and Mary gave birth to three children there. The McKechnies would eventually cross the pond to America, though not all at the same time. First, Archibald came over with three adopted sons and built a nest near Pittsburgh, in a town called Wilkinsburg. They all found employment and saved money until they could send for another family member, then another and another; federal census records show separate immigration years for each McKechnie child. Young John accompanied his mother around 1880, and two older daughters came later. Archibald and Mary continued their prolific ways in America, finishing with a grand total of 13 children — 10 of their own plus three brothers with the surname "Boyd." Ranking ninth on the age chart, Bill learned to eat quickly because food disappeared fast in that house.

The McKechnies blended in with a community developing its own distinct identity. Wilkinsburg was named either for William Wilkins, former

An early portrait of Bill McKechnie's parents in Scotland, circa 1873. The dashing Archibald McKechnie is shown with wife, Mary, and firstborn, Marion (courtesy Carol McKechnie Montgomery).

secretary of war under President John Tyler, or his brother John Wilkins Jr.,
a Revolutionary War soldier who became general of a local militia. Annexed
to Pittsburgh in the 1870s, the town fought to reverse that move, won in
court and regained her independence. In 1887 Wilkinsburg attained "borough"
status, setting the stage for a transformation from village to municipality.
Thousands of passengers rode daily on multiple railroad lines, many destined
for the seven-mile jaunt to Pittsburgh. Wilkinsburg was a religious town,
teeming with righteous Protestants who hated the demon rum; nicknamed
"The Holy City," it had banned bars and taverns since 1870, and that prohibition would continue through the generations into modern times.[2]

Like the rest of southwestern Pennsylvania, Wilkinsburg lived in the
smoky shadow of Pittsburgh. But pollution was not a pejorative in Allegheny
County, where folks walked through ashy air with blue-collar pride. It was
the by-product of something muscular and vital, something that fed the
growth of a nation. Egyptians went to the Nile for water; Americans drank
from southwestern Pennsylvania's sprawling coal beds, iron ore deposits and
massive cauldrons of molten steel. The state dripped history, with Philadelphia
and the east at ground zero of the American Revolution, while Gettysburg
and other far south sites were synonymous with Civil War carnage. Pittsburgh
was the future, and her children felt only pride, not shame.

From the very beginning, she seemed a city of destiny; overlooking the
confluence of three rivers (Ohio, Monongahela, Allegheny), Pittsburgh was
conveniently located along shipping routes and became a railroad center for
western expansion. When industry exploded, immigrants arrived in huge
numbers and took jobs in manufacturing. Many came from Scotland. Leaving
the land of the heather in 1848, 13-year-old Andrew Carnegie emigrated with
his parents and went to work in a cotton factory. Taking the American dream
to unthinkable heights, he would become founder of Carnegie Steel and the
richest man in the world. "Canny Scot" was a common descriptor for business
genius, and those same two words would one day be applied to Bill McKechnie
in an entirely different occupation.

An early population and manufacturing boom was in full swing when
McKechnie's parents emigrated. Perhaps they heard stories about the great
railroad strike of 1877, a clash that brought rioting and death. Labor battles
between unions and management were a part of the tapestry, too, a side effect
of huge company profit, long employee hours and dangerous working conditions. Professional baseball existed in the area but on a very small scale; the
major league version arrived in greater Pittsburgh a few years later.

As the decades passed, every federal census showed huge population
upswings: 156,000 in 1880, 238,000 in 1890, 321,000 in 1900.[3] (Periodic annex-
ations helped boost the statistics.) Even more impressive was the accompanying

Baby-faced Bill McKechnie is seated, second from right, in this vintage shot of his hometown baseball squad in Pennsylvania. It's either a Wilkinsburg High School or Wilkinsburg borough team, and the year is estimated to be between 1902 and 1905 (courtesy Wilkinsburg Historical Society).

growth of metals manufacturing. Fortunes were made, and culture followed the money.

Wilkinsburg took pride as little brother to a unique city that was both rugged and increasingly ornate. Entertainment and employment avenues were a short trip away — close enough for a sense of ownership, far enough to be someone else's responsibility. The McKechnies built a life in this residential community that grew to about 17,000 people during Bill's rise to manhood.

By 1900 Archibald was dead, three children had left the house and 45-year-old Mary was matron to a family of 11. A tireless bread baker and unofficial neighborhood nurse to anybody who got hurt, she did not work, but most of the older children did. The firstborn, 26-year-old Marion McKechnie, found employment at a laundry. Adopted son Thomas Boyd (32) had a job in steel works, the eldest two McKechnie boys worked as machine laborers, and 15-year-old Archie Jr. was an office boy. So the household had sufficient income while Bill (14) and three younger siblings attended school.[4] (Family legend says he was kicked out of fifth grade for bringing a snake to class.) From a young age, he felt drawn to leather and horsehide; he practically grew up on baseball sandlots, imitating local heroes who strode the hallowed fields of the professional pastime. When Bill was six, Pittsburgh's pro team got labeled with an unflattering nickname that stuck — Pirates. Officially known as the "Alleghenies," the team stood accused of stealing Louie Bierbauer from the Philadelphia Phillies — an act of piracy, some said. Secure in the knowledge that they'd signed Bierbauer fair and square, Pittsburghers dismissed the allegation but eventually embraced the colorful pejorative.

Thus one of the many things Bill McKechnie witnessed during his long life was the birth of the Pirates. As he grew up, so grew the country. Ellis Island opened in 1892, and the Wright Brothers executed the first controlled airplane flight in 1903. Between those dates, the U.S. established itself as a world power by easily winning the Spanish-American War. On the baseball front, the hometown Pirates eventually became role models of excellence for the youth of Allegheny County. After a rough ride through the 1890s, they reeled off three straight National League pennants from 1901 to 1903. With the nearby Allegheny River as a backdrop, stars now roamed the grass of Exposition Park. There was outfielder Ginger Beaumont, pitcher Deacon Phillippe and player-manager Fred Clarke. Most of all, there was batting champ Honus Wagner. Things got very exciting at the end of the 1903 season when Pittsburgh hosted four games of the first World Series. Pitted against the champs of the upstart American League, the powerful Pirates were expected to strike a decisive blow for senior circuit superiority but lost, five games to three, to Cy Young and the Boston Americans.

Bill's beloved mother, Mary Murray McKechnie. Born, raised and married in Scotland, she immigrated to America around 1880 and joined her husband, who'd come ahead of her. They raised a huge family, and Mary became sole parent when Archibald died (courtesy Carol McKechnie Montgomery).

Still, that enormous disappointment aside, it was a good time to be young and a Pirates fan. For McKechnie, it was a good time to set his own baseball destiny in motion. The game would allow him to remain outdoors in the not-so-fresh air when it came time to earn his keep. While so many others navigated the rigors and risk of underground mines and indoor steel plants, he set his sights on a career in sport. He played high school ball and played it well, though his lone surviving child says her dad never attended high school.[5] Seated three players away from his future brother-in-law, an 18-year-old Mc-Kechnie appeared in the Wilkinsburg High team picture of 1905. Everybody thought he was 17 back then; it wasn't until late in life that his true birth year was discovered in an old family Bible. Whatever his age, he helped the local boys post a decent 7–5 record that season.

When the low minor leagues beckoned, McKechnie's mother didn't object; a paycheck lent gravitas to the games. But she insisted that he never play on Sunday. Mary Murray McKechnie believed in a strict, meditative observance of the Sabbath, free from incursion by the outside world. It was a hot issue among many communities across the nation. In

This undated picture shows McKechnie in his youth, perhaps as a teenager (courtesy Tom Shontz, McKechnie's great-nephew).

1917, Christy Mathewson and John McGraw were summoned to court after leading two teams into a Sunday contest at the Polo Grounds in Manhattan. In so doing, they violated a "blue law." McGraw, of course, was manager of the New York Giants and Mathewson skippered the Cincinnati Reds. McKechnie appeared in that game and many other Sunday contests during the course of his career. Mary felt no discomfort over it; she died of a ruptured gall bladder before her son had a chance to see many Sabbath fastballs. When McKechnie began making a name for himself, there were no proud parents to share in the success. He adored his mother, and her death hurt him in a way that never fully mended. Because Mary passed away around New Year's Day, he would always feel a little sad during the holidays.

McKechnie got his first break in Butler, a city 35 miles north of Pittsburgh. Paid $75 a month,[6] he joined an independent team there in 1905 — the same year Ty Cobb debuted with the Detroit Tigers. A partner in southwest

Pennsylvania's industrialization, Butler was a manufacturing center with a population around 12,000. A wealthy playboy named Diamond Jim Brady established Standard Steel Car Company there and used his cut of the profits to bankroll notoriously voracious appetites for expensive jewels, Broadway showgirls and mountains of fine food. The local baseball team had an appetite for victory and rarely went hungry. Manning the position he would occupy for most of his playing career, McKechnie quickly established himself as a top-notch third baseman and dangerous hitter. Excellence was a common commodity on this team, with Butler becoming one of the strongest independents around. "[McKechnie] was but one of an aggregation of stars that 'Charlie' DeMoss had under his wing," wrote the *Washington* (PA) *Reporter.*[7]

The following year saw Butler backers form a stock company to finance another season. This time around, however, they strived for something bigger — Class D minor league status in the new Pennsylvania, Ohio, West Virginia (POWV) League. Butler had proved itself a good baseball town but competition for inclusion was stiff, as other area cities lobbied to join. There was competition for the services of McKechnie too; he'd reportedly received good offers from several teams. Friends believed he would ultimately sign with Washington, a charter member of the fledgling circuit and home to Washington and Jefferson College. They were correct. "They offered me more money than the $75 per month I received in Butler," McKechnie recalled in 1937. "They bowled me over by adding $100 to my Butler check and if my memory doesn't fail me, they gave me something for signing."[8] That was a lot of money in 1906, and proof that baseball men saw something special in him. Combining natural athleticism with well-honed skills, he never proved them wrong.

There was talk of baseball war; a rumor circulated that the new circuit would avoid inclusion in organized baseball's National Agreement, freeing it to raid other leagues for talent. As the area's established organization, the Ohio and Pennsylvania League seemed an obvious target. The newcomers still had to get their own house in order, however. Before a game had ever been played, teams were already coming and going. Butler replaced one of the departed, then withdrew, then decided to stay. When both West Virginia entries dropped out and a northern Maryland city joined, the fledgling circuit got a new name — Pennsylvania-Ohio-Maryland League, or POM for short. A different West Virginia team would join in midstream, too late for another acronym change.

Washington's franchise stood on stable ground. Located about 30 miles southwest of Pittsburgh, the city supported a strong independent team a year earlier and found additional investors for the better brand of baseball that organizers promised. Washington had about 15,000 people within city limits and many thousands more just beyond.[9] It was a community with extracurricular interests, and if 2,000 people attended the Washington Kennel Club's annual dog show, how many more would show up for a human spectacle? A local polo team took on all comers, horseshoe pitching was all the rage, and bowling proved so popular that Honus Wagner brought a team to compete in front of a packed house at the Washington Amusement alleys. Meanwhile, football had its faithful followers who cheered for Washington and Jefferson College in gridiron battles against Eastern powers and Pennsylvania schools.

Civic boosters touted Washington as a healthy community with fresh air, clean streets and a low death rate. Geographic elevation apparently had something to do with that. Public school buildings were large and handsome, many churches dotted the landscape, and saloons were not allowed. The big city of Pittsburgh was easily accessible via multiple, daily train routes, and a trolley line linked it to nearby Canonsburg. Detractors complained about the presence of street walkers and houses of prostitution. Others said too many

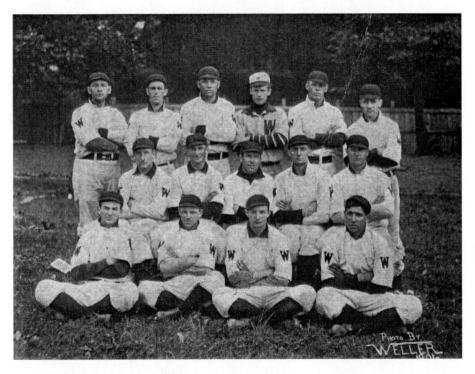

Located about 30 miles southwest of Pittsburgh, Washington fielded a minor league team in the Pennsylvania-Ohio-Maryland League. Pictured third from left in the front row, McKechnie joined the team in 1906 (courtesy Carol McKechnie Montgomery).

people were burning their trash and it caused a terrible odor. Locomotive engineers sounded their annoying whistles way too often, and when the heck was Washington going to join the 20th century and install street signs?

But all was right with the world when opening day arrived for the Senators on May 24, 1906. Optimism is always high and the sky's always the limit during those brief, innocent times when every team is 0–0. Washington was no different, with locals predicting a pennant. In this case, however, the expectations may have been justified. Keeping the best players from the previous year of independent ball and bringing in lots of new talent, the team had a nice mix. Many had minor league experience, others were former college players, and some had done both. The Senators would host home games at College Field, sharing it with Washington and Jefferson College. They had, in fact, put a 9–1 beating on the collegians in their final pre-season tune-up, and a few of the winners were former members of the losers. Senators captain Ed Murphy had two seasons of minor league ball on his resume but was probably better known as a W & J football player.

Washington opened at Braddock, which was just a hop, skip and jump away from McKechnie's hometown of Wilkinsburg. With 2,000 fans packing the grounds, he batted leadoff for the visitors and grounded out to second in the top of the first inning. The POM season was officially under way. Ninety minutes later, the Senators wrapped up a 3–2 victory. It was the first step of a bizarre pennant chase that was ultimately decided by men in suits, not men in uniforms.

In the first month of the season, Washington played nothing but road games. The home opener finally arrived on June 22, with a pre-game automobile parade headed by a brass band. Breaking the College Field attendance record, 3,000 fans turned out to greet their team and saw it drop a 9–1 decision to Uniontown. These were tough times for the injury-riddled Senators but they would rebound. By early July they stood in first place. McKechnie did not share in the good times, however; after a fair start, he fell into a terrible batting slump and his average dropped to .211. Though he still ranked among the team leaders in runs scored, he had long since been demoted from the leadoff position and usually occupied the sixth or seventh spot. Then, just when he began hitting again, a knee injury stopped his comeback. After missing seven games, he belted a double and two singles in his first game back. A 0-for-13 drought followed, however, putting him back at square one.

Washington stayed in the hunt without McKechnie's help, chasing the first-place Cumberland (MD) Giants and holding off the third-place Braddock Steel Workers. In a July 24 game against the leaders, Cumberland quickly fell way behind and stopped trying. Then a couple of Giants players assaulted the umpire over a disputed call and the game was ruled a forfeit in the sixth inning. Washington led, 10–0, at the time. The ugliness stole McKechnie's thunder—a first-inning home run that started the blowout. McKechnie had his rebellious moments, too, though nothing so drastic. He once received a $5 fine for striking an opponent in the face with his glove. Another time, he verbally attacked an umpire after grounding to deep short and getting called out at first. Fined $5 on the spot, he continued his tirade and was fined another $5. This didn't silence him either but he did finally head for the bench.

On July 25 Senators manager Budget Seaman traveled to Pittsburgh for a conference with Pirates owner Barney Dreyfuss. He returned with a deal that gave Washington the rights to pitcher Lefty McIlveen, a former Pennsylvania State College star and current Pirate. In need of minor league seasoning, the promising young hurler arrived as a welcome addition to the Senators' stretch run. Pitching was already the strength of the team, and now the staff seemed positively loaded. As it turned out, McIlveen saw more time in left field than on the pitcher's mound; a fine hitter, he moved into the leadoff spot and tried to jump-start a mediocre offense.

Complicating the pennant race were flimsy conditions of franchises at the bottom of the standings. Butler dropped out for good in July and was replaced by Piedmont (WV), which promptly folded in early August and was replaced by Charleroi (PA). Even Washington was having problems; after strong numbers in the opening months, attendance dropped to discouraging levels. Bad weather played a part, as did abrupt schedule changes that put the league on shifting sand. Or maybe it was just a matter of the novelty wearing off. What's more, the franchise backers still owed a lot of money on their promised stock investment.

The Senators were certainly doing their part, overcoming injuries and one case of appendicitis to make a run at the top. When the sun rose on August 22, three teams stood in a virtual dead heat for first place: Washington, Uniontown (PA) and Cumberland. A day later, the Senators beat Uniontown, 1–0, and moved into the lead. Led by McIlveen's three hits and two runs, they steamrolled to an 8–2 decision the next day. Over in the major leagues, the Pittsburgh Pirates stood 30 games over .500 but still trailed the mighty Chicago Cubs by ten games. Chicago also had top billing in the American League, where the White Sox enjoyed a 4½-game bulge over Philadelphia.

The POM League showcased an exciting race that would remain exceptionally close—so close that a team could drop from first place to third with a single loss. On September 6, Washington did the opposite, leaping from third to first with a 5–1 win over Cumberland. McKechnie was the hitting hero, going 3-for-3 with a run, a walk and two stolen bases.

The Senators got a break four days later when East Liverpool (OH) forfeited with a 7–3 lead at College Field. Two visiting players assaulted an umpire over a disputed call in the fifth inning and were escorted from the field by police. That left East Liverpool with only eight players, one short of the minimum. Thus the forfeit. As the season entered its home stretch, Washington stayed atop the league by a razor-thin margin. Cumberland slumped and fell out of the hunt, while Braddock got red-hot and closed on the leaders.

The Senators soon became involved in another forfeit, but this one went against them. Scheduled for games at Waynesburg (PA) on September 15 and 16, they accepted an offer from the Pittsburgh Pirates to play a home exhibition on the 16th. Washington's manager asked Waynesburg boss Sherman Grim if they could forego the second day and make it up by playing a doubleheader on the 15th. He agreed. After the home team opened with a 14–0 blowout win, Grim insisted it was getting too late to start a second game and pulled his players from the field. The Senators disagreed, as did the umpire, but Grim's decision stood. They could either return to play the next day or take a forfeit.[10] So the Washingtonians went home and played the Pirates, which seemed a sound business decision when a large, enthusiastic crowd showed up for the friendly showdown. They cared little that prices were hiked to 50 cents for general admission and 75 cents for the grandstand. A little price gouging was perfectly natural for the chance to see major leaguers up close. Honus Wagner didn't play, nor did popular player-manager Fred Clarke, and Pittsburgh used a novice pitcher. Several Pirates regulars came, however, and little Tommy Leach belted a home run in a 6–2 victory for the big boys. McKechnie went 1-for-4 and scored a run.

One day remained in the season and, even with the forfeit, Washington still led Uniontown by a game and Braddock by two. With a doubleheader and two tripleheaders slated for the final Saturday, nobody was out of the hunt. Needing a sweep to clinch, the Senators split two games at East Liverpool. Braddock swept three at Cumberland and Uniontown did the same against visiting Charleroi. When the dust cleared, Uniontown sat atop the league with a final record of 56–42 and Washington was runner-up at 57–44. The Senators had one more win but two extra losses, putting them second by the slimmest of margins — seven percentage points. Braddock came in third at 55–43, three points behind Washington.

The season may have been over but the pennant war wasn't, as teams filed protests that, if upheld, could change the final standings. For starters, the Senators challenged their forfeit loss; they said Waynesburg officials pulled a dirty trick on them. A bigger controversy revolved around game one of Uniontown's season-ending triple-header. Scheduled for the morning, it was ruled a forfeit when Charleroi didn't show up in time. The visitors later filed a protest, saying they'd never been notified about any morning contest. Further muddying the waters were stories that accused Charleroi of accepting bribe money for the no-show. The *New Castle News* wrote, "Scandal has crept into the closing hours of the P.O. & M. league and it is charged that Charleroi received $500 for forfeiting a game to Uniontown Saturday."[11]

A meeting was quickly arranged in Pittsburgh, with magnates representing their respective teams. When they couldn't agree on a decision, the matter was turned over to league president Richard Guy. He ruled against Washington, threw out Uniontown's forfeit win and also erased a Braddock forfeit loss. Taking all that into account, Uniontown and Braddock were declared co-champions with identical records of 55–42. Remaining at 57–44, the Senators finished three percentage points off the pace — a virtual dead heat but second place nonetheless. If only Guy had wiped out that disputed defeat to Waynesburg, then Washington would've been first by an eyelash. Still, the Senators didn't have the rug pulled out from under them like a certain champ turned co-champ. "The backers of the local club declare they will spend hundreds of dollars in carrying the matter before the national commission if Uniontown is deliberately robbed of a victory which had been won after such a hard struggle," wrote the *Uniontown Evening Genius*. "Furthermore if the pennant is taken away ... it will mean the last of P.O. & M. league baseball in this city."[12]

They did indeed spend hundreds of dollars, hiring an attorney named John Montgomery Ward and winning an appeal to the National Association of Baseball Clubs. Nearly four months after the 1906 season ended, a champion was crowned on January 8, 1907. Washington remained runner-up and Braddock went from gold to bronze. It put a period on an inaugural campaign that began and ended with hope. In between were the ups and downs typical of any minor league circuit, much less a brand new one. Profit margins were typically thin and some franchises lost too much money to survive. Nature weeded out the strong from the weak, the fair-weather fan base from the dependable. Umpires endured the occasional verbal or physical assault but league officials made it clear from day one that they would come down hard on offenders, and some rowdy players were banished. When gamblers became a persistent, obnoxious nuisance in the bleachers of College Park, Washington team officials arranged for a police presence to deter them.

The POM produced players who impressed major league scouts. Taking a liking to Senators southpaw pitcher Parson Rogers and Cumberland ace Nick Maddox, the Pirates bought them for about $300 apiece. Rogers never made it with the big club; Maddox became a 23-game winner in 1908. Also becoming a major leaguer was Steubenville hurler Stoney McGlynn, who recorded a league-leading 25 losses for the St. Louis Cardinals in 1907. For young Bill McKechnie, the 1906 season was a mixed bag. He reached two milestones that summer: his 20th birthday and his first taste of serious organized ball. Statistical records are incomplete but it can be estimated he hit in the .235 range and scored over 50 runs in a 98-game schedule. The numbers don't impress but McKechnie was never benched or fired, like so many other players who came and went. As the season wound down, he still won praise as one of the league's best third basemen, if not *the* best. He had a job next year if he wanted it.

Soon after that final doubleheader, Senators players began pursuing their postseason plans. College was a popular option, with four leaning toward fall admission at Washington and Jefferson. McIlveen returned to Penn State to finish up his studies, and Rogers went back to his home state of Arkansas, where he too would enter college. Team captain Ed Murphy planned to play professional football in Canton, Ohio. The slugger Walter Cariss was a physician in his other life and expected to work at a Delaware hospital, and Washington's roster also included a trained dentist from New York.[13] From medicine to midterms, it was an eclectic bunch. Some still had baseball obligations as members of a barnstorming POM all-star team. Five Senators, including McKechnie, made the squad.

In a last gasp for a struggling franchise, Waynesburg put four men on the all-stars. That city's economy took a devastating hit with the recent collapse of an important local bank, and many depositors faced bankruptcy. It was a bad time to launch a baseball franchise and the team lost money. Manager Sherman Grim was also an attorney and treasurer of the Waynesburg borough government. The financial fallout weighed on him both personally and professionally, bringing him to a point where he could barely eat or sleep. On March 4, 1907, he went to his hotel room, ingested a large quantity of morphine, slashed his left wrist to the bone with a butcher knife and gashed his neck several times. Grim was unconscious but still alive when his wife returned from a Sunday lunch and summoned help. He died the next day at the age of 41.[14]

Waynesburg did not return to the POM League in 1907.

2

More Seasoning

There isn't a player on the local outfit more popular at the present time than McKechnie. The Scotchman recently has been playing soulful ball in fair and stormy weather, testimony that he has put his heart in the work, a contribution that many of his comrades seem to have failed to make.— Canton Repository.[1]

With a mix of familiar faces and new talent, the Senators were one of several teams that did come back in 1907 for a second season. Some were champing at the bit for another shot at the POM. Like a kid writing to Santa Claus, catcher Charles Guyon sent a letter to the local paper in February: "Just a pleasant surprise to let you know that the 'Chief' is still in existence and that he often recalls the pleasant memories of Washington and his intimate friends there, and wishes that the season may soon open that shall bring me back to don a Washington uniform."[2]

Listed on the return address was Haskell Institute, an industrial and trade school for Indians in Lawrence, Kansas. Better known as "Wahoo," the speedy Native American drew notice in local baseball circles when he moved to south central Pennsylvania and played for Carlisle Indian Industrial School. Any chance of being that school's most famous alumnus evaporated a few years later when Jim Thorpe began building his legend on the football field. Washington was no stranger to Indian baseball players from Carlisle; Frank Jude followed the same path in 1905 and became a star for the city's independent league team. A year later, he wore a Cincinnati Reds uniform.

The Senators were thrown for a loop when Budget Seaman resigned as manager just a couple weeks before opening day. Hobbled by recent leg surgery, he was suffering through an agonizingly slow healing process so he called it quits, though remaining with the franchise as a member of the board of directors. He was replaced by W.E. Brown, a local businessman and longtime supporter of Washington baseball. The new boss may have lacked hands-on baseball experience but his business acumen seemed to compensate; right off

21

the bat, he proved instrumental in landing a couple of new players for the roster.

Taking over a team that had come within a few percentage points of last year's pennant, Brown had some weapons to work with. A solid pitching staff became even better when the team put its hooks into some hurlers from other minor league circuits. The infield returned intact, with the exception of a new shortstop, and the outfield had two replacements — one arriving from the Texas League, the other a favorite with the now-defunct Waynesburg franchise. There were few, if any, players more popular than smooth-fielding McKechnie.

Relatively stable, the league lost two teams from the eight that finished the previous season. Cumberland left and that meant no Maryland team in the Pennsylvania-Ohio-Maryland circuit. They kept the POM acronym anyhow, though now only two states had a stake. Representing Pennsylvania were Washington, Uniontown, Braddock, Charleroi and newcomer McKeesport. Across the Ohio border lay East Liverpool, Steubenville and another newcomer, Zanesville. The Senators opened their season on May 2 with an 11-inning, 3–2 loss at Braddock; Parson Rogers tossed a four-hit gem but was undone by a couple of unearned runs. Still, his performance marked an inspiring turnaround from the dark days of March when he was bedridden with typhoid fever. He made a full recovery.

The Senators stayed on the road for six more games, including one where they had to watch Uniontown unveil its 1906 championship banner. They made their home debut in mid–May, complete with the obligatory pre-game parade that saw players carried around the field in primitive automobiles while a band serenaded them. Twenty-five hundred fans cheered as Washington beat visiting Zanesville, 2–1, in 11 innings.

Upbeat openers aside, the 1907 season would unfold under a specter of impending collapse. As far back as early April, team directors were complaining publicly about a lack of financial support from local businessmen. They needed to raise $2,000 for startup money but got less than $800. When the Senators sold Frank McHale to Steubenville in late May, it seemed a move to recoup losses at the gate; he'd been so good the previous season. On June 17, the directors put it up to the fans — improve attendance or the franchise folds. Especially important was an upcoming three-game series with Uniontown. The *Reporter* wrote, "[The directors] want to see big crowds and assert that if they can get a large attendance at each game that the treasury will be placed in such shape that the team can continue. Otherwise there will be nothing to do but to disband."[3] The franchise did not disband.

Outside the ball park, citizens pondered a larger business-related issue: To consolidate or not to consolidate. Supporters insisted it was vital. Census reports were painting a misleading portrait of Washington, the 7,500 figure making it look like a backwoods outpost. Industry won't locate near a place like that. To correct the misconception, narrow borough limits needed to expand and envelop the many thousands who lived just around the corner. With West Washington as a pivotal target for immediate inclusion and East Washington in the near future, new city parameters might produce a figure of 25,000. Then "Greater" Washington would be taken more seriously. A decision came before the end of the year.

Around the time McHale left, the Senators lost another key player — Bill McKechnie. Sidelined by a fairly serious hand injury, he missed most of June and part of July. By the time he returned at mid-month, Washington was out of the race. His teammates had done their best, hovering around the .500 mark, and that wasn't bad considering their latest spate of injuries, but Steubenville and Uniontown ran away from the pack. McKechnie pulled a neat trick in one of his first games back, scoring from first on a single. "[It was] one of the cleverest and most daring bits of baserunning seen at College Park this season,"[4] wrote the *Reporter*. Washington still lost a 3–2 decision to East Liverpool.

A couple of days later, bad luck struck again when Catfish Creek jumped its banks and turned College Park into a placid lake. Flood waters reached into clubhouse storage areas, damaging uniforms and equipment. Sections of the outfield fences were washed away and, after the flood receded, a deposit of slimy mud remained behind. The park groundskeeper saw a significant silver lining, however; all that silt would undoubtedly fill the holes on the playing field. For the time being, though, home games had to be moved to the road, and that hurt Washington's finances even more. In early August team officials scheduled a benefit game for the Senators. They jacked up the admission to 50 cents and implored fans to do their part.

At mid-month, the franchise treasury got a boost from the sale of two players to the major leagues. Catcher William James went to the New York Giants, and the Pittsburgh Pirates purchased Bill McKechnie. The latter deal had been in the works for some time, with a secret agreement to keep young Bill in Washington through season's end. When holes surfaced in Pittsburgh's infield, the timetable was moved up to immediately. McKechnie achieved the dream of every kid who ever dirtied his shoes on a sandlot — he would play major league baseball for his home state team. Sitting 18 games over .500, the Pirates had a good team but not good enough to get a sniff of the pennant; those amazing Chicago Cubs reigned supreme with an impressive mark of 76–39. The Cubs were always great back then. Pittsburgh would achieve greatness too and, in the summer of 1907, McKechnie interacted with stalwarts such as Honus Wagner, Fred Clarke and Tommy Leach. Making his debut against mighty Chicago in game one of a September 8 doubleheader, he went face-to-face with Three Finger Brown, one of the best pitchers in baseball.

When Brown was a Hoosier farm boy, he got his hand caught in a corn shredder and lost part of an index finger. That unique hand proved quite adept at throwing a curve ball and Brown became a legend, winning 239 games over a 14-year career. This was year five, with Brown in his prime and young McKechnie overmatched. But the underdog came through in the sixth inning, driving Wagner home from third with what proved to be the winning run of a 3–2 victory. He went 1-for-4 and played a flawless defensive game at third base. Back in Wilkinsburg, nine blood siblings and three adopted brothers were about to become very proud. Also making his debut in that game was Cubs second baseman Heinie Zimmerman, a New York City native destined to lead the league in RBI twice and win one batting crown.

A few days later, McKechnie and the Pirates arrived in neighboring Washington for an exhibition game against the minor leaguers. Before that, though, he went fishing with his new buddy, Honus Wagner. Accompanied by two other players, they rode a horse-drawn carriage to a dam and cast their lines. Game attendance suffered because of nasty weather but when the storm blew over, nearly 700 watched a competitive contest with the major leaguers prevailing, 4–2. Ed Abbaticchio led the winners, going 4-for-5 at the plate, and Washington's Walter Cariss hit the only home run. Long before that exhibition, Pittsburgh brass had shown interest in making Cariss a Pirate, but he seemed lukewarm on the idea. If reports were true, the hard-hitting outfielder preferred a career in business. So the Pirates bought only one Senator contract, that of Bill McKechnie. The prodigal son later returned to Washington in a Pirates uniform, going 0-for-4 against Parson Rogers and scoring a run.

The Senators finished the POM season in fifth place with a record of 45–57, 24 games behind league champ Steubenville. McKechnie's final batting stats were weak; missing a big chunk of the season with injuries, he hit a paltry .200 and did not rank among team leaders in any offensive category except stolen bases. But the kid played a mean third base and that, more than anything, got him an audition in the big leagues. He never returned to the Senators.

In December, the consolidation crowd got its wish when a new charter expanded the boundaries of Washington. West Washington joined a municipality that now had more than 20,000 people and a valuation in excess of $11 million.[5] Meanwhile, Pittsburgh annexed Allegheny and, with a new population of over half a million, became the nation's sixth-largest city. The Pennsylvania-Ohio-Maryland League folded that same winter.

McKechnie had a brief stay with the Pirates, playing in three games, going 1-for-8 at the plate and handling five chances in the field. Also debuting that same season were Walter Johnson and Tris Speaker, taking the first, awkward baby steps on storied Hall of Fame careers. McKechnie went back to the womb in 1908 when the Pirates sent him to the Ohio–Pennsylvania League, a Class C minor circuit. He landed in the northeast Ohio city of Canton, former home of President William McKinley and future home to the Pro Football Hall of Fame. It was already a football hotbed in 1908 but baseball had deeper roots.

Home to the Canton Reds minor league baseball team, the city was better known as home of former president William McKinley. Current president Theodore Roosevelt is shown at the reviewing stand during the 1907 "McKinley Memorial Day" parade on September 30, 1907 (Library of Congress, Prints and Photography Division, Underwood & Underwood).

Rube Marquard had pitched there the previous season, winning 23 games for the city's Central League team; he'd soon join the New York Giants and begin a legendary major league career.

Proving that the region wasn't big enough for two acronyms, the POM collapse made the OP League supreme. In the scramble that followed, refugees from one tried to find safe haven in the other. McKeesport and East Liverpool joined the OP roster of eight cities but Charleroi and Uniontown were rejected. Players also arrived individually, filling openings on various teams. The Canton Reds had a particularly strong POM presence, with several former Senators filling important roles.

Once a team captain in Washington, Ed Murphy was now manager. McKechnie solidified the third base position, James Miller had a similar effect at second, and Frank McHale arrived with a reputation as the defunct league's finest pitcher. Another familiar face belonged to catcher Wahoo Guyon. While ball players shook off the rust during preseason practice and exhibition games, the city looked to shape up too. Plans were in the works for street paving and sewer improvements, and some wanted the downtown hitching posts removed. This was the 20th century, after all, and old-fashioned horse hook-ups cast a backward pall on the city's bustling business district. In a move to further modernize things, city officials announced that street lights would soon run on electricity instead of gas.

Opening day got postponed, first by snow, then by rain. On May 2, Canton lost a 3–2 decision at Akron in a game shortened to five frigid innings because of rain. McKechnie made a pivotal throwing error but redeemed himself a day later, stroking a game-winning single in the extra-inning home opener at League Park. Trying to score from second, Guyon was tagged out at the plate but the field umpire called interference on the third baseman. Blocking baserunners was common practice in those days but this infielder didn't get away with it, and Canton prevailed, 4–3. A few days later, McKechnie belted a double in another late rally that produced victory.

Guyon made headlines later that month when he was arrested in Washington and held on a $1,000 bond. The *Canton Repository* vaguely explained the source of his incarceration as "a charge preferred by a young woman."[6] His bond was later reduced to $500 and he returned soon afterward. Winning slightly more than they lost, the Reds hung around the .500 mark through the early part of the season. That wasn't good enough for management, and angry accusations of "indifferent playing" filled the air. A pitcher was suspended and manager Murphy threatened more exiles if certain players didn't show more spirit. A four-game winning streak quickly followed, punctuated by McKechnie's grand slam home run in the fourth victory. By mid–June, the Reds occupied fourth place but were only 2½ games out of first.

On June 24, the nation mourned the loss of former president Grover Cleveland, who died of heart failure at his home in Princeton, New Jersey. The only chief executive to serve two non-consecutive terms, Cleveland had endured declining health for years but his passing still came as a shock to those around him. He would be remembered forever as the 22nd and 24th president of the United States. Long after death, his name lived on in sports pages because of a famous namesake — Grover Cleveland Alexander, the fourth pitcher elected to the Hall of Fame. Alexander was a novice in 1908, playing semi-pro ball far from Canton. He would play for McKechnie one day.

Staying in the top four of an eight-team league, the Reds remained a better-than-average team but fell further out of first. The "spirit" issue hadn't completely gone away, though some players were beyond criticism. Fans gushed over Kaiser Lichtenbach, a control pitcher who won game after game in the early stages of the season. Before batters figured him out, some called him the best hurler in the OP. Already known as a good hitter, Bill Bailey raised his profile even higher by drilling home runs in three consecutive games, a rare feat in those days. Also singled out as a hometown favorite was Bill McKechnie, a superb fielder and base stealer, whose hitting had begun catching up with the rest of his game.

By the end of July, the financial situation got so bad that there wasn't money to pay the players. Twelve thousand dollars in the hole and unable to secure loans, the Canton Athletic Club petitioned for temporary protection from creditors and got it. A Common Pleas judge placed the corporation in receivership, giving control to an attorney who would try to fix the mess.

There was talk that the Cleveland Naps might buy the franchise to use it as a farm team. If the Reds lacked old-time fundamentals, that wouldn't necessarily preclude promotion to the majors. According to a sports column in the *Repository*, big league baseball wasn't a game of skill any more: "'Inside ball,' the quintessence of team work, has ... been neglected by various managers, who seem to want every batsman to 'kill the ball,' to bang it 'all over the lot' regardless of what the particular situation may be. This has brought about a falling off in the much needed sacrifice hitting."[7]

In the same year that Henry Ford introduced the Motel T automobile, traditionalists were already singing that familiar tune. It was also the same summer and autumn that the Wright Brothers won further fame by refining their invention and pushing the boundaries of flight. Over in France, Wilbur broke time-aloft records that were first set by him and his sibling. Meanwhile, Orville made demonstration flights for army brass at Fort Myer, Virginia; military minds were already contemplating warfare applications for the airplane. The Canton area had a love affair with flight of a different kind, as newspapers carried stories about the adventures of balloon aeronauts. When the Aero Club of Ohio spearheaded races and exhibitions, Canton was a common starting point, and local Labor Day celebrations always included a popular balloon race.

The OP baseball season concluded September 8, with Canton dropping a doubleheader in front of nearly 4,000 fans at Akron, Ohio. McKechnie stroked two hits in the morning opener, then sat out most of the afternoon game. He ended the season as owner of a solid .283 batting average, third highest on the team. At 65–56, Canton finished a distant third, 18 games behind league-champion Akron and 9½ back of runner-up East Liverpool. Maybe things would've been different if the Reds could have kept pitcher Buff Ehman in town, but the Canton native won a league-leading 25 games for Akron. Still, third place wasn't bad in an eight-team circuit.

With local baseball finished, sports fans turned toward football. Jim Thorpe would play there professionally one day, but for now the gridiron menu consisted of interscholastic, college and semi-pro. Come late September, Akron won bragging rights in a second sport, as its semi-pro squad notched a 6–0 victory over Canton. Football still faced competition from the national pastime, where two major league pennant races wound toward a thrilling close. Area fans had a couple of contenders to root for — the Pittsburgh Pirates in the National League and the Cleveland Indians in the American. At the end, both failed by razor-thin margins and a Chicago Cubs–Detroit Tigers World Series was born.

On the day of Game 1, Canton welcomed a guest speaker who was as blunt and charismatic as any baseball manager in history. She showed no interest in the national pastime, however; Carrie Nation gained widespread fame as both a preacher for prohibition and hands-on saloon smasher. Representing the Women's Christian Temperance Union, she pulled no punches while addressing 2,000 people at the city auditorium:

> This afternoon I went into a few of your saloons.... At the gambling table I saw your men of Canton pouring down their throats hell's poison. And I said, "Canton is rotten: someone is to blame for all this rottenness." Who, then, is the responsible party? I'll tell you straight.... The most lawless man in your city is your mayor. And the police come in as a good second.[8]

Nation blasted the immigrant German brewers Schlitz, Pabst, Anheuser and Budweiser. She attacked Republicans, then turned on applauding Democrats, saying their party hadn't done anything for the temperance cause either. She hoped a Prohibition Party would replace both on the national stage. All this from a 63-year-old woman who would not live to see Prohibition become the law of the land in 1920. Bill McKechnie did not return to "rotten" Canton. He continued his minor league climb the following year, landing in Wheeling, a historic Ohio River city on the northern panhandle of West Virginia. With a population of about 40,000, it was smaller than Canton but bigger in base-ball prestige. Here, McKechnie played for the Stogies, a Class B franchise in the Central League. This was the big-time. While lower minors fretted about travel costs and shaped their leagues around nearby regional cities and afford-able train fare, the Central ventured much farther. It stretched across Ohio into the far reaches of Indiana and also included Lower Michigan. Wheeling was the farthest point east.

Major league teams dipped into the Central League for replenishment, and some big leaguers wound up there on the way down. Wheeling's industry had grown at the end of the 19th century, with iron and steel mills dotting the landscape. Other industries flourished, too, and the team name "Stogies" was a tribute to the thriving cigar business. As a huge manufacturer of cut iron nails, the city became more famously known as "Nail Capital of the World."

With a diversified industrial economy and large accompanying workforce, Wheeling seemed more than capable of supporting a baseball team. Child of a southern state (Virginia) and sandwiched between two northern ones (Ohio and Pennsylvania), the area's peculiar geography gave it an unusual history. Wheeling remained loyal to the Union during the Civil War and became cap-ital of a new state when West Virginia separated from secessionist Virginia in 1863. Perhaps some of the city's older residents still talked about those days. The capital eventually moved south to Charleston, leaving Wheeling as a ven-erated but remote outpost on that northern sliver of West Virginia. It grew strong, and baseball grew alongside of it.

As the 1909 season approached, America welcomed a new president named William Howard Taft and said goodbye to his predecessor, Teddy Roosevelt. Wheeling said goodbye to its theatrical season, though vaudeville shows would continue a while longer. Outdoor entertainment arrived in the form of Stogies baseball, with fans hoping to see a better show this time; their team had finished dead last the previous year. The job of rebuilding the fran-chise fell to 41-year-old manager Bill Phillips, a respected Pennsylvanian who'd seen a lot of baseball. He was a promising young pitcher at one point, posting a 17–9 record with the Cincinnati Reds in 1899. Three years later he recorded a strong 2.51 earned run average while going 16–16. Exiting the majors after the 1903 campaign, Phillips finished his career with 70 wins and 76 losses.

Now he was building a second career as minor league manager, and the early results looked promising. The old pitching wing still had some magic left, too. Motivating without intimidating, he was both a players' manager and a manager-player. "I would rather play under Phillips than any other manager in the country," McKechnie said upon his arrival in camp on March 29. "The same goes here too," added Will McClelland, who'd served under Phillips the previous year at East Liverpool.

As the calendar flipped to April, the Stogies prepared for an exhibition game against baseball's greatest living legend, Adrian "Cap" Anson. One of the founding fathers of the National League in 1876, Anson became the game's first transcendent star. He spent his entire tenure with the Chicago White Stockings, quitting after 22 years with 3,000-plus hits and a .329 lifetime batting average. Now pushing 60, he headlined a strong semi-pro barnstorming squad called Anson's Colts and put Wheeling on the schedule in 1909.

Anson needed the money; he was a year away from bankruptcy. Before game day he dropped in at the *Register* newspaper office to regale reporters with tales of yore. He said modern baseball had no players to compare with stars of the 1870s and 1880s. Then came a history lesson that went even further back:

> When I first played ball it was then known as town ball, when the runner was "swiped" with the ball, and if it struck him about the face it certainly hurt some. Then came the change of rules that only required the ball to be thrown in front of the runner. Along in the early seventies the rules were again changed, which are used today, requiring that the runner shall only be touched with the ball.[9]

Anson's team rolled to a 10–4 victory over the Stogies, with the old guy going 1-for-5 and scoring a run. It was an ugly debut for the home team but nobody read much into it. They hadn't been together long, the roster was incomplete and most were playing out of position. Anson's boys had more game experience. McKechnie delivered one hit in four tries, scored once and threw out two baserunners.

No sooner had Anson left town than the New York Giants arrived for another exhibition. A couple of major leaguers switched sides to bolster the local squad, and a crowd of 1,288 gawked at the legs of Giants catcher Chief Meyers, who was wearing a pair of those newfangled devices called "shin guards." The majors beat the minors, 7–2. After a 3–0 loss to the Philadelphia Athletics, Wheeling finally broke through on April 8, edging Philly, 5–4, in front of 250 fans at Island Park. The Giants and A's weren't champions just then but both would win more than 90 games in 1909. Though they didn't bring all their best players, several regulars took the field for these preseason contests. At the tender age of 23, Bill McKechnie had already locked horns with some of the best players in the world.

As the Stogies rounded into shape, locals liked what they saw; this team could be a winner. Keeping his cards close to the vest, manager Phillips refused to make a pennant forecast. "The Wheeling team will make a better showing than the aggregation of 1908, of that I am certain. More I will not predict now."[10]

About 2,000 paying fans descended on Island Park for the season opener and watched the Stogies drop a 4–0 decision to Grand Rapids. Earlier that afternoon, a large opening day parade went through the city, first on traction cars, then by automobile. West Virginia's governor took part in it and later threw out the ceremonial first pitch from his grandstand seat. The ensuing loss proved deflating but fans could take heart that pundits believed nobody would run away with this year's pennant — the league was too balanced for that. After a slow start, the Stogies got hot and climbed into first place on May 23; McKechnie led the way with a sizzling average over .370, nearly 50 points better than the next best Stogie. As usual, his defense earned rave reviews, too.

Winning eight straight games at one point, Wheeling still couldn't pull away from the field. Zanesville further closed the gap, courtesy of a disputed 3–0 victory on June 1. With two runners aboard in the eighth inning, fleet-footed McKechnie sent a grounder to the second baseman, who bobbled the ball. "Mac" was called out at first. "Mac beat Lloyd's throw easily and astonishment reigned supreme when the substitute umpire declared the speedy Stogie infielder was in the down and out class. Mac kicked so vigorously that he was ordered out of the game."[11] Balance was restored the following day, as McKechnie blasted a game-winning double in the bottom of the ninth. Wheeling spent lots of time in first place during those opening months but never got much separation from Zanesville and Grand Rapids.

In the midst of it all, the future arrived in Cincinnati when the Reds' ball field played host to a night game under crude lighting. The June exhibition game between two amateur Elks Club teams was deemed a success. "I don't believe that night baseball is destined to rival the daylight article but I will say that I am much surprised at the ease with which the game was played tonight," said Reds manager Clark Griffith. "Under improved lighting it will grow more popular."[12]

In early July, the Central League staked claim to organized baseball's first night game. It happened in Grand Rapids with the home team pulling out an 11–10 triumph against Zanesville. Many pioneers were planting their flag that summer; headlines carried news that a French pilot flew across the English Channel, a Wright brother broke the altitude record, and Frederick Cook claimed he'd conquered the North Pole. Meanwhile, the Pittsburgh Pirates opened state-of-the-art Forbes Field and announced that the first-game attendance mark (30,338) was a world record. About 400 folks from the Wheeling area attended that one.

Winners of six straight games, Zanesville pushed the number to nine with a three-game home sweep of Wheeling. When the Potters took two more in Stogies territory, it seemed clear who had the Central's best team. It centered on the pitcher's mound, where a dominant staff held Wheeling to just two

The Wheeling Stogies were surprise contenders in the 1909 Central League. This caricature was published during an early-season surge into first place (*Wheeling Register*).

runs in five games. Phillips stopped the bleeding with a five-hitter, leading his "Smokes" to a 7–1 win in the series finale. The offense would continue to struggle, however, and Wheeling dropped farther from the top. As the team's best hitter, McKechnie certainly bore little blame for the free-fall, but his average had dropped steadily since the glory days of May. Topping out at .378, he was barely above .300 by early July.

Zanesville did not capitalize on Wheeling's woes, so the race remained tight. Then, at the same time McKechnie went on the disabled list with a leg injury, the Stogies got hot. Pitchers crafted shutouts and batters put crooked numbers on the scoreboard. The streak continued when McKechnie got healthy; beginning the last week of July and lasting deep into August, Wheeling won and won and won. Robert Tarleton blasted two home runs in a 4–3 win at Grand Rapids, Phillips tossed a no-hitter against visiting South Bend, and McKechnie popped a two-run single during a 2–0 triumph at Dayton. When McKechnie drilled a double and triple in another triumph on August 21, it gave him 100 hits for the season. Now sporting a 65–39 record, Wheeling led Zanesville by two games, with Fort Wayne a distant third.

Around this time came word that the Pirates had just purchased two Stogie stalwarts: Tarleton and McKechnie. They would complete the Central League season first, though. Wheeling kept rolling to the very end, finishing at 83–50 and winning the pennant by 7½ games. In the September 16 season finale at Zanesville, McKechnie capped things by hitting for the cycle, smacking a home run, triple, double and single. That big finish pushed his final batting average to .282, not an eye-popping figure but 32 points better than his nearest teammate and good enough for tenth in the league. Only four Central League hitters eclipsed the .300 mark. It was a pitcher's league and Wheeling's staff rose to the challenge by twirling 26 shutouts; John Fisher won 25 games, Phillips went 12–3 and Rufus Nolley was 18–14.

On September 19 the champs hosted the Pittsburgh Pirates in a much-ballyhooed exhibition contest. Cheered on by the biggest baseball crowd in city history, the hometown boys rolled to a 9–1 victory. Many fans still left disappointed, though, because the major leaguers loaded their lineup with back-up players.

Wheeling saluted its champions with a banquet, sponsored by the local Business Men's Protective Association. Included on the menu were oysters, green turtle soup, spring chicken, vegetables, cake and ice cream. Asked to make an impromptu speech, manager Phillips praised fans, players and executives. An evening of music and merriment closed with everybody singing "Auld Lang Syne," a song particularly fitting for players like McKechnie who would never return to Wheeling or the Central League.

3

In the Company of Champions

Honus Wagner had the most to do with my success as a ball player by teaching me where different players hit and their habits. — Bill McKechnie

On a late January day, Pittsburgh Pirates owner Barney Dreyfuss was talking to a sports reporter when the mailman arrived and dropped a batch of letters on his desk. A large envelope caught his attention. "That's coming [back] fast, only sent it out a few days ago," Dreyfuss remarked in his signature German accent. Wearing a Wilkinsburg return address, it contained a contract signed by one William B. McKechnie. He'd wasted no time putting his name on the dotted line. "The contract didn't have far to go but even then this promptness is commendable," Dreyfuss continued. "McKechnie is a big lad in uniform. He has filled out over his form when he was a Pirate three years ago. Big fellow now. Played fine ball in 1909. [Manager] Fred Clarke will give him a trial this spring, that's sure."[1]

A Jewish German immigrant, Barney Dreyfuss became the poster child for the American Dream. Born in the last year of the Civil War, he came to the United States at age 17, took a menial job at a distillery and worked his way up to the front office. Dreyfuss had a head for figures and a passion for baseball. He bought stock in the Louisville team during the early years of major league baseball and eventually became owner. A move to Pittsburgh followed near the turn of the century, when he bought into the Pirates and brought along his best Louisville players — Honus Wagner, for one. A pioneer baseball magnate with big dreams and an ego to match, Dreyfuss would serve 32 years as Pirates president. In 1910, he liked the kid from Wilkinsburg.

It was no small achievement when the kid went to spring training and made the team. Things had changed since he had that cup of coffee in 1907; the Pirates were champions now, having won 110 games before beating Ty Cobb and the Detroit Tigers in the 1909 World Series. Yet they still saw a need for a rookie named McKechnie. By April, other teams wanted him too.

Team secretary Will Locke said, "That's right, McKechnie is in demand. John Harris, of the Bostons, says he wouldn't mind taking the man off our hands. A club in California also seeks him. Clarke looks for a first-class performer in the local man."[2]

A lot of men had come and gone since McKechnie last wore a Pirates uniform. Mainstays remained, guys like outfielder Tommy Leach, pitcher Deacon Phillipe and, of course, Honus Wagner. Now 36 years old, the legendary Dutchman would become a mentor to young McKechnie, showing him the ropes and offering advice on the finer points of the game. "Honus seemed to take a fancy to me when I first came up," McKechnie would remember. "Maybe it was because Honus, like I, came from the outskirts of Pittsburgh. He taught me to watch other National League ball players, see where they were most likely to hit, and other peculiarities."[3]

Son of a German immigrant, Wagner left school at age 12 to work

After a successful tour on the local minor league circuit, McKechnie became the property of Pittsburgh Pirates magnate Barney Dreyfuss. The German immigrant lived the American Dream, working his way from manual labor to management before becoming president of the Pirates (National Baseball Hall of Fame Library, Cooperstown, New York).

in the coal mines. Baseball gave him a way out. A stocky figure with bowed legs and a lantern jaw, Honus looked and acted like an "everyman" but played like nobody else. He was surprisingly fast, predictably strong and exceptionally skilled. In 1908 he played hardball at the negotiating table, holding out for the princely sum of $10,000, double his previous salary. When management finally met his demands, he became an owner's dream thereafter, gladly accepting the same pay year after year. A genial, big lug, Wagner did not own an ego proportionate to his talent; it was hard to find anybody with a bad thing to say about him. Excluding good looks, he had it all.

With both his parents dead, McKechnie appreciated the gentle guiding hand of men like Wagner. Things had certainly changed back at McKechnie's household in Wilkinsburg; once as large as 15, it now numbered five. Though she held no job, 21-year-old Margaret was listed as household head in the 1910 federal census. Bill still lived there with his sister, as did a younger blood

The great Honus Wagner became mentor to young Bill McKechnie when he broke into the majors with the Pittsburgh Pirates (Library of Congress, Prints and Photography Division).

brother and an older adoptive one. New to the house was an eight-year-old niece. Other family members were carving out their own lives, much as their brother was doing in professional baseball.

The lid came off the 1910 season at Washington, D.C., where President Taft started a durable tradition when he threw out the ceremonial first pitch.

Walter Johnson tossed a one-hitter, leading the Washington Senators to victory over Connie Mack's Philadelphia Athletics. It was *not* a sign of things to come; Philly won the American League pennant that year and Washington finished 36½ games out of first.

Trying to defend their National League title, the Pirates faced stiff competition from a loaded Chicago team. These were the Cubs of Tinker, Evers, Chance and Three Finger Brown. Before Pittsburgh dethroned them, they'd won three straight pennants and two World Series. Though placing second in 1909, Chicago still won 104 games. Pittsburgh had most of its championship pieces in place but there was flux on the infield; a new starter occupied third base and a new teammate stood on first. Dots Miller returned to second base but his bat was missing in action. Though Wagner provided a steadying influence at shortstop, he couldn't strap the entire infield on his broad back.

Enter Bill McKechnie. The eager 24-year-old didn't hit much, but he

The defending world champion Pittsburgh Pirates posed for this 1910 spring training picture in Hot Springs, Arkansas. Sitting in the center of the front row, wearing black, is their rookie infielder, Bill McKechnie (National Baseball Hall of Fame Library, Cooperstown, New York).

filled an important role as versatile substitute. He played every infield position at some point, even four games at first base. When Miller missed several contests with a knee injury in July, McKechnie moved into the starting lineup, and most observers agreed that he was an upgrade defensively. If only the sandlot boys could see him now.

Pulling in $1,500 per season[4] on his contract, McKechnie used part of the income to finance a Wilkinsburg team in a local independent baseball league.[5]

The Pirates were good in 1910 but not championship caliber. They spent several days at the top of the standings in May before the Cubs blew by them and put a permanent stranglehold on first. Mark Twain died that spring, his soul following Halley's Comet into the great beyond. Pittsburgh pennant dreams lived a bit longer but fell on a deathbed in mid–June and expired long before the final bell. Some fans didn't take it well; worn down by persistent catcalls and badgering, player-manager Clarke announced he would play no more. The final straw came in an early September game versus the New York Giants, when vocally abusive critics demanded that Clarke replace himself with a better outfielder. Hardnosed John McGraw was the opposing manager that day, and he practically shed tears over the ugliness:

> Never, never in my connection with baseball, extending over a period of 21 years, did anything ever transpire to hurt me so much as did the demonstration against Fred Clarke in the second game of yesterday's doubleheader. How the people of Pittsburgh, for years renowned as game baseball fans, would hiss and jeer at the man who brought the city of smoke its first pennant and first world's championship, is beyond my comprehension.[6]

A longtime veteran outfielder, aging Clarke finished the season with a .263 average and was second on the team in RBI. Though greatly curtailing his playing time for the remainder of the season, he did not quit entirely, and a year later made the critics eat their words. The Pirates placed third at 86–67, 17½ games behind Chicago and 4½ back of the Giants. Wagner did his part, Leach was solid and Bobby Byrne enjoyed a breakout season at third base. Team batting ranked about the same as in the championship year, but Pittsburgh fell from first to fourth in run scoring. Pitching was the biggest culprit, with the team ERA jumping from 2.07 to 2.83.

McKechnie hit .217 for the season but his modest debut generated enough local name recognition to get him an off-season endorsement. He provided a newspaper testimonial for "Meyer's Specific," a household remedy for rheumatism, bruises, sprains, cuts, burns, sore throats and more. He claimed the substance cured his injured ankle during a barnstorming tour.

The next season would bear a striking resemblance to the last. The Philadelphia Athletics captured World Series glory again and Pittsburgh finished a distant third in the National League, winning one less game than in 1910. McKechnie again served as a jack of all positions, though this time he played 57 games at first base. The "initial sack," as some reporters called it, had long been a source of frustration; management just couldn't find the right player for the job. In 1911, it was split evenly between McKechnie and a rookie who soon fell out of the big leagues and never returned.

Injuries hit the infield hard, with some starters forced to sit and others playing in pain. Their pain was McKechnie's gain; at one point he took Wagner's place at shortstop when the legend reluctantly agreed to move to first base. The Pirates certainly had their bright spots; Wagner captured his eighth batting crown, Babe Adams and Howie Camnitz won 20 games, and future Hall of Famer Max Carey joined the outfield. Meanwhile, Clarke enjoyed a bounce-back season, hitting .324. Once again, Pittsburgh had a good team but not good enough; with a record of 99–54, New York ran away from the pennant field, beating Chicago by 7½ games and the Pirates by 14½.

Appearing in 104 games, McKechnie hit .227, scored 40 runs and stole nine bases. In affairs of the heart, however, he was batting a thousand; he married his hometown sweetheart in mid–June. The first time Beryl Bien

In 1911, Bill married his hometown sweetheart, Beryl Bien. Here, they're shown on their honeymoon (courtesy Carol McKechnie Montgomery).

spoke to him, he got so flustered that he swallowed his chewing tobacco. After that, nuptials always seemed inevitable — at least to the future groom.

The national pastime paled in comparison to national headlines of 1912. This was the year Wilbur Wright died, Teddy Roosevelt got shot, the Titanic sank, Jim Thorpe dominated track at the Stockholm Olympics and Woodrow Wilson won the presidential election. Still, a protracted World Series got its due in October and the outdoorsman Roosevelt surely took notice of it after the failed assassination attempt. Winning their second straight NL pennant, McGraw's Giants went on to lose an eight-game heartbreaker to the Boston Red Sox. Though finishing far behind New York, Pittsburgh put together a fine season that generated 93 wins and runner-up honors. McKechnie did not partake in much of the fun; credited with just 24 appearances through mid–August, he was shipped north to St. Paul (MN) of the American Association.

"McKechnie's transfer to St. Paul wasn't surprising. Though playing fair ball, the local lad this season suddenly developed into a leggy fellow. He piled on masses of meat around the thigh. Seemed to be lumbering and slower than in stripling days," reported *Sporting Life*.[7]

Recently turning 26, McKechnie was no longer a stripling; he was a St. Paul Saint. Though home to a famous winter carnival that featured giant ice castles, the city could not be mistaken for a frozen outpost. It was the capital of Minnesota and one of the biggest meat packing centers in America. It also had a mammoth railroad clearing house called Minnesota Transfer Station.

St. Paul attracted business and professionals just as its ball team attracted quality athletes. A charter member of the American Association minor league, the city had a long tradition of pastime excellence. So did Minneapolis, its neighbor and chief rival. Forget Milwaukee, Kansas City or Toledo; above all else, the twin cities wanted to beat each other. The AA earned respect as a high-class circuit, a springboard to the majors for some and a soft landing for others who'd fallen from up high. McKechnie joined a struggling Saints squad and fit right in with struggles of his own. The glove remained airtight but he just couldn't hit. It was a fairly common condition for St. Paul swatters, though McKechnie took it to extremes.

The team did produce a few good hitters here and there; eclipsing the .300 mark, outfielder Walter Rehg would soon graduate to the majors and stay there awhile. McKechnie's hitting improved, though too late to give him a decent average; he finished at .234. With a record well below .500, St. Paul wrapped up the season in sixth place and, to make matters worse, Minneapolis won 104 games and the pennant. Looking toward next year, Saints Nation pushed for a talent infusion — perhaps a couple of hard-hitting outfielders and a pitcher or two. Was there any room for a good-field, no-hit infielder? The Boston Braves thought so and drafted him back to the majors.

The following winter, McKechnie returned an unsigned contract to Braves management; unhappy with the terms, he preferred to remain in the American Association at his current salary. He did play major league ball when the season opened, occupying the unfamiliar position of center fielder. On a cold April 10 that saw Boston's mayor throw out the first pitch, he went 0-for-4 at the plate, scored once and caught three fly balls in an 8–0 home win over the New York Giants. Then McKechnie vanished in a puff of smoke, claimed off waivers by the New York Yankees. A story circulated that the Braves didn't mean to make him available and wanted him back, but the Yankees refused. Another source said the Braves purposely made him available because they had no openings for an infielder.

Either way, the Wilkinsburg boy had to relocate to Manhattan — home of Broadway, Pennsylvania Station, the Polo Grounds and now William Boyd McKechnie. At this point in history, the Yankees were ugly kid brothers to the ruggedly handsome New York Giants. One rarely contended, the other was a perpetual powerhouse. The Giants had won 103 games and an NL pennant during the previous season, while the Yankees lost 102 on their way to dead last. Nothing changed much in 1913.

In some ways, though, it was a time of tremendous change. This was the season that the nickname officially changed from "Highlanders" to "Yankees" and the address changed from Highlander Park to the Polo Grounds. It was also a time of growth for McKechnie, earning his keep in the center of the universe; he appeared in 44 games as a utility infielder, mostly at second base. It wasn't an entirely positive experience, as some New York newspaper men tagged him with the unflattering nickname of "134 Bill McKechnie" — a dig at his anemic batting average. In spite of his failures at the plate, McKechnie had a powerful supporter in new manager Frank Chance. The former Cubs star admired his baseball IQ and kept him in the lineup longer than anybody expected. Asked why he was so partial to McKechnie, Chance reportedly snapped, "Because he is the one man on this ball club who has an intelligent idea of what this is all about. He knows more baseball than all the rest of this team put together."[8] Another version of the same story has the boss delivering a detailed tongue-lashing to underlings who grumbled about the teacher's pet relationship: "You fellows say I'm always talking to McKechnie. That's true. You say I tell him all my best plans and say nothing to you. That's true, too, and I'll tell you why. It's because Bill McKechnie is the only man on this club who is smart enough to think for himself. He knows more about baseball than the whole lot of you thrown together. And that goes."[9]

But the prize goes to a third retelling of the tale: "Because he's the only son-of-a sea-cook on this club who knows what it's all about. Among this bunch of meatheads, his brain shines like a gold mine."[10] Regardless of the exact words, it was high praise coming from a man with an impeccable pedigree; beginning his Cubs career in 1898, Chance went on to win four pennants and two World Series as a player-manager. The praise was all the more impressive considering that grouchy Chance wasn't exactly a positive-reinforcement guy. His nickname of "Peerless Leader" sometimes got parodied to "cheerless leader."

If Chance seemed particularly testy in 1913, he had good reason. Losing 12 of their first 14 games, his diamond dimwits were on their way to a 57–94 season and seventh place. These weren't yet the Yankees of Babe Ruth, Lou Gehrig or even Wally Pipp; they were a team of Birdie Cree, Roy Hartzell and Harry Wolter. Uber-wealthy Jake Ruppert (old money) and Colonel Tillinghast Huston (new money) were still a couple of years away from taking the ownership reins. For the time being, the franchise remained in the dirtier hands of gambling mogul Frank Farrell and his old associate Bill Devery, an ex–police captain.

For winning baseball games, McKechnie did not arrive at a good time; for making a major league roster, it couldn't have been much better. Embarrassed by their triple-digit loss figure of 1912, management flushed out the old and brought in the new. Of course, newer didn't necessarily mean better. The team did have one strong drawing card, however, and his name was Hal Chase. A California boy who became immensely popular in New York, the talented first baseman was an eight-year Highlander veteran. He even managed the team in 1911, though the experience didn't instill any great respect for authority. Chase mocked Frank Chance behind his back, aiming words of ridicule toward his deaf ear. The bench would erupt with laughter and the boss inevitably became angry. It was just one example of the contempt that Chase felt for his manager, and the feeling was mutual.

They actually had a lot in common; both were first basemen, native Californians, and spent their entire careers in the spotlight of major metropolises. The age difference was only five calendar years (35 and 30) but success separated them by light years; Chance still wore that championship aura from the Cubs dynasty. When he returned to Chicago as a visiting manager, Comiskey Park welcomed him with Frank Chance Day. Nearly 36,000 enthusiastic fans turned out to pay tribute, and that figure disappointed owner Charles Comiskey, who expected to break the major league attendance record of 38,281. He'd boosted capacity by adding temporary seating, but four poorly-constructed sections collapsed under the weight of too many bodies. Though hundreds tumbled to the ground and several were injured, mayhem did not overshadow the guest of honor. Chance was that popular in Chicago.

A pre-game parade saw more than 700 automobiles trekking to the park, where about 25,000 fans arrived an hour before game-time. Many carried Chance Day pennants. Entertaining the early-arriving crowd were acrobats, cabaret singers, trained dogs, band concerts and fireworks. Moving-picture men captured the scene when the Illinois governor presented Chance with a huge floral horseshoe. The whole thing must have made Hal Chase sick.

Their dugout conflict lasted 39 games; claiming that Chase was trying to throw games, Chance insisted on trading him. Ownership eventually gave in, sending the popular infield artist to the Chicago White Sox for two non-descript players. Suffice it to say that Frank Chance would take one Bill McKechnie over a hundred Hal Chases. Neither would finish the season in New York, however. McKechnie had a few highlights; playing shortstop, he went 2-for-4 and scored twice in a 3–3 tie against the defending world champion Boston Red Sox, and also delivered two hits during a loss to Ty Cobb and the Detroit Tigers. In a win over Cleveland he had the privilege of throwing out the great veteran Nap Lajoie, still a heck of a hitter in his 18th season and closing in on 3,000 hits.

For the most part, though, McKechnie did not deliver — especially at the plate. He battled an injury in mid-summer but that was small excuse for a man who looked overmatched when healthy. Even on a dysfunctional team like the Yankees, .134 was slim sledding and, in August, McKechnie got a ticket back to St. Paul, where he appeared in 32 games and hit .245. He joined a team with more major league talent than the last time he swung through. Some had already been to the bigs and would never return; some were on the way up for brief, inauspicious careers. Shortstop Everett Scott went on to set a major league record for consecutive games played. Other American Association cites owned talent, too, and the Saints finished fifth out of eight teams.

With the season done, McKechnie had unfinished business to settle. Assured that the Saints would fulfill payment provisions on his major league contract, he was disappointed to find his salary cut. What's more, he had to play a longer season at that reduced rate. Calculating the difference, McKechnie insisted that somebody owed him $450, no small sum in 1913. When Yankees executives ignored his demand, he declared himself through with baseball. As of November, he had a job with a fabric importing business, owned by his in-laws. As of October 13, he also had another mouth to feed — Bill McKechnie Jr. The baby boy would inherit much of his father's smarts and some of his athletic ability. For now, he was entirely helpless.

Retirement didn't last long for the senior McKechnie, and he soon cast his lot with a new circuit that trumpeted itself as a third major league. They called it the Federal League.

4

Reaching New Heights
with the Feds

Bill McKechnie gave an exhibition of broncho busting that brought rounds of applause from the cow men, especially when Bill, bouncing high in the air, declined farther to ride and dismounted with considerable grace and great speed.—Indianapolis Star[1]

By 1914, McKechnie's brief career had already seen its ups and downs. He'd reached the mountaintop when playing big league ball in his own back yard with the Pittsburgh Pirates, but success proved fleeting. Twice demoted to the minors, the 27-year-old had reason to worry about his future in the big time. Then, out of the blue, opportunity knocked on his door and its initials were F.L.

The Federal League debuted the previous year as a modest minors circuit, although it did invade four major league cities. With one season under their belt, the Feds suddenly got ambitious and declared themselves major. They hired a new, aggressive president, brought wealthy businessmen into the ownership fold, declared the reserve clause invalid, and tried to lure major leaguers with promises of big salary hikes. Also dipping into high-level minor leagues, they stripped the American Association and International League.

It was basically the same game plan the American League employed when breaking up the National League monopoly starting in 1903. Thirteen years later, AL president Ban Johnson saw things from an entirely different perspective and threatened to ban any player who jumped to the so-called outlaw league. Most of the big stars stayed put in both major leagues but a couple of aging legends jumped ship, bringing name-recognition and credibility to the Feds. Both were former Cubs teammates—Joe Tinker and Three Finger Brown. Taking a position as player-manager of the Chicago Whales, Tinker returned to the city that once adored him; he played there from 1902 to 1912, winning two World Series along the way. Now approaching the twilight of his long career, he still had some pop left in the bat, hitting .317 as player-manager for Cincinnati in 1913.

Like Tinker, Brown was approaching the end of a memorable career. Pitching for the Cubs from 1904 to 1912, he'd won lots of games and a couple of championships, though the victories had slowed to a trickle. After going 5–6 with a 2.64 earned run average in 1912, Brown was traded to Cincinnati, where he compiled marks of 11–12 and 2.91. Then came an offer he couldn't refuse — take a pay raise and become player-manager of the Federal League team at St. Louis. The Feds also landed a young pitching phenom named Tom Seaton, who was coming off a 27–12 season for the Philadelphia Phillies. But in the end, they failed to sign any stars in their prime and even got turned down by a minor leaguer named Babe Ruth.

Several solid, second-tier players took the money and made the switch, however. Then there were the third-tier guys like Bill McKechnie, for whom the choice was pretty easy. He took the money and the starter's job. What's more, he got to return home to play with the Pittsburgh Fed team — or so he thought; the "Pittfeds" soon turned him over to the "Hoofeds" of Indianapolis. Whatever disappointment he felt must've been mitigated by the presence of his old Wheeling manager Bill Phillips, who held the reins in Indiana's capital city and led the Hoosiers to a pennant in 1913. That was minor league ball, however, and Phillips didn't bring many of his champions back when the league went major. Like everybody else, he looked for upgrades from above.

The Hoosiers landed veteran Cy Falkenberg, a 33-year-old pitcher coming off a fantastic 23–10 season with the Cleveland Indians. An ordinary hurler for most of his career, the tall stringbean reached new heights when he learned the art of scuffing baseballs with an emery board. Also arriving was Vin Campbell, a former teammate of McKechnie's during the Pirates years when both were wet behind the ears. In 1912, Campbell hit .296 and scored 102 runs for the Boston Braves. Second baseman Frank LaPorte eclipsed the .300 mark twice for the St. Louis Browns in 1911 and 1912, then sank to .252 the following year in part-time duty for the Washington Senators. Indianapolis brought in minor league left fielder Benny Kauff, who hit .346 for a Connecticut team in the Eastern Association, and right fielder Al Scheer, who made 22 plate appearances for the Brooklyn Dodgers. Bill Rariden had five years' catching experience with the Braves, and first base seemed locked up by 33-year-old Biddy Dolan, a minor league veteran with graying hair and a powerful bat. Dolan was one of the few holdovers from Indy's 1913 squad.

The baby of the family was Edd Roush, a 20-year-old outfielder who ranked lowest on the experience odometer. Accumulating ten at-bats for the 1913 Chicago White Sox, his cup of coffee could've fit in a thimble. But the kid had spunk and loads of raw talent. He also had a date with Cooperstown.

One of McKechnie's St. Paul teammates signed a contract with Indy but immediately had second thoughts. Outfielder Everett Booe finally agreed to come, providing that someone took his place as baseball coach at a small college in Clinton, North Carolina. In the strangest of trades, Indianapolis sent utility infielder Carl Vandergrift to college and put the coach to work.

As spring training approached, the baseball war heated up. It wasn't just entrenched powers that felt robbed; the newcomers yelled "thief" too. Accusing the majors of stealing players with binding Fed agreements, league president James Gilmore threatened to return the favor: "If the American and National Leagues ignore our contracts and fail to appreciate the spirit of sportsmanship we have shown, we will start the biggest of baseball wars. When it is over, the Federal League will have the stars of the old leagues and will be the strongest in the game."[2]

On the same day Gilmore's threats were published, local press hyped a basketball story from nearby Bloomington, where Indiana University beat Purdue, 30–28, on a last-second shot that sent supporters into a frenzy. "The 2,000 men and women who occupied the bleachers jumped from their seats, rushed on the floor, and members of the victorious team were carried to their dressing rooms," wrote the *Indianapolis Star*. "A procession was formed, headed by the band, and a snake dance and nightshirt parade followed on the downtown streets till a late hour."

Even as early as 1914, Indiana was basketball country. It was a baseball state first, though, with a long tradition of raising corn, tomatoes and major leaguers. Indianapolis owned pioneer status, fielding National League entries in 1876, 1887, 1888 and 1889. Now big-time baseball was back, according to Federal League promoters, and locals couldn't wait to take a look at their new team. The unveiling would have to wait until Bill Phillips put one together at spring training out west.

Nestled in the Panhandle Plains of north-central Texas, Wichita Falls hosted two Fed teams — the Hoosiers and Kansas City Packers. It was an island of civilization in a sunbaked sea, with a cowboy charm that quickly presented itself when locals welcomed both squads with a genuine Texas barbecue. Held at a ranch outside town in late March, the event was sponsored by the local chamber of commerce. Ball players started their adventure early, piling into automobiles for a 25-mile drive through the wind-swept prairie and working up an appetite along the way. They arrived at an oasis of outdoor cooking, complete with fresh beef and camp coffee.

A few urbanites soaked in the atmosphere by going jack rabbit hunting, while more adventurous types rode wild horses. Two particular city boys displayed a surprising knack for the latter: "[McKechnie] and Vincent Campbell really did show considerable class on the ponies. Each has a firm seat, a steady hand and a love for riding."[3]

Later on, the real cowboys showed them how it was done. When the party moved to the ranch house, Benny Kauff needed some taming too. More than a little tipsy, he was about to show his silk underwear to the lady of the house when teammates intervened.[4] Ever the diplomat, McKechnie defused the situation with soothing words to the hostess. Young Edd Roush helped put out the fire. Meeting for the first time that day, he and McKechnie began a lifelong friendship.[5] Fate put them in the same dugout for years to come, and unspoken affection bonded them outside the stadium.

Weather played havoc with spring training, and the Hoosiers left Wichita Falls with only 17 workouts under their belts. Indy still had a chance to iron out some wrinkles on the way home, however, and scheduled a stop in Oklahoma City, where they could work out with a local team of the Western Association. Rain hindered those plans too. To make matters worse, Bill Phillips got food poisoning from a bad hamburger and Cy Falkenberg announced that his three-year-old daughter had symptoms of measles. The manager made a quick recovery and put his team through one last practice. The little girl was bundled up by her father and taken to St. Louis, where Vin Campbell's physician father would take a look at her.

Back in Indianapolis, the city was abuzz with talk about the Indianapolis 500. A monumental rules change made time trials determine not only the final field but the starting order. (Lineups were previously determined by draw.) The move was designed to make things safer at the beginning, where 30 cars thundered at incredible speeds of 60 to 80 miles per hour. Race day was still over a month away, however, and baseball openers were just around the corner. Predictions rolled in from the experts, most picking the New York Giants to take National League honors and the Philadelphia Athletics as AL kings. American Association prognosticators leaned toward the Louisville Colonels and labeled the Indianapolis Indians as a middle-of-the-pack team. The Indians' biggest competition would come from the Hoosiers, with attendance and admission dollars as grand prize.

Wholesale roster upgrades made this infant Federal League hard to forecast, and many newspapers wouldn't even hazard a championship guess. Still, there was praise for the teams in St. Louis, Chicago, Brooklyn and Baltimore. Indy's defending champ status counted for very little. "Indianapolis has two good pitchers and a fair [catcher], an indifferent infield and an experimental outfield as first-class teams go," said the *Brooklyn Eagle*.

The Hoosiers also lacked a ball park, or at least one that was ready for use. Like so many Fed franchises, Indy built a new, major facility when the league went major. Contractors were cutting it close, though, and "Federal

Park" remained incomplete when the season opened. Fortunately, the team began with seven road games. An April 12 open house saw team officials greeting throngs of anxious fans, and franchise president J. Ed Krause sang praises for the new league, saying there was a big demand for a third option in the majors. He believed the Feds gave Indianapolis a chance of hosting a World Series one day. Locals yearned for something like that, something to put their metropolis back on the national baseball map.

About 23,000 fans attended Indy's April 16 opener in St. Louis, and all were treated to a ceremonial first pitch between Missouri's governor and the local mayor. Actually it was four pitches, only one of which came close to home plate. Cy Falkenberg enjoyed better success, hurling eight scoreless innings, and Biddy Dolan belted a three-run homer in a 7–3 Indy victory. With McKechnie as their starting third baseman and hitting second in the lineup, the Hoosiers went 3–4 on their first road trip. Now all eyes focused on Indy's home opener, with lavish ceremonies planned for day one at the new Kentucky Avenue facility. Hordes of workmen hustled back and forth in a last-minute sprint to have Federal Park ready. In addition to the typical stadium trappings, they'd added a touch of class by installing a suite of "comfort rooms" for lady patrons. Handsomely furnished and serviced on game days by a corps of maids, the section included both reception areas and bathrooms. Federal League officials made a point of targeting the fairer sex, and "Ladies Day" contests were staples of their schedules.

Indianapolis met its new team at the newborn ballpark on Thursday, April 23. Earlier that day, the city launched a welcoming parade that traveled through the downtown business sector for more than an hour. Cheering fans lined the route on both sides and, when game time approached, a stream of motorcars and trolleys headed toward the stadium. Foot traffic was heaviest of all, as thousands of residents crowded the sidewalks for a pastime hike. More than 15,000 passed through the gates; some had seats in the horseshoe grandstand, some headed for the pavilions on either side, and a bleacher behind left field provided an entirely different vantage point.

A couple of notable Democrats arrived for the first four-pitch ceremony, with Indiana governor Samuel M. Ralston throwing to local mayor Joseph E. Bell. Dressed in a frock coat and square-top derby hat, the governor delivered four low ones to the vicinity of the mayor and home plate. Falkenberg soon ambled to the mound and christened the stadium with its first real pitch — a ball — and then threw the initial strike. But the first shutout went to St. Louis pitcher Hank Keupper, as Indy lost a 3–0 decision. The hometown fans never gave up, staying in their seats through the bottom of the ninth and rooting for a rally.

Though they lost a battle, the Hoosiers won the war — one for credibility and hometown support. Folks seemed to enjoy the product at Federal Park. Perhaps it provided something to take their minds off the deteriorating situation in Mexico, where America seemed poised for war. Irate over detention of U.S. sailors, the country rallied around President Wilson's push for reprisals. By a vote of 337–37, the House of Representatives passed a joint resolution backing armed intervention. Two worlds collided when President Wilson pointed to the Mexican crisis as the reason he would not throw out the first pitch in the AL opener between Boston and Washington. It touched Federal Park, too, causing officials to remove the Mexican entry from a display of world flags.

Spring showers hit the city in early May and cancellations became commonplace as the diamond turned into an ugly quagmire. To avoid any fan confusion, the Washington Hotel raised a red flag when Indy planned to play and no flag when a game was cancelled. Regardless of weather conditions, the city eagerly awaited the arrival of a particularly exciting team whose roster included elephants, camels, zebras, monkeys and a battalion of horses. The world-famous Ringling Circus and its long yellow train were scheduled to arrive in Indy for a May 6 extravaganza. Thirty years earlier, five Ringling brothers ran a traveling wagon show with a trained horse and dancing bear. By 1914 they employed well over 1,000 people and about the same number of beasts.

The Hoosiers finished May in fourth place, six games behind league-leading Baltimore. Looking for a boost, the team acquired veteran Charlie Carr, an aging first baseman who was seven seasons removed from a mediocre major league career. His high-water mark came in 1903 when he hit .281 for the pre–Cobb Detroit Tigers. Speculation soon emerged that Carr might take over more than first base — he could have been in line to replace Phillips as manager. With the team now floundering in seventh place, it seemed entirely plausible, but team officials dismissed the rumor in an official statement. Carr smacked a triple and a single in his June 9 debut.

Word came from Fed headquarters that additional major leaguers stood poised to jump. Among them was southpaw pitcher Reb Russell, a White Sox starlet who leaned toward the Hoosiers. Also perched to bolt was Hal Chase, his roving eye now focused on Buffalo. Whether trying to launch, enhance or resurrect baseball careers, more and more players found themselves attracted to the Federal League stage. Carr certainly seemed to enjoy himself; on June 14, he went 4-for-4 and scored four times in an 11–4 triumph over Pittsburgh. Two days later, McKechnie crafted a 3-for-3 outing and Falkenberg struck out ten in a 4–1 triumph. Winners of seven straight, the hard-hitting Hoosiers were turning things around. Hitting over .400, Benny Kauff had emerged as the league's biggest star, and his teammate Campbell was right on his heels

McKechnie sits on the Indianapolis Hoosiers bench during a Federal League game at Chicago's Weeghman Park. He blossomed into a superb all-around player in Indy (SDN-059578, Chicago Daily News negatives collection, Chicago History Museum).

in the batting race. McKechnie hit in the .270 range, scored lots of runs and played airtight defense.

Now nipping at the heels of league-leading Chicago, Indy twice came from behind to sweep a doubleheader against the visiting Brooklyn Tip-Tops. As a crowd of 5,500 went crazy, the home team stretched its winning streak to 11 and took over first place. When the number reached 15, the *Star* paid bizarre homage by framing its game story in "Sambo" broken English, under the pseudonym byline of "Zebediah Crabbit."

> I wuz a coming' in from beddin' down the hosses t'other ev'nin,' down to my home in Brown County, w'en Sister Sophiry, she says to me, sezshe: "Zebbie, I see's how that Injanap'lis team's a-goin' like a house afire."
> "Du tell!" says I.
> "Yep," she says, sezshe, "they'e up an' won fo'rteen straight games."
> ... An I swan, ef it warn't true, ev'ry las' word uv it. So I makes up my min' to take th' fu'st train er the' fu'st tourin' kyar I see an' cum to town to see how they was a doin' it.

The plot takes Zebediah to the site of the 15th win, where a beat writer asks him to cover the game. That's how readers got to see such homespun gems as "Well, th' Packers kept a-tryin's an' Kaiserling he kep' a flingin' and' th' result was that them fellers in th' gray unnyforms didn't do no more scorin' until the eighth innin'."[6]

The streak ended a day later with a 5–3 loss to the fellers in the gray uniforms, also known as the Kansas City Packers. What a great ride it had been; a few weeks earlier Indy looked dead in the water, and now it led the Federal league — barely. Playing some winning ball of their own, the Chicago Whales pulled within a few percentage points of first. Joe Tinker knew a thing or two about conducting pennant races in the Windy City. Around the same time, news came from overseas that Serbians had assassinated an Austro-Hungarian archduke in Austria. The domino effect would lead to world war. Geographically separated and politically neutral, America could still enjoy carefree days at the ballpark for a while longer.

The Whales moved four games ahead of Indy by early July, setting the stage for a pivotal mid-month series in Chicago, where the Hoosiers took the opener, 3–2, on "German Day" at Weeghman Park. Few dared to promote German pride when America entered World War I, but for now, people did it with pride. Prior to the game, a parade moved across the field, complete with band, mounted police and about 1,500 marchers from German clubs. At a flagpole in center field, the band halted and played both "America" and "Der Wacht Am Rhine" while flags from both countries were raised. Needless to say, Old Glory went solo when the nation went to bat against the Kaiser.

The teams split a doubleheader the following day, with Kauff producing five hits, four runs and two homers; when the Hoosiers left town, they trailed the "Chifeds" by three games. The big winning streak became a dim memory as Indianapolis dropped into fourth place, six games out. There was still a lot of season left, though.

On August 18 McKechnie rapped five hits in six at-bats, leading his team to an 8–7 win against the Pittsburgh Rebels. Roush tied the game with a lucky two-run homer in the eighth, circling the bases when his "Texas Leaguer" fly ball bounced over the head of outfielder Davy Jones and rolled to the fence. Finding a niche as super-sub, Roush had become a great pinch-hitter and spot starter. His emergence coincided with Indy's re-emergence into the pennant hunt. Led by an explosive offense, the Hoosiers found themselves back in first place by late August. Down to the wire it went, with the contenders trading places over and over.

Chicago pulled out to a 2½-game cushion with about a week left in the season, but Indianapolis swept Kansas City and came within a half-game. As the schedule ticked down to three games, it all came down to this: Indy had to beat cellar-dwelling St. Louis more than Chicago beat sixth-place Kansas City. Both contenders owned better talent and a home field advantage.

Facing the same pitcher who shut them out on opening day, the Hoosiers pounded 12 hits in a 7–4 win on October 6. Then came wonderful news from the Windy City; the Packers beat Chicago not once, but twice. Gene Packard tossed a five-hit shutout in KC's 1–0 opening victory and the underdogs rapped nine hits during a 5–3 success in game two. With the 1914 campaign nearly complete, Indy was back in first and one win away from clinching.

Boss Phillips went with his ace, Falkenberg, in the next contest, and St. Louis selected Dave Davenport, a so-so rookie with raw talent. The Hoosiers manufactured four runs with help from shoddy defense, and that was more than enough support for Falkenberg, who faced only 30 batters in a dominating shutout. He threw a one-hitter through eight innings, surrendered a couple of harmless singles in the ninth, struck out eight batters and walked one. When catcher Bill Rariden caught a foul fly for the third out, fans swarmed the field in celebration. Indianapolis was champion of the Federal League.

One more game remained on the schedule but with pre-game running and throwing contests, it seemed more like a company picnic. Roush made headlines by winning the bunt-and-run event in so-called "world record" time, going from home to first in a sizzling 3.2 seconds. Campbell won the longer race that day, reportedly equaling Ty Cobb's best time when he circled the bases in 14 seconds, and Earl Mosely took the baseball toss with a throw of 122 yards, two feet, six inches. Preventing a picnic sweep for the home team, a St. Louis catcher grabbed first in the "accurate throwing contest."

Looking back on the season, McKechnie had a lot to smile about. He was the first player to hit a ball over the right field wall in Brooklyn, and among the first invaders to hear cheers from Pittsburgh fans, who remembered his days with the Pirates. More than anything, though, 1914 went down as the year he mastered every phase of the game. If this was truly a major league, then his name could now be mentioned with the game's greatest stars. The good-field, no-hit label died in the wake of a .308 batting average, as he became one of the Feds' best offensive players. He had always been quick, aggressive and clever; he just didn't get on base enough to exploit his talents. Once the batting average clicked, he owned the base paths. If Benny Kauff hadn't been born, McKechnie would've led the league in both runs scored (107) and stolen bases (47).

But Kauff was, indeed, born on January 5 of 1890, a date that would become significant to jewelers, sportswriters and fancy underwear salesmen. As a minor league standout, the former Ohio coal miner had already tasted baseball celebrity and liked it. By the end of the end of the 1914 season, he was a full-fledged superstar. Commonly referred to as the "Ty Cobb of the Federal League," Kauff led the circuit in hitting with a .370 average and also took top honors in runs (120), hits (211), doubles (44) and stolen bases (75). He ate up the accompanying adulation and brought additional attention to himself with flamboyant attire, set off by diamond rings and stickpins. Benny Kauff was a show, but he wasn't the whole show for Indy. Get past him and opposing pitchers still had to face a Hoosier murderers row, with four other starters batting better than .300 and a couple knocking on the door. Pitching was in shorter supply, so Falkenberg may have been the team's most valuable player; he posted a 25–16 record and 2.22 earned run average. Indy finished at 88–65 —1½ games better than Chicago's 87–67 and 4½ better than Baltimore. Rounding out the pecking order were Buffalo, Brooklyn, Kansas City, Pittsburgh and St. Louis.

Players, press, team officials and community leaders all gathered for a celebration banquet at the Washington Hotel. When telegrams of congratulations were read out loud, one stood out from the rest. Addressed to Bill Phillips from American League president Ban Johnson, it read, "I congratulate you upon your great victory and am working diligently to get together a team that can compete with you. I am for you and always have been."[7] The message was a joke and everybody knew it; Ban Johnson had nothing but contempt for the Hoosiers and every other Fed team. Despite that, there was a very serious movement to arrange a series between champions of the Federal and Major leagues. Sometime around mid–September, Fed president James Gilmore mailed a letter of challenge to big league leaders:

> While it may be true in your national agreement we are classified as an
> enemy of organized baseball, the phrase cannot survive the force of time
> and the demands of the sport-loving public.... Before either of the two
> clubs in organized baseball who win pennants ... can claim the world's
> championship, they must in some manner play the winner of the Federal
> League pennant.

At season's end, the champion Hoosiers sent a cockily-toned challenge
but both bow shots were met with stony silence; the majors could not be
baited into a three-tier series for the championship of the world. Without
official sanction, however, the matter was being discussed on a franchise-to-
franchise basis, and Indianapolis newspapers reported that several notable
Philadelphia Athletics were in favor of the proposal. The games would supposedly begin in Indy, then hop to different cities of the Federal League. It
sounded like an absolute cash cow. First, Philly had to beat the NL champion
Boston Braves in the World Series, but that was a foregone conclusion. Surely,
Boston had used up all its divine intervention in an unlikely pennant run.

Mired in last place on July 18, the Braves ended up winning the pennant
by 10½ games. Their amazing turnaround did not inspire postseason confidence
among most baseball folk, however. Ranking third in team ERA and fourth
in team batting average, the Braves seemed a very ordinary NL team, while
the mighty Athletics were defending world champs. Historians know the rest
of the story; in an upset of monumental proportions, the Braves not only won
the World Series but did it in a four-game sweep. Contacted by Fed officials,
team captain Johnny Evers shot down any notion of an Indianapolis-Boston
series. Turning down a check for $17,000, he said, "If you offered me $25,000,
it would make no difference to me. I will not consent to violate the rule of
organized baseball that prohibits a team that has competed in a world's championship series from playing any more that season. We are not permitted to
play, except as individuals."[8]

With those words, baseball came to an end in 1914. Rumor mills still
operated full force, though, and talk spread that John McGraw was trying to
lure three Hoosiers to the Giants—McKechnie, Campbell and Roush. Kauff
supposedly heard offers from the Athletics but planned to honor his three-
year deal with Indy, assuming that there was a team to return to. Some insiders
said the champs were leaving town, and an October newspaper report from
the Federal League conference did nothing but fuel the gossip. It said Indianapolis might be too "small fry" to maintain its franchise. Hoosiers officials
disagreed.

Exciting news arrived in December, when Walter Johnson said goodbye
to the Washington Senators and signed a contract with Joe Tinker's Chicago
Whales. Here was a great player in his prime, on the way to one of the greatest

pitching careers in baseball history. What a coup for the Feds, and it resonated well beyond the Windy City. Hoosiers president Krause boasted, "It is just one more of the bombs we have fixed to toss into the ranks of Organized Ball, and there will be others to follow in the near future.... It surely will be a treat for Indianapolis fans to see such players as these in action at Federal League park next summer. The fans here have long wanted major league ball. At last their hopes have been realized."[9]

Johnson reneged on the deal and remained with Washington. He felt bad about breaking his word but nonetheless bowed to guilt-trip pressure from Senators owner Clark Griffith. Indianapolis fans would not see "The Big Train" in action unless they visited an American League city. They might not live in a Federal League city much longer; hardly a day went by without press speculation about a peace treaty in baseball's costly war. An outright merger seemed unlikely but so did total surrender. Regardless, Indy officials promised their fans that the Hoosiers would return in 1915.

It was a promise soon broken.

5

Garden State Peppers

Do you realize that a decision in this case may tear down the very foundations of this game, so loved by thousands, and do you realize that the decision might also seriously affect both parties?[1]— Judge Kenesaw Mountain Landis

After filing an anti-trust lawsuit against Organized Baseball, the Federal League got a bad draw when the case ended up in the court of federal judge Kenesaw Mountain Landis. A huge fan of the major leagues, he was sympathetic to the men who ran it and considered their monopolistic policies to be necessary evils. Five years later, those men made him the most powerful man in baseball. After attorneys wrapped up arguments in January, the baseball world anxiously awaited his decision — an endless wait, as things turned out. In effect, Landis delivered a pocket-veto.

Back in Indianapolis, winter passed without any official change but everybody knew something bad was brewing. Stockholders sued the cash-strapped Indy franchise, asking that it be placed in receivership, and league officials mulled over strategies to keep it solvent. Under that cloud, the Hoosiers headed south for spring training in Valdosta, Georgia. By the time they returned north, they had a new name and a new home; the champs were moving to Newark, New Jersey. Taking over as owners were P.T. Powers and Oklahoma oil baron Harry Sinclair, the latter becoming famous as part of the Teapot Dome bribery scandal of 1923. By the end of March it was official — the Indianapolis Hoosiers were now the Newark Peppers.

It made good business sense to relocate to a more densely populated area. In addition to the greater Newark region, officials believed they could also draw fans from nearby New York City. The kings of the Federal League were a championship product that, with proper marketing, could reach a huge pool of pastime consumers. Also lending gravitas to the franchise was super-wealthy Sinclair, whose worth was estimated at $10 million. For all his wealth and influence, however, he could not prevent the loss of his team's best player. A pre-existing Hoosier transaction had sent Bennie Kauff to the Brooklyn Tip-Tops, and Sinclair's vociferous objections went for naught.

The Feds added more major league star-power with the defections of Athletics pitchers Eddie Plank and Chief Bender. The longtime veterans weren't getting any younger but they hadn't lost much either; Bender went 17–3 in 1914 while Plank was 15–7. Also switching circuits were a pair of National League hurlers with solid resumes, Hooks Wiltse and Ed Reulbach. Though past their primes, both brought name recognition from 20-win seasons of yesteryear. Some other moderately talented big leaguers made the switch, too, as the Feds continued to upgrade.

The rumor mill churned out one about legendary third baseman Home Run Baker coming to Newark, but insiders believed the owners wouldn't poach a player with a binding big league contract. Besides, why break the bank on a high-mileage model when they had a sleek new car in the garage? As *Sporting Life* put it, "Even if [Home Run] Baker were free Powers does not need him, as he has a most efficient young man named McKechnie at the third corner. He is not only a speedy fielder, but is good at the bat and can bat from either side of the plate."[2]

With training camp winding down toward its final days in early April, boss Phillips told his Hoosiers-turned-Peppers to take Monday off. Most embarked on a fishing trip, traveling in autos furnished by local merchants. Perhaps they talked about that day's big boxing bout in Cuba, where hulking Jess Willard squared off against the great black champion, Jack Johnson. Newspapers would bark the news from coast to coast when Willard won the crown on a 26th-round knockout. In a front-page story, the *New York Times* claimed the fight restored pugilistic supremacy to the white race. Willard believed he won because he lived right, unlike the boozing Johnson. Though quoted with cordial comments immediately afterward, Johnson later insisted that he threw the fight. If so, he did a poor job of it, thumping Willard at will for most of the bout. Some thought Johnson punched himself into exhaustion and the younger, fitter Willard had more energy at the end.

Back in New Jersey, workers scrambled to complete the new baseball field in Harrison, which lay just outside Newark. It was the same last-minute formula the franchise followed in Indianapolis and, once again, it proved fortunate that they opened on the road. Catching an early-morning train on the Atlantic Coast Line, the Peppers left Valdosta on April 8. Well-wishers arrived to see them off and encourage a return the following year; most were merchants or city officials, who connected spring training to dollar signs and civic distinction. It seemed quite an honor to host a genuine poor man's version of a major league baseball team, and the Indianapolis vs. Newark hubbub provided an unexpected bonus. Whether calling them Hoosiers, Peppers or homeless waifs, all newspaper reports made some reference to where those players rode out the storm — good old Valdosta. It was like free advertising for a nation-wide tourism campaign.

Departing the Deep South, the "Peps" traveled to Baltimore, where they took a 7–5 decision in their season debut on April 10. Maryland's governor threw out the first pitch, one of the few that Newark batters didn't tear into. It was a great beginning but team executives must've been grinding their teeth over the news from Brooklyn: Benny Kauff was already a Big Apple hero. In his second trip to the plate, he blasted a three-run homer that propelled the Tip-Tops to a 13–9 victory over Buffalo. The Peppers went on to sweep their three-game series, then headed for their new home. Perched near the mouth of the Passaic River, Newark was about ten miles west of New York City and its huge pool of potential customers.

The area bubbled with history. A few miles east lay the site where Aaron Burr shot Alexander Hamilton in their duel of 1804, and the first organized baseball game was held in nearby Hoboken in 1846. A sickly child named Stephen Crane spent the first eight years of his short life in Newark, long before achieving fame with his 1895 novel *The Red Badge of Courage*, and Thomas Edison produced some of his early inventions in a Newark office. The old genius was still alive in 1915, running a sprawling laboratory just a few miles outside the city.

Newark witnessed lots of baseball through the years but nothing at the major-league level. The Indians won an International League championship two years earlier and seemed strong enough to contend in 1915 but would never dream of calling themselves major league. Excited by the notion of top-flight ball, locals quickly took the Peppers into their hearts. On the night before the opener, 900 boisterous fans attended a welcoming banquet, where they cheered the words of local dignitaries and team officials, and hailed the very sight of Peps players. League president James Gilmore told the crowd, "I wish my friend Ban Johnson were here to take a peek into this room. He would see something to convince him about a thing or two. We are perfectly willing to talk peace with the other fellows but nothing will ever be done which will eliminate the Feds as a major league."[3]

After sitting through five hours of frivolity, Gilmore exited Krueger's Auditorium, wiped a handkerchief across his brow, buttoned his coat tight and exhaled, "Gad! That was the greatest celebration banquet I ever attended. It beats anything I've ever heard of."

Opening day saw thousands line the streets to view a mile-long welcom-ing parade, with eight mounted policemen leading a procession of bigwigs in motorcars. Players from both teams rode along too. Things were less jovial back at the still-unfinished ballpark, where workers fought against the clock. Construction would continue for weeks but vital projects approached completion and officials promised that fans would not be inconvenienced. Most notable on the to-do list was completing the grandstand. Several laborers had worked through the previous night arranging seats, and the task was complete by morning, when a new crew arrived to begin decoration duty.

The Peppers lost to Baltimore in that April 16 debut but were victorious in all other respects. Setting a Federal League record for attendance, 26,032 fans paid admission and thousands of paraders slipped in for free. President Gilmore was there, proclaiming Newark a "big league city in every sense of the word." A couple of weeks later, the city celebrated another season debut, this one for the Newark Indians. Showing no favorites, Mayor Thomas Raymond called for another half-day holiday on April 29 and agreed to throw out the first pitch at Wiedenmayer Park.

Benny Kauff soon drew attention in all the major newspapers, but not the kind he wanted. Deserting his Brookfed team, he joined the New York Giants and appeared in uniform for a game against the Boston Braves, a move that infuriated everybody except John McGraw. The Braves protested, saying Kauff belonged to the Feds and was ineligible for National League contests. The Brooklyn Tip-Tops said Kauff jumped a binding contract with them, and Federal League powerbrokers raged over the audacity of McGraw to poach a Fed player. Kauff, meanwhile, insisted he never signed a binding contract with Brooklyn and was free to play wherever he wanted. It was a tangled web of recrimination.

Maybe the Peppers were lucky to be rid of him. Bill Phillips gently chided the wayward one in the press: "Benny is a good ballplayer but he has been ill-advised and his desire for publicity has got him into trouble. When I lost Kauff I believed that I had lost a good man but after looking over my outfield material I came to the conclusion that it was best for the team that Kauff should go to Brooklyn."[4] The firestorm died down when officials banned Kauff from the National League and sent him back to the Feds. Everyone agreed that the blame rested with Kauff; he'd deceived John McGraw and abandoned binding obligations to the Tip-Tops. The major leagues and Federal League didn't agree on much but both claimed to detest contract jumpers.

Kauff filed a lawsuit against organized baseball, claiming it blocked him from receiving his signing bonus and $1,000 a month salary — the terms for his cancelled Giants agreement. "My contract with the Giants is iron bound and states very clearly that I am to be paid whether or not I am able to play," he said.[5] "They signed this paper with their eyes open and I insist that they live up to the agreement. I cannot be held to account for any bungle the New York Club might have made.... I am not caring for anybody but Kauff and you can bet I am interested in his welfare." His defiant tone soon disappeared when he pleaded for reinstatement into the Federal League. On May 6, the *New York Times* published a conciliatory letter from Kauff, expressing regret for his actions and blaming the situation on bad advice from older men. He returned to the Brookfed dugout a couple days later.

On the day of Kauff's "mea culpa," a story came out of Chicago that the Feds would join the National Agreement as a full-fledged major organization and World Series participant. The next day, a German submarine sank the British ocean liner Lusitania while it traveled off the coast of Ireland. As the death count of Americans climbed, former president Teddy Roosevelt called for an immediate U.S. response while the current chief—Woodrow Wilson—calmly weighed his options.

On the baseball front, Newark was locked in a tight five-team pennant race. Through May 18 the Peps sat in second place, 1½ games behind league-leading Pittsburgh. Few Newark fans doubted that their peerless leader would guide the team back to championship glory for a third straight year. Bill Phillips was portrayed as a father figure and shrewd tactician, who got the most out of his boys. In the *Newark Evening News*, an artist sketched a well-crafted portrait of the manager, dressed in formal wear and a lit corncob pipe hanging from his mouth. "Corncob Bill" was one of his nicknames, though he also carried Perfecto cigars to distribute among friends.

Phillips was a winner, with an incredibly high success rate; since becoming a minor league manager in 1904 he had delivered eight pennants in five cities, with the last two coming back-to-back at Indianapolis. Newark was thrilled to have him. That five-star resume counted for nothing, however, when the Peppers struggled. They did okay in April and May but a June swoon put them a game under .500 in sixth place. They weren't the same team without Kauff, and McKechnie's bat disappeared as well. Loaded with .300 hitters while in Indy, the franchise barely produced two in Jersey. Over the course of a few short months, Phillips' reputation fell from "genius" to "clueless." When the Peps lost their fifth straight game in a 12–2 blowout, that was the last straw; on the morning of Saturday, June 19, P.T. Powers fired Phillips and promoted Bill McKechnie to manager.

It was sad to see a legend turned into a scapegoat, but what an opportunity for the brainy 29-year-old. Later that night, the McKechnies and Roushes celebrated with a five-cent pitcher of beer at a tavern across from their apartment house. The two married couples had become quite close, and good news for one was good news for the other. From the standpoint of winning games, the Newark experience had been disappointing thus far. Off the field, it was an entirely different story; in their first tour as traveling baseball gypsies, small-town newlyweds Edd and Essie Roush treasured their time out east. Ah, to be young, in love and sampling new culture in exotic, big-city surroundings. "That year in Newark was the best in our lives," Essie remembered. "The McKechnies were a big part of that."[6] Meeting for the first time in Newark, the wives became fast friends and stayed close after one husband became boss of the other.

Roush was one of the few former Hoosiers to flourish in a Peppers uniform. Limited to part-time duty a year earlier, the speedy, 22-year-old became a premiere outfielder and a .300 hitter. As manager, McKechnie would lean on him and Vin Campbell, who was tearing up Fed pitching at a .354 clip. But what would he do about that guy at third base with the terrible batting average? Since the guy's name was Bill McKechnie, he probably wouldn't get cut, even if he *was* hitting .217. Under his own self-tutelage, McKechnie improved his batting average 40 points by season's end. Two days after the promotion he led by example, scoring the winning run in a 3–2 win over Pittsburgh. The Peps won four of six under their new manager, then lost a close one to Kansas City. When they returned to action June 25, Ladies Day turned into a Suffrage rally at the ballpark.

Sponsored by the Women's Political Union of New Jersey, the event featured some nationally-renowned speakers who performed before and after the game. Their eloquence and diction stood out among monosyllabic sportsmen. One particular speaker—Mrs. Ella Reeve Bloor—picked out a spot where men had gathered, hopped on a chair and bellowed her beliefs. Nobody left her presence and many more gathered around. According to *Evening News* accounts, the stands were full of "suffragists who want to vote, many other women who don't know whether they want to vote ... quite a number of gentlemen who think women should vote and are not afraid to say so, and a varied collection of fans and fanesses who wanted to see the Suffs in action."[7]

With suffrage banners waving in the wind and promotional balloons bobbing in the stands, Newark beat Kansas City, 6–1. It was a breakthrough of sorts because the Peppers hadn't beaten the league-leading Packers all season, and they usually lost on Ladies Days too. Now perceived as jinx beaters, the suffragettes were welcome to come back whenever they liked.

Around that same time, a Cornell University professor was planning a more radical approach to influencing national policy. At issue was United States involvement in providing funding and munitions to the enemies of Germany in World War I. The scholarly linguist went to Washington, D.C., where he bound together three sticks of dynamite and used a knife to hollow out space on one of the sticks. He filled the hole with a few match heads, then attached an upside-down, corked bottle of sulfuric acid. Placing the makeshift bomb in a Senate reception room on July 2, he calmly departed the Capitol Building and went into the city. Hours later, acid ate through the last pieces of cork and ignited the matches. Fortunately, the room lay empty; Congress was not in session and sightseeing tours were done for the day. Hearing the impressive explosion from afar, the professor immediately boarded a late train for New York City, where he shot filthy-rich financier J.P. Morgan Jr. at his summer home.

The professor called himself Frank Holt, though he was better known to old associates as Eric Muenter, a former teacher of German language at Harvard. He changed his identity and fled Massachusetts after becoming a suspect in the poisoning death of his first wife. Muenter was thought to be a German immigrant, though he never admitted to it. Regardless, he held Morgan responsible for helping finance death and destruction in the Fatherland. The burly millionaire emerged as a heroic figure, running through gunfire to tackle the intruder and disarm him. Muenter was then battered senseless but not by his intended victim — it was the butler, with a lump of coal, on the stairway. Morgan made a complete recovery and Muenter committed suicide in jail. Things sure were exciting in the Big Apple; nothing like that ever happened in Newark.

Still hovering around .500 at the end of June, the Peps got hot in July and won six out of seven. Good news was tempered by bad, however, as word emerged that the franchise might fold soon. After that glorious opening day of packed stands, attendance had dwindled to painfully low levels, especially at weekday games. If the turnout didn't improve drastically, the team wouldn't even last the rest of the season. The city had already lost its American Association team, when the Indians transferred to Harrisburg, Pennsylvania. With a weekend series scheduled for July 10 and 11, locals needed to show their support or risk losing another team. One report said Indianapolis wanted the franchise back.

Newark did not rise to the challenge, as about 1,000 turned out for the Saturday contest and 3,000 on Sunday. Maybe it was because the Peppers weren't really Newark's team. Peps powerbrokers had thought it a good idea to locate in nearby Harrison, which provided easy train access to fans from New York but made local entry difficult. No trolley lines traveled near the park's entrance, and other forms of public transportation seemed inadequate.

When players left on a road trip the following Monday, they couldn't know if they'd ever return. With his team treading water toward the end of July, McKechnie shook up the batting order. He moved himself from sixth to the second slot, dropped Jimmy Esmond from second to third, and pushed Roush from third to the cleanup spot. It worked like a charm, as the Peps put together a five-game winning streak, then took three of four in Chicago and knocked the Whales out of first. Sitting just 3½ games from the top, the Newfeds were suddenly contenders again. Around the same time, Sinclair and

Powers announced the franchise would stay in Newark permanently and they were going to drop ticket prices too. Adding to the love-fest, county officials voted to permit a railway company to lay tracks over the Jackson Street Bridge, making the Harrison ballpark more accessible from all parts of Newark. Things were looking up for the Peppers.

On August 9, 18,000 fans took advantage of the bargain prices for a Sunday doubleheader. Concessionaires followed the bargain theme too, resisting temptation for ballpark gouging and selling liquid refreshments at a reasonable price. Other Fed owners looked at what happened in Newark and realized less was more; price reductions soon spread throughout the league.

Cut-rate prices were a great motivator but not the only reason for making a trip to Harrison's ballpark. Winning ten of 11 games, the Peppers became the hottest team in the circuit, and their next opponent was league-leading Kansas City. Newark won the first game, 3–1, while the second was rained out. Catcher Bill Rariden made the game's critical play during the second inning, picking off a runner at second base with two outs and the bases loaded. Earl Mosley faced few mound challenges after that and finished with a six-hit gem.

The park police chief failed to make a catch in the ninth inning while rain fell on the ten-cent fans in uncovered areas. When one wet youngster made a dash across the field for dryer seats, the cop tried to stop him but proved too slow for the task, all to the delight and derision of the viewing audience. Other than that the home team made every play, as the Peps improved to 54–44 and pulled within 1½ games of first. They swept a doubleheader the following day, knocking Kansas City out of first and creeping within a few percentage points of the lead.

Thus began a crowded sprint to the finish, with four horses going neck and neck. On August 16 Newark pulled off another sweep and moved into a first-place tie with Chicago, capping an amazing turnaround for a team that only recently looked hopeless. Bill McKechnie could've run for mayor of Newark.

Down the stretch went Pittsburgh, Chicago, Kansas City and Newark; then St. Louis joined the cluster, too, making it a fivesome. In an August 22 doubleheader against Pittsburgh, the Peppers won the opener on a Roush home run in the bottom of the tenth inning. Esmond smacked a solo homer in game two, highlighting a victory that put his team in first place ... barely; Kansas City stood second by one percentage point (.563 to .562), while Pittsburgh and Chicago trailed by 1½ games.

As August turned to September, the Chifeds took the top spot and built a little breathing room. Meanwhile, Newark struggled against lower-level teams like Buffalo and Brooklyn. The slump reached its painful peak on September 8, when those Brookfeds wrapped up a five-game sweep with a twin-bill triumph. The day pushed Newark's losing streak to eight games, four of which were shutouts. It knocked the Peps right out of the race. Not coincidentally, their worst struggles came after a shoulder injury knocked McKechnie out of the lineup; he would sit out the last six weeks of the season.

Pittsburgh took over the lead and stretched it to 3½ games before Chicago and St. Louis chipped away. The pennant came down to the season's final game, the second half of a doubleheader between Steel Town and the Windy City. After losing the opener, the Chifeds clinched the title with a win in game two. Nobody played the same number of games, so winning percentage determined the final order. At 86–66, the Whales posted the highest fraction: .565789. In St. Louis, the numbers were 87–67 and .564935, while Pittsburgh registered at 86–67 and .562091. It went down on a short list of baseball's most exciting pennant races of all time. Newark finished in the dreaded "second division," fifth from the top and fourth from the bottom.

Once again, Federal League officials issued a World Series challenge to the majors, and once again it was ignored; ditto for the Chicago Whales and their similar offer. The Feds stayed in the news during the off-season, with Kansas City reporting it was $35,000 in the hole and Buffalo needing to raise $100,000 or risk losing its franchise. Newark had its own financial travails, but officials seemed optimistic about the future, as Powers predicted great things for 1916 and promised to upgrade the talent. He said transportation problems would soon be solved, with new trolley lines bringing fans near the ballpark. Negotiations were ongoing to widen footpaths across the Center Street Bridge, thus alleviating congestion on a pedestrian artery to Harrison.

Executives from both sides of the baseball fence claimed there was no truth to further rumors about a shutdown and settlement with the Federal League. The Peps conducted business as if there would be another season, signing a couple of veterans from the West Coast in November. McKechnie was slated to return as manager, and a report came out that he was trying to sink his Fed hooks into major leaguers Heinie Groh and Ray Chapman. Toward the end of November, the outlaw league announced the purchase of a Manhattan site for its long-awaited New York invasion. Home Run Baker would reportedly be named manager.

It was all a ruse. By threatening to take a bite out of that cash cow named New York City, Gilmore and gang hoped to gain leverage at the bargaining table. Putting on their best poker face, the Feds were bluffing; they'd lost tons of money, two franchises were dead in the water, and the entire circuit teetered on the edge of collapse. Could bravado camouflage frailty? Apparently so.

Reeling from decreased attendance, increased payrolls and diminishing profit, the majors couldn't afford a third year of high-stakes poker. They didn't dare call the raise. Still, big league magnates essentially got what they wanted when the two sides met in late December; the Federal League folded and agreed to drop its antitrust lawsuit, and owners once again held "take it or leave it" power over players at the bargaining table.

Some Fed bosses made out pretty well in the peace settlement. Chifed president Charles Weeghman bought controlling interest in the Chicago Cubs and moved them to his former Fed ballpark, while Phil Ball took over as St. Louis Browns owner. These were significant concessions, opening closed ranks to new blood. The majors also compensated Fed franchise holders with cold hard cash, not to mention the purchase price for selected players. It seemed an equitable deal for just about everybody except the guys holding bats and gloves. For loyalists and defectors alike, salaries were soon slashed back to pre–Fed levels.

6

Back to the Majors

The features of our winning streak have been the batting of [Dave] Robertson and the general work of McKechnie. Bill seems to have found himself at last. He is hitting hard and timely and his fielding is brilliant. — John McGraw[1]

Along with about 200 other former Feds, McKechnie was out of a job. How many would the major leagues take back, if any? For the cream of the crop, those banishment threats were just a lot of hot air; management couldn't wait to put them to work. But what about a sore-armed, .257 hitter like Bill? Did his magnificent 1914 season count for anything, or would teams focus solely on his latest results? Even in a best-case scenario, he certainly couldn't expect to find another manager's job in the bigs.

Exercising a geographic prerogative, John McGraw went shopping at Federal League going-out-of-business sales in the New York area. The grand prize was Benny Kauff, the Brookfed malcontent who led his league in hitting (.342) and stolen bases (55) despite missing time while suspended or AWOL. Various sources list the purchase price at $25,000, $30,000 or $35,000. Fast, strong, skilled and confident, Kauff proved he could do everything on a baseball field. He was a "can't miss" star for a Giants team that desperately needed one after finishing dead last the previous season.

Continuing his talent infusion, McGraw bought catcher Bill Rariden from Newark and reluctantly took Roush too. Germany Schaefer practically twisted the manager's arm to get him to grab the southpaw center fielder. As a former Pepper, Schaefer had insider knowledge and saw enormous potential in young Roush. "He's a better ball player than Kauff," Schaefer told his friend, McGraw. "He's not as colorful as Kauff but he can play rings around him."[2] With three strong outfielders on the roster, there seemed no reason to add another, and few truly believed Roush was better than Kauff. But Schaefer wouldn't shut up and, with nobody else beating a path to Roush's door,

When the Federal League folded, John McGraw stocked his New York Giants with former Feds. He eventually got around to signing McKechnie (Library of Congress, Prints and Photography Division, Bain News Service).

Wearing a New York Giants uniform, McKechnie poses at his defensive position
of choice — third base. The Giants signed him after their starting third baseman
went down with an injury in a preseason exhibition (Library of Congress, Prints
and Photography Division, Bain News Service).

McGraw could get him cheap. So he did. Desperate to upgrade a weak pitching staff, the Giants also grabbed 19-game winner Fred Anderson from the Buffalo Feds.

Nobody wanted McKechnie. He did find a spring training home, thanks to former Feds Phil Ball and Fielder Jones, who were now owner and manager of the St. Louis Browns in the American League. It was a loose association with no official ties between player and franchise, though they surely would've signed McKechnie if he'd set the pre-season circuit on fire. Joining the Browns in Palestine, Texas, he worked to stay sharp and be ready for possible job openings in St. Louis or anywhere else.

The talk of camp was a 23-year-old phenom named George Sisler. He came to the Browns as a promising pitcher in 1915 but it quickly became apparent that he needed to be on the field every day. Over in Boston, Red Sox management hadn't yet figured that out with young Babe Ruth, who went 18–6 the previous season while pitching for a World Series champion. Sisler had that kind of potential but was too good at everything else to stay on the mound. The *St. Louis Post Dispatch* wrote, "He is inherently a ball player, fortified with speed, good hands and the intuitive knack of making the right plays. He is one in a thousand. Ty Cobb is his predecessor."[3]

Though a historically poor team, the Browns generated some rare pre-season optimism. As manager of the St. Louis Terriers, Fielder Jones had turned around a tail-ender franchise and come within an eyelash of delivering a Federal League championship to the city. He took the 1906 Chicago White Sox to a World Series title and finished out of the top three only once in a seven-year managing career. Jones expected to win and he raised eyebrows by publicly stating that the Browns were better than his champions of 1906.

The everyday lineup hadn't changed much from the previous year, but Jones upgraded his pitching rotation by transferring his top Federal Leaguers to the Browns' rotation. Included in that mix was Eddie Plank, the former American League star. Throw in a blossoming Sisler and the team seemed primed to improve on last year's 63–91 record. For the very optimistic, pennant contention was a possibility too.

Listed as a second baseman in box scores, McKechnie hit .247 during the early practice games of spring training but raised his average to .303 by late March. During that same span, Sisler started out at .389 and finished at .361; several teammates hit far better. McKechnie tagged along as the Browns broke camp and returned home, but his future looked grim when half of April passed with no job offers.

A day before their season opener, the New York Giants traveled to New Haven, Connecticut, for an exhibition game with Yale University. Trying to leg out a triple, third baseman Hans Lobert slid into third base and blew out his left knee. His back-ups weren't battle-ready or completely healthy either, so McGraw picked up the final leftover from the Federal League — Bill McKechnie. A month later, the straight-talking skipper reflected on his decision: "I knew Bill was not much of a hitter, but he was always a good fielder and what we needed most was steadiness at third."[4] On day three of the season, McKechnie started at third base for the Giants. With a mind more impressive than his talent, he was soon selected to serve as manager for Sunday exhibition games in New Jersey. (New York did not allow baseball on the Sabbath.)

Despite a terrible 1915 showing, the team had some good players in the fold. Second baseman Larry Doyle came off a tremendous season, leading the National League in hits and doubles; Fred Merkle was decent at first base and pitcher Jeff Tesreau won 19 games. The strong 1916 outfield featured George Burns' knack for run-scoring, Dave Robertson hitting for average and leading the league with 12 home runs, and Kauff imitating Cobb. As predicted, Roush was the odd man out. He rated higher than the world's greatest athlete, however, as Jim Thorpe didn't even make it out of spring training. Winner of the decathlon and pentathlon at the 1912 Olympics, he entered big league baseball a year later, not long after being stripped of his gold medals. At issue was his amateur status and past payment for playing low-level minor league baseball. Nowadays, he openly pursued a major league salary and didn't care who knew. Unimpressed by his spring showing, the Giants sent him to Milwaukee of the American Association.

The Giants' biggest star did not shine so bright any more. After a dozen years as baseball's greatest pitcher, Christy Mathewson went 8–14 in 1915 and it was obvious he didn't have much left. With 369 wins on the career ledger, however, he'd earned the right to keep trying. McGraw would sooner cut his own throat than cut a New York City hero like Matty.

Perhaps the second-biggest star was the stadium they played in — the Polo Grounds. With the park hosting both Giants and Yankees, every major leaguer competed on that odd-shaped field at one time or another. Its outfield dimensions were comically skewed; short fences beckoned power hitters down the lines in left and right, while center field acreage deserved its own zip code. Viewed from overhead, the stadium looked like a giant bathtub. With its imperfections embraced as personality quirks, the Polo Grounds became a national landmark and its reputation had grown since McKechnie played there in 1912. Back then, he worked for the Yankees under Frank Chance and never had to deal with the National League tenants. In 1916 he became property of the fiery McGraw and took little notice of the Yankees.

Over the course of 13 seasons at the Giants helm, McGraw had won five pennants and finished second five times. Next came that 1915 meltdown and a final record of 69–83. It did not seem like an anomaly when New York began the current season with 13 losses in 15 games. The ugly opening started with several close defeats, then deteriorated into a series of blowouts; barely out of the starting gates, the Giants already looked doomed.

Out of nowhere, they took a 180-degree turn and launched a long winning streak, beginning with a 13–5 demolition of old Honus Wagner and the Pittsburgh Pirates. Another win followed, then another. In a 3–2 triumph over Pittsburgh, Mathewson came through with six strong innings. Looking like his old self, he later threw a complete game in St. Louis and pulled out a ninth-inning save at Cincinnati. The streak stretched to double figures and kept going strong; when Mathewson tossed a four-hit shutout at Boston, the number was 17.

A few weeks earlier, the Giants were given up for dead, and now they sat 1½ games out of first place with a 19–13 record —17 straight wins and all of them on the road. As McGraw pointed out, McKechnie played a big role in the historic streak. Not only did he provide a defensive anchor at third base but he hit .319 over those 17 games; his bat proved particularly potent between wins six and 16, when it generated a .432 average. Things sure had brightened since the dark days, when McKechnie went 1-for-20 during a seven-game losing streak and was briefly benched.

The glorious victory string finally ended May 30 in the morning game of a doubleheader at Philadelphia; playing the role of spoilsport was Al Demaree, a Giants castoff who shut down his old mates in a 5–1 triumph. The Giants returned to earth and, by mid–July, were out of the race with a record hovering around .500. Their third baseman was still getting rave reviews, however. *Sporting Life* wrote, "McGraw was on the verge of handing him his release, when McKechnie started to play real ball. Today he is by far the best third baseman in the league and is not only a remarkable fielder, but a great batter who seems to have developed the knack of hitting only when a blow is productive."[5]

His emergence was soon overshadowed by monumental news that shocked the nation's biggest city: Christy Mathewson was going to be traded to Cincinnati, where he would take over as Reds manager. To New Yorkers, it was akin to trading the Statue of Liberty; neither was getting any younger but both were beloved Big Apple icons. It wasn't just that "Matty" won more games than any National League pitcher in history; it was the way he carried himself while doing it. Handsome, smart, kind, charismatic, athletic, hardworking and successful at everything he tried, Mathewson was to Manhattan what Superman became to Metropolis. Only Matty was real.

One *New York Times* sports column read like an obituary: "On his shoulders Manager McGraw rested a great responsibility, and Matty carried it with dignity and honor.... Big Six, as he was affectionately known to every New

Yorker, will be sadly missed at the Polo Grounds. As long as the strong concrete pillars stand at the Brush Stadium, the fond memory of Matty will remain."[6]

Similar sentiments did not emerge about the other two Giants included in the trade — Edd Roush and Bill McKechnie. In return, McGraw would receive player-manager Buck Herzog and outfielder Wade Killefer. Though not yet official, it seemed like a done deal.

The devil was in the details, however, and the two sides reached an impasse over a controversial provision. The Giants wanted an option on Mathewson that allowed them to reclaim him after two years. Reds executives flatly refused; they'd take all of Matty or none of him. On July 20, a *Cincinnati Enquirer* sports cartoonist addressed the trade controversy with a drawing that depicted Mathewson as a flower atop a rocky cliff; the top rock was named "Unfair Terms." On the ground was another flower with Hal Chase's face surrounded by petals. A fan was shown, telling Reds management, "I say, old chap. There's no need to climb way up there for a manager when you've got a daisy like this right in your front yard."

That daisy would go down as one of the most crooked players in baseball history, but his gambling and game-throwing weren't yet common knowledge. Chase joined the Reds after the Federal League collapse, took over first base, and made a good impression with strong hitting and superior defense, rare traits for Cincinnati's bottom-feeder franchise. What's more, Chase had managing experience from 1911 when the Yankees presented their fox with the keys to the henhouse. On July 22, the cartoonist cast Mathewson in an entirely different light; this time he rode a galloping horse toward an unseen battlefront, carrying an upraised sword while leading a Reds charge. The trade was complete. Cincinnati got the return-option thrown out and secured a drawing card for its last-place team, while McGraw upgraded his infield with Herzog, who was a shortstop in Cincinnati but had played third base during a previous two-year stint with the Giants.

A benevolent motivation also existed on New York's end; Mathewson wanted to manage someday and he got an immediate opportunity with the Reds. The trade would go down as one of the greatest in Reds history, not because of Mathewson but because of Roush; allowed to play every day, he soon became a star. McKechnie carved out a niche as a solid back-up at third base, playing behind talented Heinie Groh.

Cincinnati was no New York and the Reds didn't compare to the Giants, but opportunity beckoned at Redland Field, not the Polo Grounds. A bad team typically has more job openings than a good one. It certainly wasn't a bad city, however; Cincinnati had a rich tradition, dating back to its days as a rollicking river town and stopover on the Underground Railroad. By 1916, it was home to a symphony orchestra, art museums and a music hall; a couple of skyscrapers towered downtown and beyond the city limits lay Cincinnati Motor Speedway. There was no Broadway or Waldorf-Astoria Hotel, but locals created their own definition of culture.

With the Ohio River and national canals as commerce routes, Cincinnati seemed destined for greatness during the early decades of the 1800s. Industry exploded, population grew and slaughterhouses became so plentiful that the city was dubbed "Porkopolis," in honor of its reputation for prolific hog processing. River trade shrank when railroads became prime movers and municipal growth slowed; Cincinnati would not become a huge metropolis like Chicago later did. Instead, it became Midwest royalty, small when compared to America's major cities and quite large compared to its neighbors.

When it came to baseball pedigree, nobody topped Cincinnati; the city hosted history's first professional baseball team in 1869. Traveling across America, the "Red Stockings" went 57–0 that year and 67–6–1 the next. Six seasons later, Cincinnati became a charter member of the National League. Admittedly, precious little success followed in the wake of those illustrious beginnings.

The Reds produced one championship over the next four decades, and that came in a watered-down version of major league ball called the American Association. They spent eight seasons as an AA entity, joining it in 1882 after parting ways with the National League in a dispute over ballpark beer sales. Cincy occasionally crafted strong seasons against the big boys: 77–50 in 1896, 92–60 in 1898, 88–65 in 1904, but had no title to show for it. Failure continued into the 20th century and, with a 35–50 record, the team was halfway through its seventh straight losing season when Mathewson, Roush and McKechnie rolled into town.

They went to work for Garry Herrmann, a product of ward politics who climbed to a position of influence in city government. A high-ranking aide to corrupt Republican Party boss George Cox, he got in on the deal to purchase the Reds in 1902 and was named team president. Untarnished by his shady past, Herrmann became a respected, charismatic figure in baseball circles. His lavish parties were legendary and, with his unnatural addiction to sausages and love of cold beer, he appealed to the blue collar men of Cincinnati. He was the perfect host-entertainer-publicist, all rolled into one. Herrmann also wielded great power as swing vote on the three-man National Commission, which ruled baseball before the commissioner's position was invented. The Reds hadn't seen much success under his watch, but fans finally felt a dose of optimism when Herrmann brought a legend to town.

Redland Field fans roared their approval when Mathewson made his managerial debut on Friday, July 21. With a small shift in the winds of fate, they could've been cheering him for the past 16 years; the Reds had Mathewson

in 1900 but traded him to the Giants before he ever pitched a major league
game. In return they got sore-armed legend Amos Rusie, who never pitched
another game in the major leagues. Better late than never, Mathewson finally
wore a Cincinnati uniform, though his pitching days were pretty much
finished. He would take the mound if needed but hoped it wouldn't be necessary; at the ripe old age of 36, history's best NL hurler didn't have much
left in the tank. As a rookie manager, however, he glowed with energy and
planned to lead the Reds for at least three seasons, the length of the contract
he signed earlier that day. Rainy weather diminished the turnout but 2,500
people saw a great game that went to extra innings.

Sixty-four years later, Edd Roush reflected on that day, "We was two
runs behind and there was two on and I got a three-base hit. God dammit,
in the tenth inning we beat 'em. So they thought I was a hell of a ball player
in the league."[7]

A dramatic debut victory for Mathewson, with the new centerfielder
blasting the pivotal blow; what a way to start for the new-look Reds. If only
it were true. The Reds actually lost in the tenth inning but Roush got everything else right; facing Philadelphia's southpaw sensation Eppa Rixey, he
drilled a two-run triple that tied the game at 4–4 in the bottom of the ninth.
Going for the kill, Roush kept running and got thrown out at the plate. The
Phillies scored twice in the top of the 10th and won, 6–4.

Even in defeat, observers noticed a positive difference among Reds players; they showed energy and optimism, rare commodities for non-contenders.
The *Cincinnati Post* said, "Such hustling by a Cincinnati team hasn't been
seen around here for a long, long time. Every player worked as tho he was
satisfied with his boss. And that sort of spirit is bound to show results."[8]

Matty received a royal welcome on July 26 when the Reds opened a
series at the Polo Grounds. So strong was their affection for him that many
home fans switched allegiance and rooted for the Reds. They had plenty to
cheer about, as the visitors took a 4–2 victory over the Giants. McKechnie
got his first start at third base that day and delivered three hits.

Losing on the following day, Cincinnati then made a short trip to Brooklyn's Ebbets Field for the next stop on its eastern swing. Mathewson was the
star of the show there, too, and there seemed no limit to the love for New
York's still-favorite son. Rarely using the word "Reds," Manhattan press typically called them "Matties" or "Matty's Reds." Whatever folks called them,
they still weren't very good. The Reds continued struggling in those early days
of Mathewson's reign, but he never lost the enthusiastic support of Cincinnati;
nobody expected him to rebuild the team overnight. He was laying the foun-
dation for next year by studying his boys and forming relationships with them.
Sometimes he was the teacher and sometimes he was just one of the guys,

joining players for meals and card games, or talking baseball in the evenings. Little did they know that their sainted boss would turn them into criminals.

On August 19, the Reds and Giants broke a New York "blue law" by playing a Sunday game at the Polo Grounds. It was a blatant violation of Section 2145 of the Penal Code. Among the 25,000 spectators who saw the Giants drop a 5–0 decision to the Reds was a police detective, who'd won the plum assignment of witnessing the alleged infraction. A day later, Mathewson and John McGraw were issued summons to appear before a judge in Washington Heights Court.

Baseball executives were not naïve; they knew the law but also felt they had a way to get around it. The first home Sabbath contest in Giants history was scheduled as a "benefit game" for dependents of the Army's 69th Regiment. Highlighted by performances from two brassy bands, a concert preceded the baseball. When game time approached, officials closed the gates and denied admittance to a large crowd outside, a move calculated to put them in accordance with the law. About 2,000 uniformed soldiers settled in for a fun diversion at the ballpark, and several thousand dollars were deposited into the families fund.

It would've seemed downright unpatriotic to prosecute two men who helped make it all possible. One judge still saw enough evidence to issue the summons, but another sided with the managers when they appeared in court. This particular Sunday contest did not distract from, or impinge on, anybody's religious liberty. Magistrate F.X. McQuade wrote, "There is not a scintilla of evidence of any one in the vicinity being disturbed. Instead of McGraw and Mathewson being summoned here to answer a charge of this kind, the public owe to each of them a vote of the highest commendation for lending their services to this patriotic cause. The motion to dismiss by counsel for the defense is granted."[9]

Mathewson took the mound one last time on September 4, going against Three Finger Brown at Wrigley Field in Chicago. It was a contrived matchup of former greats-turned-graybeards, and attendance hit a season high that day. Facing each other for the first time since 1912, they couldn't get anybody out—even each other. When the dust cleared the two teams had combined for 34 hits and 18 runs. Around that same time, the New York Giants launched a winning streak that would reach 26 by the end of the month. It crushed the old major league record of 20, set by Providence in 1884, and made Mathewson very happy for his old teammates. "It is the most remarkable feat in years," he told the New York Times. "McGraw has a great team and I am tickled to hear that he has broken the record."[10]

McGraw still didn't come close to the pennant; seven games out of first, his team finished in fourth place with an 86–66 record. The Reds tied for last with St. Louis, both posting marks of 60–93. Providing Cincy fans at least one speck of pride, Hal Chase won the NL batting crown with a .335. Roush hit .287 as a starter, and McKechnie batted .277 in 37 games.

What could the Reds accomplish with a full season under their new manager? Fans would have to wait awhile to find out, but spring training was only five months away.

7

Getting Better

The Reds are underway. Our boys, led enthusiastically by their able commander, Christy Mathewson, took up their labors for the season of 1917 at the Louisiana State Fair Grounds this morning and continued desperately at work until the bright southern sun was sinking toward the far Texas horizon.—Cincinnati Enquirer[1]

The writers were refining their strokes at spring training, too, and Jack Ryder's "game" approached midseason form. Reporting from Shreveport, Louisiana, he also informed readers about an absentee list that included Edd Roush. It provided little cause for alarm because nobody expected perfect attendance during the early days of training camp. A few days later, alarm bells sounded at ear-splitting decibels when Roush announced he didn't want to play baseball anymore. Still a Hoosier farm boy at heart, he disliked all the traveling and hated living in the big city. After missing most of March, he finally decided to accept his big league destiny.

Ty Cobb asked for permission to train with the Reds in April, and Mathewson welcomed him with open arms; young players could learn much from watching the great one up close. Though he offered no detailed explanation on why he wanted to leave his own team, baseball folks knew all about his fistfight with former Red and current Giant Buck Herzog. It happened while the Giants and Detroit Tigers paired for an exhibition tour of Texas. Cobb won the fight and insulted McGraw, which led some New Yorkers to grumble about retaliation. Rather than look over his shoulder for the rest of that tour, the "Georgia Peach" chose to relocate.

Several old warriors went out on their shields in 1917; it was the last season for Honus Wagner, Johnny Evers, Eddie Plank and Sam Crawford. They'd already lost standing to baseball's current standard-bearers, and a new group of starlets stood poised to become even greater. The latest crop included names like Babe Ruth, Rogers Hornsby and George Sisler. Also ready to break out was Mr. Roush, who would win his first batting title that year. McKechnie's talents were far more modest, and it remained unclear whether he'd see much playing time or even make the roster. He maintained a positive outlook, however. "I've been pushed off two or three ball clubs by fast young fellows who looked better than I did and I have pushed some other folks off ball clubs," McKechnie told reporters. "And I was never sore when I got the hook, nor were the other fellows sore when I beat them out. If any kid player can chase me to the bench, he's welcome and I'll root for him every time he comes to bat."[2]

Baseball entered uncharted territory when the United States entered World War I toward the end of spring training. The dead had been piling up in Europe for years, but those were other people's sons and fathers; now Americans were lining up to die. Never before had the major leagues opened play with the nation at arms, though they came close with the Spanish-American War. The 1898 season was a few games old when that lopsided conflict broke out, and victory arrived before the end of the year. In 1917 the enemy was a hundred times deadlier, and nobody knew how the potential carnage would affect the national pastime.

"In a general way [executives and owners] believe that baseball is facing a fairly prosperous season but expect the receipts and attendance to fall below estimates made before the developments of the past few weeks," said the *Cincinnati Enquirer*. "Precedents ... are few. During the Spanish-American war baseball experienced little if any setback. Last summer the International League clubs in Canada enjoyed marked prosperity, notwithstanding that a large proportion of young Canadians were in or training for the trenches."[3]

Baseball and war proved more than compatible, with ballparks hosting patriotic tributes and fundraising drives. Twenty-five thousand energetic fans poured into Redland Field on opening day, April 11, and many of them waved American flags. Thunderous cheers erupted when a band performed "Yankee Doodle Dandy" and the "Star Spangled Banner" during a pre-game concert, and Army buglers periodically played reveille plus other calls from a station near the Reds bench. Fueled by patriotic fervor and opening day optimism, the crowd excitedly settled in for a game between the Reds and St. Louis Cardinals. Never mind that these were the same two teams that tied for last the previous season.

McKechnie got the honor of starting at third base, with Heinie Groh moving to second. It was the last full game he would play until mid–July. Twirling a complete-game four-hitter, Pete Schneider led Cincinnati to a 3–1 triumph; one of those hits went to 21-year-old Rogers Hornsby. McKechnie started a two-run uprising in the fourth when he singled and scored on a Groh triple, and Chase followed with an RBI single. It was a lonely day in the field for McKechnie, with no balls hit or thrown to him.

In addition to his roles as pitching legend and rookie Reds manager, Christy Mathewson was also a patriot who supported wartime charities. Here, he poses with women of the Red Cross. Matty would later go overseas to serve in World War I (Library of Congress, Prints and Photography Division, Bain News Service).

Roush went hitless that day but caught fire afterward and owned a .429 average by April 22. An ankle injury then sidelined him and the Reds bought Jim Thorpe from the Giants as a replacement. Seeing little major league time during his first three seasons, "Big Jim" played in the American Association in 1916; now he had another opportunity to make it in the big leagues. Greasy Neale moved to center field and Thorpe took over in right. Perhaps they found time to talk football now and then, for both are enshrined in the Pro Football Hall of Fame — Thorpe as a player and Neale as championship-winning coach of the Philadelphia Eagles. Neither has a plaque in Cooperstown.

Starting strong, Thorpe was an adequate fill-in and stayed in the starting lineup after Roush's return. His hitting weaknesses eventually caught up with him, however, and playing time became scarcer. When Mathewson dealt him back to the Giants in August, Thorpe left Cincinnati with a .247 batting average.

Though the Reds didn't make any pennant push during the early months, they were still having a season to remember. Most notable was the May 2 double no-hitter at Chicago, with Cubs pitcher Hippo Vaughn bested by Cincinnati's Fred Toney. Vaughn held Reds batters hitless until the top of the tenth, when Larry Kopf drilled a solid single and eventually scored on a Thorpe dribbler in front of the plate. Toney went the whole ten innings without surrendering a hit.

John McGraw threw a famous punch after an early June game at Redland Field but it didn't strike anybody in a Reds uniform. It landed on the nose of umpire Bill Byron, who had supposedly offended the sensitive one. "I hit Byron because he insulted me," McGraw later explained. "We had some words and he said something about me talking big for a fellow who was run out of Baltimore.... I hit him. That's all there is to it and I don't see any reason for anybody to get excited about it."[4]

July first was supposed to be Honus Wagner Day, with Cincinnati the latest stop on the Dutchman's farewell tour. Toney stole the spotlight, however, pitching both ends of a doubleheader sweep over Pittsburgh. Still, it was a special day for Wagner, who delivered two hits and seemed genuinely touched when Reds fans cheered him upon every plate appearance. And if *he* was feeling emotional, then the scene must've had a powerful effect on his former protégé in the home dugout. McKechnie did not play that day.

Sparked by Toney's double triumph, the Reds won seven of eight in early July. A doubleheader sweep at the Polo Grounds improved their record to 45–39 and pulled them within one game of second place. Cincinnati had become a genuine contender, and its manager earned high praise for turning things around. The *New York Times* cooed,

> For many years it has been generally known that the Reds had a life lease on the second division, but now along comes Big Six who breaks the lease and takes a fine apartment in the first division. It may be due to Matt's soft, soothing words or it may be due to some kind of Hindu magic that he is exercising, but whatever it is, the Giants' former boxman has the Cincinnati team playing the best ball that any N.L. crowd has shown here this year.

In addition to lauding Reds pitching and hitting, the writer said Cincinnati's infield performed "like a troupe of Jap acrobats." High praise, indeed.

The Reds later swept five straight at Brooklyn to move into sole possession of second place; New York sat in first, leading by only one in the win column but with far fewer losses. With bad weather cancelling several games in Manhattan, the Giants had played 14 fewer games than Cincinnati. Stretching their latest winning streak to seven games on July 27, the red-hot Reds looked forward to a 10-game home stretch. Then the bottom fell out: Philadelphia won two, Brooklyn exacted four games of sweep revenge and McGraw's boys took three of four. Throw in the next day's defeat to Boston and it made for 10 losses in 11 games. Now sitting in fourth with a 55–53 record, the Reds' pennant hopes were dead.

The only remaining drama rested in the race for NL batting champion, where Roush led the field. It eventually became a two-horse race between him and Rogers Hornsby. The young Red never blinked and topped the younger Cardinal by 14 points, .341–.327. Heinie Groh had a memorable season, too, hitting .304 while leading the league in hits (182) and doubles (39), and placing second in runs scored (91). He played 154 games at third base; nobody was going to move him from that position. McKechnie took part in 48 games, most of them at second base, and hit .254.

Cincinnati placed fourth at 78–76, 20 games behind pennant-winning New York. Overhauling his infield and bringing in new pitchers, McGraw had transformed his team into a winner again. Coming through with big seasons were the guys who'd once kept Roush on the bench; Dave Robertson belted a league-leading 12 home runs, George Burns hit .302 and led the NL in runs scored, while Benny Kauff somewhat lived up to his Federal League hype by placing fourth among league hitters with a .308 mark.

The Giants went on to lose the World Series to a Chicago White Sox team with most of the same players who later appeared in the Black Sox series of 1919. The Fall Classic wasn't the only postseason baseball series, however; back in those days teams often fought it out for bragging rights in a particular city or state. Cubs battled White Sox in Chicago, Yankees and Giants tangled in New York, Cardinals met Browns in St. Louis.... Every two-franchise territory had somebody pushing for a showdown. In Ohio it was north vs. south, Lake Erie vs. Ohio River, the Cleveland Indians against the Cincinnati Reds. Scribes focused on the centerfielder showdown, with rising star Roush against venerable Tris Speaker, the only man to beat Cobb in a batting race and the gold standard for outfield defense.

Such exhibitions are unthinkable in modern times but they made perfect cents at the time — as in dollars and cents. Nobody got rich in the old days, so anything that generated extra revenue was usually worth the trouble. Cleveland had just completed a strong season, going 88–66 while placing third in the American League. In addition to Speaker, the lineup featured Ray Chapman — the AL's stolen base leader and hardest-hitting shortstop — plus a great one-two pitching punch of Jim Bagby and Stan Coveleski. Though their own record stood ten games worse, the Reds bowed to nobody; they had just completed one of the finest showings in franchise history, placing a sturdy stepping stone for future success. Cincinnati hadn't seen a season this encouraging since 1905.

The encouragement continued when the Reds won four of six games and

were crowned champions of Ohio. Both center fielders lived up to their billing, with Roush hitting .444 over six games and Speaker batting .542. The teams still had one more stop: an October 11 exhibition game for soldiers at Camp Sherman in Chillicothe, Ohio. Recruits gathered on a hill behind home plate, while officers reserved special seating inside roped barriers. A group of Cleveland players greeted the divisional commander with a synchronized marching drill.

The contest came to an abrupt halt in the eighth inning because of an acute supply shortage; in laymen's terms, they ran out of baseballs. A special military-friendly rule encouraged soldiers to keep any foul balls that came their way. Officials brought five dozen balls to the fray but many were thrown into the crowd prior to the first pitch. When Hal Chase fouled off the last three in stock, the game ended with Cleveland leading, 3–1. Now the season was over.

Opposite: Edd Roush quickly became a star after landing in Cincinnati. Along with McKechnie, he was part of the historic trade that sent Christy Mathewson from the Giants to the Reds (Library of Congress, Prints and Photography Division, Bain News Service).

8

Homecomings

I'll drive east to my old home at Factoryville, Pennsylvania, then go wher-ever they send me. I'm not thinking about coming back as a general or with any added decorations: that's just the luck of war opportunities and help from the boys around you. All I'm thinking of is just the chance to do whatever I can and do it to the best of my ability.[1]— Christy Math-ewson

The good news came in March of 1918: McKechnie was going home to the Pittsburgh Pirates, and they didn't pay the Reds $20,000 to have him sit on the bench. He would become a major league starter once again. Things had changed since he had left; business was booming in Steel Town with fac-tories operating around the clock to feed the country's war machine. Mean-while the baseball team had gone bust, losing 103 games in 1917, and some pundits were calling for the head of Barney Dreyfuss. The Pirates went through three managers in the previous season alone, and only one everyday position player (Max Carey) was still around from 1912 when McKechnie last played a home game at Forbes Field. Coincidental or not, the team had recorded only one winning season since then, a far cry from its days as a contender during McKechnie's time there. It lost 103 games in 1917.

There was a hole in the team's heart where Honus Wagner used to be. At the age of 43, he finally retired from the game that prevented an entirely different career path in Pennsylvania coal mines. Manager Fred Clarke was gone, too, replaced by Hugo Bezdek, a man as burly and Bohemian as his name suggested. Wagner, Clarke, Claude Hendrix ... none of those old-time stars wore Pirates uniforms anymore. Tommy Leach did but he was a shadow of his former self and played little; he left the team around the same time as McKechnie and was just now returning too. If the locker room felt hollow to McKechnie, he probably wasn't alone; war produced a similar effect nation-wide. When America entered the fray a year earlier, it was still in parade mode and hadn't yet dirtied its uniforms. By the spring of 1918 doughboys had arrived in force overseas and fought bloody battles along the Western Front. Back home, folks wondered out loud whether baseball should even play its season under such a cloud.

In May, the provost marshal released a "work for fight order," commanding all draft-age men to join the military or work for war-related industry. It would go into effect on July 1. Baseball failed to win exemption, was classified "non-essential" and had to end its season by Labor Day, about a month earlier than usual but a two-month extension on the original work-or-fight date. They could've continued with aging or underage athletes, but Uncle Sam had dibs on everybody else.

Whether drafted or enlisting, a steady stream of ball players went into military service. Some teams were affected more than others, and Chicago served as the prime example of fate's fickleness. Up on the north side, the Cubs took few significant roster hits and won a pennant. Down south, the world champion White Sox imploded after losing most of their best players to the military or industry. Lots of Pirates departed the Forbes Field fold during the season, leaving management scrambling for fill-ins, but few had contributed much in 1918 and most were replaceable. As sole provider for his wife, son and a newborn daughter named Bea, McKechnie was a longshot for conscription. Four of the top five NL hitters never got the call from Uncle Sam, so Roush and Hornsby were free to stage a rematch for the batting crown. Kauff was the only one who traded his bat for a rifle.

All told, about 175 players answered their country's call. Ballparks continued to host patriotic tributes that somewhat validated the gaiety of games during such serious times. Back in Cincinnati, Mathewson donated $10,000 to a Liberty Loan Day event in May. Fresh-faced Yanks bolstered the weary Allies but paid a heavy price along the way; by war's end, more than 100,000 Americans lay dead and another 200,000-plus wounded.

For players and fans alike, baseball provided some escape from the pressures of the times and, despite losing so many men to military service in midstream, both leagues did their best to put on a memorable show. Three teams went down to the wire in the American League pennant race, with Boston barely holding off Cleveland and Washington. Red Sox pitcher Babe Ruth showed his potential as a batter, leading the league in home runs, slugging percentage and, yes, strikeouts. Through May 18 he was first among AL hitters with a batting average of .476.

The Chicago Cubs ran away with the NL championship but there was a nip-and-tuck battle for the batting title, with Brooklyn's Zack Wheat edging Edd Roush, .335-.333. Some Pittsburgh people argued that the crown should've gone to Pirates youngster Billy Southworth, who hit .341, but officials decided that even in a shortened season, 64 games weren't enough to qualify. The left-handed outfielder had 163 fewer at-bats than Wheat. Eight seasons into a Hall of Fame career, Max Carey batted 67 points lower than the surprising Southworth but led the team in runs scored (70) and led the entire league in stolen bases (58).

The Pirates had a decent season, finishing in fourth place with a 65–60 record, but compared to the previous year's debacle, it was a sensational turnaround. Their pitching staff led the way, with three starters recording earned run averages below 2.40 and one more at 2.60. Earl Hamilton went 6–0 with a 0.83 ERA before joining the Navy, and veteran outfielder Casey Stengel owned a .293 batting average when the Navy called him. If Pittsburgh could get those guys back, the future might be bright.

The season was nearly done when Christy Mathewson handed over the Reds' managing reins to Heinie Groh and prepared to do his part overseas. He returned alive but did not return healthy. A captain in the Army's Chemical Warfare Service, he inhaled mustard gas and never managed another game. Around the same time he left Cincinnati, baseball received official permission from the provost marshal to hold a World Series. Without it, Babe Ruth couldn't have extended his Fall Classic record for scoreless innings — 29⅔ — before the Cubs pushed a run across in Game 4. The mark stood for 43 years. More importantly, Ruth's Red Sox seized the opportunity to win their third World Series in four years; 86 years would pass before they won another.

In these uncertain times, major league baseball seemed uncertain too. If the government could end the season early this time, what would it do next year if the war went badly? Bill McKechnie didn't want to find out so he quit baseball and joined the business world. Moving his family to Toronto, Ohio, he went to work in sales for a sewer pipe company.[2] When the war ended in April, McKechnie stuck by his decision.

By late January, reports were circulating about him being hired as player-manager of a Toronto semi-pro team that had games on weekends. The recently retired Honus Wagner agreed to play for him on Sundays. By mid–March it had become official that McKechnie would not return to the Pirates or any other team. Content with his new job, he sat out a season that ended with a World Series that remains the most notorious in history. Roush's star shined even brighter that year; he won his second batting title while leading the Reds to a pennant under new manager Pat Moran. When Mathewson didn't report from Europe in timely fashion, Moran got the job and masterfully merged his pieces into a National League powerhouse.

The rest is well-known history: Cincinnati upset the Chicago White Sox in the World Series and several Sox players took bribes to lose. Gamblers promised much money but delivered little, or perhaps none at all, according to an aged Roush. "I don't think they got anything if you want to know what I think about it. That's what a [White Sox] pitcher said.... A fella told me, 'We was tryin' to win after the first ball game. We didn't get the money so we was tryin' to win it.'"[3] Missing all the excitement by a couple of years, McKechnie had played alongside most of the Cincy players, and it doesn't take an over-active imagination to picture him in that Series, perhaps starting at second base. Henie Groh had a lock on third but second and shortstop were perceived weaknesses in the Reds lineup. What wonderful first-hand stories McKechnie would've had to tell about the scandal Series. Instead, he worked in sales.

It was an eventful sports year, highlighted by Babe Ruth's new home run record of 29; most teams didn't hit that many. Sports pages also trumpeted the achievements of new heavyweight champion Jack Dempsey and the great race horse, Man O' War. Front page news hit harder in 1919, with the nation caught in a whirlwind of historical highlights and lowlights. Congress passed suffrage and prohibition legislation, race riots broke out, labor strikes popped up everywhere, a "Red Scare" saw government crackdown on suspected Communists, and a flu epidemic continued its deadly trek across the globe. Working regular hours on a regular job, McKechnie must've had plenty of time to put his feet up and read all about it.

When the new decade arrived, McKechnie went back where he belonged and rejoined the Pirates. The post-war climate proved financially healthy for major league business, and the occupation of ballplayer seemed stable again. The city's population was now approaching 600,000, with about one-fifth of them foreign-born, and baseball had many supporters among the mass of industrial worker bees. They may have felt subservient to the elite class of wealthy industrialists and financiers, but everybody was equal in the bar, voting booth or ball park. And green grass was a refreshing change of pace, compared to the residue of large-scale manufacturing. Appalled by what he saw while traveling through Pittsburgh and surrounding towns, author H.L. Mencken wrote a scathing critique:

> Here was the very heart of industrial America, the center of its most lucrative and characteristic activity, the boast and pride of the richest and grandest nation ever seen on earth — and here was a scene so dreadfully hideous, so intolerably bleak and forlorn that it reduced the whole aspiration of man to a macabre and depressing joke. Here was wealth beyond computation, almost beyond imagination — and here were human inhabitations so abominable that they would have disgraced a race of alley cats. I am not speaking of mere filth. One expects steel towns to be dirty. What I allude to is the unbroken and agonizing ugliness, the sheer revolting monstrousness, of every house in sight.[4]

The famous social critic should've paid a visit to McKechnie, who rented a charming home in Wilkinsburg. No longer living at the old family commune, he was now head of an abode that included his wife, two small children and a teenaged maid. From there, he commuted to work at cavernous Forbes Field in a pastoral, not monstrous, part of the city.

McKechnie did not return to the same status as in 1918, when starting every game for Pittsburgh; he was a back-up again, seeing limited action under new manager George Gibson, a 12-year Pirates veteran who started at catcher for the 1909 world champions. Occupying McKechnie's old spot at third base was "Possum" Whitted, an average journeyman who'd arrived via mid-season trade the year before.

It was an uneventful season at Pittsburgh, where the Pirates once again finished a few games over .500, in the middle of the National League pack. Serving as a utility infielder, 33-year-old McKechnie saw action in 40 games, half of them at third base. His batting average sank to .218, his lowest since the "134" days in New York. Rookie shortstop Pie Traynor hit even worse, but the 20-year-old played only 17 games and that wasn't much of a sampling. With more seasoning, he might make a decent player.

The World Series scandal broke into the open in September, with a Chicago grand jury hearing testimony. Eddie Cicotte, Shoeless Joe Jackson and Lefty Williams all confessed to taking bribes, while Happy Felsch confirmed his own guilt in a newspaper interview. As the White Sox sat one game out of first place with three games to play, owner Charles Comiskey suspended his seven disgraced players. (The eighth, Chick Gandil, had not returned for the 1920 season.) There was still a glimmer of hope for repeating as AL champion, but those suspensions made it unlikely.

Praising Comiskey's actions as a monumental sacrifice for the integrity of the game, the New York Yankees owners immediately put their entire roster at his disposal. In theory, the Sox could replace Shoeless Joe with Babe Ruth or Cicotte with 26-game winner Carl Mays; or maybe they could just go into battle with an entire lineup of Yankees. Comiskey politely declined, saying league rules forbade any such transaction. The gesture may not have been entirely altruistic; it was the only chance any Yankee had of making the World Series in 1920.

On September 30, Buck Herzog was stabbed after a Chicago Cubs exhibition game in Joliet, Illinois. It happened when a fan accosted him, saying, "You're one of those crooked Chicago ball players. When are you going to confess?" Was Buck Herzog mistaken for White Sox third baseman Buck Weaver? Not necessarily. Though he had no connection to the Black Sox, the former Red and current Cub did stand accused of National League crookedness. Herzog was in the process of thrashing the fan when a knife-wielding ally joined the fray, slashing Buck's left palm and opening minor cuts on his knuckles and calf.[5]

Losing more prestige with every passing day, the national pastime was in trouble. If fans couldn't trust players, they might stop coming to the ballpark. Baseball magnates had one ace up their sleeve, however, and were about to be dealt another. Signing with the New York Yankees during the previous winter, Babe Ruth hit more home runs (54) in 1920 than every major league team but one. That kind of revolutionary star power could take the sport to another level. In November, owners hired Kenesaw Mountain Landis for the new position of baseball commissioner. Ruling with an iron fist, he set out to restore baseball's honor.

The Pirates sent McKechnie back to the minors in 1921, and that was not a good sign for somebody his age; now 34 years old, he had seen his major league stock drop to an all-time low. He landed with the Minneapolis Millers of the American Association, not far from where he played as a much younger man in 1912 and 1913. Back then, he was a St. Paul Saint.

Local media announced in early January that McKechnie, "a third sacker of some fame," had been added to the Millers roster. By the end of the month, there was talk of him returning to Pittsburgh but it never happened, and that was probably for the best because, professionally and personally, he enjoyed a great year in Minneapolis. It all began in Oklahoma City, site of the team's spring training, where he joined a bunch of other guys with the same first name. A Keystone Cops skit broke out during practice one day when four Bills occupied the infield and chased the same pop fly. Each followed the order of his manager, who created mass confusion by yelling for "Bill" to make the catch. The *Minneapolis Tribune* described what happened next: "It was high enough so all of them had a chance to get under it. Bill Rose and Bill James got out of the running first when they tangled in front of the [batter's] box. Bill McKechnie and Bill Conroy, rushing in from opposite corners of the diamond hit head on and the ball landed peacefully on the ground just outside of the tangle of arms and legs."[6]

Similar difficulties existed among the team's "Macs"—McKechnie, McDonald, McLaughlin and Mack Allison. As an outfielder's throw headed toward the unaware McKechnie, someone yelled, "Look out behind you, Mack," and four men ducked. When the Millers left Oklahoma City for an exhibition game in Kansas, McKechnie asked to stay behind so he could sing in a special Easter church service. For at least one day, he had "Bill" and "Mack" all to himself.

Almost everybody agreed that the Millers looked much improved over last year's fourth-place team, and manager Joe Cantillon claimed he had the best ball club in the league. McKechnie was selected captain of that club and would occupy the leadoff position in the batting order. A few days into the season, the Millers had a game cancelled in Milwaukee because a foot of snow lay on the ground. An uncommonly strong blizzard had swept through the area a day earlier, but snow cancellations were not all that uncommon during early spring baseball in the ice belt. Neither were games played in bone-chilling cold.

As the two teams waited for a break in the weather, perhaps McKechnie pondered on what his children were doing back in Pennsylvania. It wouldn't be long, though, before he could bring them to work at Nicollet Park. The *Tribune* wrote, "Bill McKechnie received good news here today. It was that his wife and family would join him Friday in Minneapolis.... All persons having furnished houses to rent are asked to communicate with McKechnie."[7]

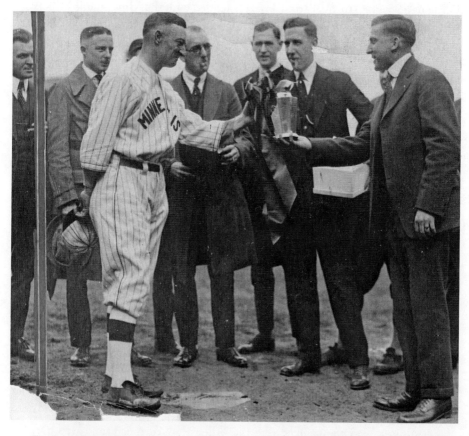

During a home-plate ceremony at Nicollet Park in Minneapolis, a group of well-dressed, former Pittsburgh residents gathered to honor McKechnie. This *Minneapolis Morning Tribune* photograph, published on May 24, 1921, shows him accepting a gift from the Steel Town delegation (courtesy Minneapolis Public Library).

They made him feel right at home in the twin city; on April 23, he was honored in a pre-game ceremony by a group of former Pittsburgh residents.

McKechnie hit well during those early months. Maybe he had struggled against major league pitching but, at this stage of his career, the veteran was more than a match for minor league hurlers. The Millers had another ex–big leaguer tearing the cover off baseballs; his name was Reb Russell and he shared certain traits with the great Babe Ruth. Like Ruth he was a former pitcher of note, winning 22 games for the Chicago White Sox in 1913. Also like Ruth, he could hit the ball a long, long way; an outfielder in Minneapolis, Russell played every day and smacked home runs in bunches. He launched a signature shot during a July 2 home game, sending the ball over the right field wall and through the plate glass window of a shop on Nicollet Avenue. For good measure, McKechnie belted one over the left field scoreboard in the same game. All was right with the world that day, as Minneapolis recorded a 4–1 victory over evil twin, St. Paul.

Time and again, the Millers proved themselves superior to six other AA teams. Problem was, there were seven others, and the seventh made a nest in first place. With McKechnie, Reb Russell and fellow power hitter Rip Wade leading the offense, Minneapolis managed to stay within striking distance of the league-leading Louisville Colonels. On July 28, Russell closed out a 5–4 victory at Toledo (Ohio) by throwing a runner out at the plate; and not just any runner — it was Jim Thorpe, finishing his baseball career in the minors. The win pulled Minneapolis within one game of first. Commissioner Landis grabbed headlines in early August when he hit the eight "Black Sox" with a lifetime ban. His announcement came on the heels of their acquittal by a Chicago jury; a former judge himself, he had no qualms setting that verdict aside and pursuing his own agenda.

Russell's home-run pace picked up as the season progressed. He drilled three in one day during a doubleheader split at Kansas City, and two in one day during a home loss to Toledo. As of August 20 his total stood at 26, two off the league lead. McKechnie came up big at the end of the month, going 3-for-5 and scoring three runs in a 12–8 win against Louisville. Then he stroked a game-tying, two-run single in the eighth inning of the following day's contest. Trailing by seven runs at one point, the Millers won in the tenth inning on an RBI hit by Henri Rondeau. Victim of a questionable strike call on the first pitch, he'd muttered some epithets in French but apparently did not violate the American Association's no-profanity rule. Or if he did, nobody knew. Rondeau smacked the next pitch down the third base line between bag and fielder, culminating an unlikely comeback that pulled the Minnesotans within two games of the league lead.

A longtime Millers outfielder, Rondeau had a resume that included brief and mediocre stints as major league part-timer. The Connecticut native was on the downside of a notable minor league career but still showed flashes of his former self now and then. Minneapolis's explosive offense could get by without major offensive contributions from its aging left fielder. In the same game that Rondeau delivered his game-winner, second baseman Bob Fisher extended his consecutive-game hitting streak to a league-record 36. Also bolstering the attack was 37-year-old outfielder Sherry Magee, a longtime standout of the Philadelphia Phillies.

On September 10, the Millers sat 1½ games out of first and, by midmonth, trailed by two. The race would get no closer, however, as Louisville pulled out to a comfortable lead with a strong stretch run. Two wins over Minneapolis put the margin at 6½ and allowed the Colonels to coast to the finish line, where they ended up 4½ lengths ahead of the Millers.

Completing the season on a positive note, Minneapolis swept a doubleheader at Toledo on the final day. McKechnie went a combined 3-for-8 with four runs and a double, while Jim Thorpe was 4-for-9 with one run, a triple and two stolen bases. Posting a final record of 98–70, Louisville would represent the American Association in the Little World Series against International League champion Baltimore. A whole lot of talent graced the field for that eight-game showdown; Baltimore featured a young Lefty Grove, destined for future greatness as a Philadelphia Athletics pitcher. More famous at the time was his teammate Jack Bentley, another one of those former major league pitchers who became a prolific home run swatter in the minors.

Louisville had a manager (Joe McCarthy) whose future included eight World Series appearances as skipper of the Yankees, and a team captain (Buck Herzog) who had already played in four for the Giants. But the best batter was a big league washout who reached unprecedented heights with the Colonels. A solid hitter during his best years as part-time player and full-time journeyman, Jay Kirke averaged 49 hits over a seven-season stint in the majors. In 1921, he fed his .386 batting average with a league record 282 hits. Granted, the AA season lasted about 12–15 games longer than the big league version, but his numbers still astonished.

The Colonels topped Baltimore, five games to three, prompting Louisville to celebrate for a second time. Not content with mere contention and a runner-up record of 92–73, Millers management promised roster upgrades in 1922. Team president George Belden was determined to overhaul the pitching staff but he probably wouldn't dare tinker with the rock-solid offense, where Bob Fisher hit .351 and Rip Wade compiled a .327 mark with 31 home runs. Best of them all was Reb Russell, who belted 33 homers and hit .368. If it weren't for a certain Kansas City Blues legend, Russell's star would've shone even brighter. But nobody could top American Association superstar Bunny Brief, a jazz-age blaster whose career bore a striking resemblance to that of "Crash Davis" in the movie *Bull Durham*.

Like Kevin Costner's character, Brief washed out of the majors and then earned the somewhat dubious title of minor league home run king. After recording a grand total of five homers in four years and 184 big league games, he smashed well over 300 during a long and decorated minors career that ended in 1928. Brief captured his fifth of eight home run crowns in 1921, belting 42 round-trippers while batting .361. Those weren't even his most impressive stats, he also led the league with 166 runs scored and 191 RBI. In a hitter's league, Brief set the standard.

McKechnie was no Bunny but he had a dazzling final stat line just the same — 140 runs, 212 hits, and a .321 batting average — and his sparkling defense drew just as much praise. A rumor circulated that he would be the shortstop in 1922 but he did not play there, third base or any other position. Stupendous statistics aside, his playing days were over. Minneapolis certainly wanted him back, and he did return the following season, but only briefly and in an entirely different capacity. Now a Pittsburgh Pirates coach, he arrived in early May with hopes of securing a deal for Russell. He left empty-handed but did not give up on the idea.

It was a great day when McKechnie got the call from Pittsburgh. His new career shift brought him home and blazed a path toward his true calling of strategist and leader. What's more, he landed on a pennant contender that went 90–63 the previous season, finishing four games behind the mighty New York Giants. Pirates pitchers led the league in team earned run average. The combined batting average ranked low but three future Hall of Famers dotted the lineup along with two high-average hitters and a catcher who led the NL in putouts, assists and fielding average. Manager George Gibson had a lot of weapons to utilize.

McKechnie played with most of them in 1920 but he saw new faces too. The colorful veteran Rabbit Maranville was shortstop now, one year after a big trade that brought him over from the Boston Braves in exchange for three players and $15,000. To get him, Pittsburgh parted with significant talent, most notably Billy Southworth, who'd cooled off since his breakout season of 1918 but still wielded a solid stick. He batted .280 in 1919 and led the league in triples, then hit .284 the following season. His numbers ranked better than most major leaguers but worse than most major league outfielders. Also sent packing were Fred Nicholson, who hit .360 in 58 games, and Walter Barbare, who produced a .274 mark in a similar small sampling.

Maranville did not come cheap, especially considering that he'd never hit better than .267 during nine years with the Braves. But he'd been a good run producer and provided a strong defensive presence at shortstop. He also projected a championship aura, still glowing after playing a crucial role in the "Miracle Braves" World Series run of 1914. Despite a lowly .246 average, he made the most of his hits that season, leading the team in RBI and stolen bases and placing second in runs scored.

Statistics can never tell the full story of Walter James Vincent Maranville, master of the basket catch and of turning managers into basket cases. The colorful one could be a reporter's dream interview or a boss's nightmare of hyperactive immaturity. But Maranville was a mostly harmless, rascally Rabbit that everybody liked and some even loved. No matter how annoying, there was something innately appealing about a childish jokester, and his antics were usually forgiven in a business where grown men played a boy's game.

Beyond the pranks was a man of tremendous experience and knowhow, attributes that the Pirates hoped could improve the team. They should've won the pennant in 1921 after taking a 7½-game lead into late August, but a monumental collapse followed and the Giants raced past them as if they were standing still. That led to an all–New York World Series, where the Giants topped the Yankees, five games to three. Pirates fans believed it should've been their team dispatching the American Leaguers. Feeling like the pennant rug had been pulled out from under them, many questioned their players' character and manager's leadership. Maranville hit a career-best .294, so he certainly wasn't to blame.

Lost in the recriminations was the memory of talented Pirates playing magnificently for most of the season. The best of them were coming back for another shot in 1922, and they craved vindication. The lineup became even stronger with a personnel change at the hot corner, where Pie Traynor began his long trek to Cooperstown. Seldom used in his first couple of tours on the roster, the 22-year-old was finally handed the keys to third base. With Traynor augmenting an already formidable attack and the return of an elite pitching staff, Pittsburgh seemed ready for another title run. Maybe this time they could finish the job.

The Giants were loaded and loomed as favorites, a common condition during the franchise's dynasty of the early 1920s. With Babe Ruth redefining the game, his Yankees emerged as an elite team, too, making New York the capital of baseball and the Polo Grounds its state house. The American League tenants had overstayed their welcome, however, and were looking for a place of their own. Around the same time the 1922 season opened, they hired a firm to build Yankee Stadium. Before long, the Pirates would look for somebody to rebuild fading pennant hopes. Still cursed by the hangover of 1921, they came out flat and looked entirely mediocre. The disappointing start fueled more recriminations from fans and press, with many revisiting the troubles

Opening in 1909, Forbes Field was a modern marvel of concrete and steel. McKechnie made his major league debut when the Pittsburgh Pirates still played at ancient Exposition Park but spent a vast majority of his hometown career at Forbes (Library of Congress, Prints and Photography Division).

of the previous year. Some said the players turned yellow at crunch time and management was weak on discipline. It all grated on manager Gibson, and by July, he'd had enough. With his team sporting a 32–33 record, he resigned, then slipped quietly out of town. Ownership handed the reins to Bill McKechnie, launching a second career that would dwarf his first.

9

Start of Something Special

Say, I've got a man on my bench who is going to make one of the best managers in baseball. He's not a regular but he has it all up here [pointing to his head]. That's Bill McKechnie. You'll hear of him winning pennants some day.[1]— Barney Dreyfuss

The Pirates owner saw it coming as far back as 1918; he knew Bill McKechnie would someday become a skipper and a great one. The only question was when and where. Thanks to George Gibson's demise, the answer was here and now. Bursting with pride over their fellow townsman's promotion, several hundred Wilkinsburg friends and neighbors organized a parade and walked behind a marching band — all the way to Forbes Field. In a pre-game ceremony, a delegation presented a jeweled watch to the man who had brought so much positive publicity to their hometown. McKechnie was often referred to by the nicknames "Wilkinsburg Bill" or "Wilkinsburg Will."

With a promising season slipping away, there wasn't time to ease into the job. On paper, the Pirates had the look of a contender, and fans expected to see a quick transition from potential to performance. Near the top of McKechnie's to-do list was reining in his team's hell-raisers, most notably the hard-drinking duo of Maranville and Mose Yellow Horse. The latter was a proud Pawnee whose parents were children when the tribe endured forced relocation from Nebraska to Oklahoma. The children became adults in foreign territory, married and raised a son who threw stones at small game to help feed the family.[2] Stones were later replaced by baseballs, and Yellow Horse fed himself with a pitcher's paycheck. Upon joining the major leagues, he quickly bonded with Maranville, a good friend and bad influence; some said those two put George Gibson out of a job. Prior to his first eastern road trip, Bill was called into the owner's office.

"Well, have you figured how to make your players behave?" Dreyfuss asked. "I suppose you realize you have a couple wild Indians on your club — Yellow Horse and that Irish Indian, Maranville."

One of McKechnie's first tasks as Pirates manager was to get control of rascally Rabbit Maranville. The veteran infielder was hugely popular among fans and bartenders (Library of Congress, Prints and Photography Division, Bain News Service).

"Everything is hunky-dory, Mr. Dreyfuss," McKechnie responded. "I'm going to room with that pair."[3]

Before the team's opener at the Polo Grounds, he called players together for a meeting and told them what to expect from their old coach turned new skipper. He would not rule with an iron fist, but he *would* rule and expected as much respect as he gave. He also demanded a reasonable level of discipline. With Prohibition in its second year as law of the land, McKechnie announced his own ban on bootleg liquor and set a midnight curfew. He surely didn't expect 100 percent compliance, but perhaps a new voice of authority could assert more control than the last.

Maranville and Yellow Horse seemed to fall in line at the start of the eastern swing, beating curfew by a mile. Sharing a suite with them at New York's Ansonia Hotel, McKechnie was pleasantly surprised when he returned one night to find the pair snoring in bed. Relief turned to shock, then anger, when he opened a closet door and was nearly toppled by a flock of escaping pigeons. Stirred by McKechnie's startled shout, Maranville rose up and said,

"Hey Bill, don't open that other closet. Those pigeons that got out belong to the chief—mine are in that one over there." From an outside window perch, they'd used popcorn and crumbs to entice the birds indoors, all the way to McKechnie's closet. It became one of those legendary baseball stories, retold for generations. Another version has Rabbit saying, "Don't open the other closet, Bill. The chief's got his pigeons in there and, boy, he'd really be mad if you let 'em out."[4] It hadn't taken long for the pranksters to haze their rookie manager properly.

McKechnie bolstered his lineup by jump-starting negotiations to bring holdout catcher Walter Schmidt back into the fold. Rookie Johnny Gooch had filled in admirably with a .300-plus batting average, but the team missed the all-around game of its longtime backstop. McKechnie also urged the bean counters to spend a few on Reb Russell, his former American Association teammate in Minneapolis. Four years since Russell's last big-league tour as a Chicago White Sox pitcher, he'd reinvented himself as a destroyer of minor league hurlers. Major league mound men would fare little better against his powerful bat.

Could Schmidt and Russell spark an underachieving team? Or more importantly, could McKechnie? The Pirates had been slumping terribly over the past few weeks and little changed in the early stages of the new leader's reign. The *Philadelphia Evening Public Ledger* said,

> The sudden and hectic downward rush of the Pirates is the topic of conversation whenever two smoke-begrimed citizens meet. A month ago today George Gibson had the team up there fighting in second place. Today they are falling so fast that a new concrete bottom will have to be poured to prevent them from falling out of the league.... Bill McKechnie has found already that his new post as manager is anything but a bed of roses. One game has been won since he took the drooping reins from George Gibson's bleeding hands. The team has cracked under the strain.[5]

Not long after that dire depiction hit news stands, the Pirates began playing good baseball. Steadily moving up the standings, they took over second place on September 3. The New York Giants put a stranglehold on first but there was honor in the runner-up position, too, especially considering how far Pittsburgh had come. With Bill McKechnie at the helm, a sinking ship straightened up and sailed right. The Pirates stayed in second place until the final day of the season, when Cincinnati edged ahead and pushed them into a third-place tie with the St. Louis Cardinals. Pittsburgh finished 85–69: 32–33 before McKechnie and 53–36 after.

In a year that saw headlines about Mahatma Gandhi's imprisonment by British authorities and Benito Mussolini taking power in Italy, Pittsburgh sports pages focused on the fall and rise of Wilkinsburg Will's Pirates. Their

Mose Yellow Horse was a Pawnee Indian who left the reservation to become a major league pitcher. He bonded with Rabbit Maranville, a good friend and bad influence (Library of Congress, Prints and Photography Division, Bain News Service).

.308 team batting average not only led the National League but also set a club record. Big numbers came from small names: Carson Bigbee hit .350, Cotton Tierney .345 and Johnny Gooch .329. Reb Russell showed he was much more than a minor league mauler, batting a team-high .368 in 60 games. Just imagine what he and the Pirates could do with a full season under McKechnie.

But did the power brokers want Bill back? He must've had his doubts in September when a report circulated that the team's veteran catcher was in line to take over. McKechnie had been instrumental in breaking the holdout deadlock that had kept Walter Schmidt off the roster; now a story made the rounds that Schmidt wrote a letter to a friend, claiming he would become manager next year. Wasting little time in squashing that erroneous rumor, Barney Dreyfuss signed McKechnie for the following season before the current one was complete. He liked how his players had responded to new leadership and absolutely loved that McKechnie had more wins than losses against the mighty New York Giants. John McGraw's boys took the pennant by seven games and swept the Yankees in the World Series, but they did not get the best of Mr. McKechnie.

Optimism ran high in 1923, with Pirates fans expecting bigger and better things. McKechnie's wife was expecting, too, and, unlike the team, she delivered. On May 12, Beryl McKechnie gave birth to another son and named him James. He would become an entertainer, socialite and something of a play-boy — the antithesis of his father. Bill Jr. was a lot like his dad, but Bill Sr. could never quite figure out son number two. The mystery did not yet exist in 1923, however, as infant Jim provided little distraction beyond diaper rash and late-night feedings. The loudest crying came from disappointed fans, who watched their Pirates finish the same as they had in 1922 — third place, behind the Reds and well behind the Giants. There were signs of better days ahead, however. Young Pie Traynor emerged as a star, hitting .338 and eclipsing the 100-mark in both runs and RBI; Max Carey won his second straight stolen base title, and future Hall of Famer Kiki Cuyler got an 11-game introduction to the Pittsburgh outfield.

More promising greenhorns arrived the following season, further bolstering a team that seemed ready to make a serious pennant run. Though ace pitcher Johnny Morrison had an off-year, dropping from 25–13 to 11–16, Pittsburgh welcomed two talented rookie hurlers who made up the difference and then some. Bursting onto the major league scene with a 16–3 win-loss record, southpaw Emil Yde led the league in winning percentage (.842) and tied for first in shutouts (four). Meanwhile, right-hander Ray Kremer went 18–10, led the NL in appearances and joined several other finalists in that tie for most shutouts. McKechnie had a personal investment in Kremer's signing and success; unable to secure the services of a couple of can't-miss infielders while scouting in California in late 1923, he didn't want to disappoint Dreyfuss by coming home empty-handed so he recommended Kremer, a longtime minor league hurler who had flown under the major league radar. Along with 20-game winner Wilbur Cooper, the two newcomers led Pittsburgh's staff to the league's second-best earned run average.

The pitchers prospered from an improved defense, with rangy rookie Glenn Wright excelling at shortstop and Rabbit Maranville moving to second base. The prodigy and the proven became a great infield combo and, with speedy Max Carey in center field, Pittsburgh was tough up the middle. Cuyler exploded from his cocoon, hitting a sizzling .354 in his first full campaign on a major league roster. Pittsburgh's outfield was well-stocked with solid veterans but, by June, McKechnie had to admit the gifted youngster deserved a regular spot in the starting lineup. Though some came close, no other Pirate broke .300 and the team batting average ranked in the middle of the NL; they scored more runs than most, however, and that probably had something to do with leading the league in stolen bases.

New York's National Leaguers had shown small chinks in the armor when losing the previous year's World Series to the Yankees, but still basked in prestige brought by three straight pennants. In 1924, they would pair the league's best offense with a deep, though unintimidating, pitching rotation. Still, the gap was narrowing between Giants and not–Giants: Chicago made an early run at the top before losing Grover Cleveland Alexander to injury, but the Pirates and Brooklyn Dodgers stayed in the hunt until the end. Coming off a sixth-place finish in 1923, Brooklyn was a surprise contender, and much of the credit went to the best one-two pitching punch in baseball: Dazzy Vance and Burleigh Grimes.

After a mediocre start to the season, Pittsburgh eventually found its groove and nipped at the Giants' heels through late summer. Next, Brooklyn joined the race, thanks to a 15-game winning streak. The Pirates' charge died in late September, courtesy of a three-game sweep by McGraw's boys at the Polo Grounds. When the dust settled at season's end, New York emerged with a fourth straight flag; its 93–60 record was a game-and-a-half better than Brooklyn's and three above Pittsburgh's. Once again, the Pirates were third, but at least it was a close third. The Giants would lose the World Series to baseball's latest miracle team — the Washington Senators. A charter member of the American League, the franchise was best known for perpetual non-contention and wasting the remarkable talent of Walter Johnson. Through 17 seasons, 350 victories and 3,000 strikeouts, the flame-throwing Kansan never even got a whiff of the postseason. Then came the unexpected in 1924, when the Senators put it all together and took the pennant by two games over the mighty Yankees.

Babe Ruth continued his assault on the lively ball that year, posting typical power numbers but also winning his only batting title with a .378 average. For the first time in four years, he would not make the World Series his personal playground. And for the first time ever, Walter Johnson had his moment in the ultimate spotlight. Whatever disappointment the country felt over The Bambino's absence was offset by universal goodwill toward the venerated pitcher. His best days lay behind him but the old lion still had claws and he was as good as anybody in 1924; putting together his finest season in five years, Johnson led the league in victories (23), winning percentage (.767), earned run average (2.72), shutouts (six) and strikeouts (158).

Squashing the notion that they were a one-man team, the Senators won the Series without much help from their superstar. Johnson lost both his starts, then returned as a reliever in Game 7 and tossed five shutout innings. Washington won in the bottom of the 12th when a routine grounder hit a pebble and bounced over the Giants' third baseman for an RBI single. It seemed like divine intervention, aimed directly at Sir Walter.

Barney Dreyfuss probably saw it as poetic justice for the Giants. He believed a recent scandal made the New Yorkers unfit and unfair representatives of the National League in the Fall Classic. A coach and player stood accused of bribing a Philadelphia Phillie to take a dive. American League President Ban Johnson said Brooklyn should replace New York in the Series, and Dreyfuss suggested they cancel the whole thing. Pittsburgh's placement could've been affected if somebody were trying to lose that late September series between the Phillies and Giants. Plus, Dreyfuss heard stories that somebody offered bonuses to opponents who went all-out against the Pirates.

The Pittsburgh owner was becoming a real buzz killer at World Series time, and Commissioner Landis didn't like it. He'd taken decisive action by blacklisting the suspected crooks, but Dreyfuss wouldn't let it die. Supposedly armed with additional evidence about the scandal, he traveled to Washington, D.C., before the Series and sought an audience with Landis. The judge refused to meet him but was later cornered by the persistent one at a hotel elevator or corridor, depending on who told the story. Bill McKechnie accompanied his owner there and played a significant role in the confrontation that followed.

"When will you be in? I came all the way from Pittsburgh to talk to you," Dreyfuss asked.

"I will *not* be in," answered Landis.

Angered by the commissioner's dismissive attitude, McKechnie shouted, "Why won't you be in?"

Landis became angry himself and went nose to nose with his questioner. "Who are you? I have nothing to do with you!" As he walked away, McKechnie called him a "front runner."[6] A year later, the commissioner would not be able to avoid the Pittsburgh brain trust.

That 1924 title looked less like an upset when Washington repeated as American League champs in 1925. This time, the Senators took their pennant with room to spare, pulling away in late summer and finishing 8½ games better than second-place Philadelphia. Babe Ruth fell off his perch and the Yankees tumbled with him, all the way to seventh place and a 69–85 record. His excesses finally catching up to him, the Bambino's body rebelled at a steady, sleepless diet of booze, broads, beef, bratwursts and big cigars. Thus was born the spring training "bellyache heard 'round the world," with stomach surgery the reported treatment for an intestinal blockage. Others have speculated that he contracted venereal disease or alcohol poisoning. Whatever the cause, Ruth missed the first couple of months of the season and wasn't himself after returning. Accustomed to magnificence from the great one, Baseball America felt robbed. Of course, New York disillusionment ran high but at least the city could still lean on its defending National League champs. With the emergence of budding star Bill Terry, the Giants looked even better in 1925.

Dreyfuss did not stand pat in Pittsburgh. Looking to push his Pirates over the top, he made an unpopular, preseason trade that sent away everybody's favorite scamp, Rabbit Maranville. Also departing for the Chicago Cubs were fun-loving first baseman Charley Grimm and southpaw pitcher Wilber Cooper, who'd won 20 games in four of his last five seasons. In return, Pittsburgh got 15-game winner Vic Aldridge — a solid hurler but an apparent downgrade from Cooper — and second baseman George Grantham, who had hit 50 points higher than Maranville but struggled on defense. The Cubs also threw in prospect Al Niehaus, a good minor league first baseman who hadn't carried his success to the majors and never would.

Pirates fans blasted the deal. Not only did Dreyfuss trade away two popular players and a successful pitcher, but he asked for little in return. The boss man knew what he was doing, though; this team needed less personality and more discipline. "I got rid of my banjo players," he told sportswriter Fred Lieb.[7] The thoroughly professional Cooper did not fit into that category and was considered a casualty of war. The opening battles went to John McGraw, as his Giants spent most of spring and very early summer in first place. Never far back, the Pirates made their move in late June, taking over first and keeping it for most of July. If the recent past was any indicator, New York would probably sprint past them soon and hold its lead to the finish line.

But these weren't the same old bridesmaid Pirates; their offense put up numbers that eclipsed anything the Giants ever did. From top to bottom, everything clicked for a lineup with no weaknesses. If young second baseman

Eddie Moore had hit two points higher, the entire starting eight would've belonged to the .300 club. Kiki Cuyler, Max Carey, Pie Traynor and Clyde Barnhart were all magnificent. So was 24-year-old shortstop Glenn Wright, who led the team in RBI. Maybe there was something in the Forbes Field water because even old Stuffy McInnis — a waiver wire castoff — hit .368 in 59 games.

Grantham's first year in Pittsburgh proved a memorable one as he pitched in with a career-high .326 average. Still, the trade was more about subtraction than addition, and everybody got straight A's after the class clowns were expelled. No longer hindered by adolescence interruptus, principal McKechnie got the most out of his boys. Over the course of the summer, they went from contenders to leaders to dominators, and won the pennant by 8½ games over New York. Posting a final record of 95–58, Pittsburgh led the league in every major statistical category except home runs. It was a season for the ages.

History better remembers 1925 for the Scopes "Monkey Trial," the publication of Adolf Hitler's *Mein Kampf,* and F. Scott Fitzgerald's *The Great Gatsby.* Approaching Ruthian levels of stardom, Red Grange dominated college football as a University of Illinois running back, and Big Bill Tilden ruled tennis. In baseball, Yankees shortstop Everett Scott ended his record string of consecutive games played and Lou Gehrig began his. Rogers Hornsby hit .403, won the Triple Crown and spent most of the season as St. Louis Cardinals manager. There was also a World Series worth remembering.

Not so long ago, it seemed Walter Johnson would conclude his remarkable career without a single post-season appearance. Now the "Big Train" was gearing up for his second consecutive Fall Classic and, a month away from his 38th birthday, still had enough zip on the old fastball to carve out a 20–7 record against AL opponents. Johnson finished one win off the league lead, placed second in strikeouts and third in earned run average. Several elder statesmen sparked Washington's charge to the top, and they would remain in the spotlight during an age-versus-youth showdown against the Pirates.

A winter trade brought in 36-year-old pitcher Stan Coveleski, a longtime Cleveland star who was coming off the first bad season of his ten-year career. Costing only a couple of washout players in return, it was the deal of the century for Washington; Coveleski went 20–5 and led the league in ERA. The Senators' best batting average (.350) belonged to their oldest starter — 35-year-old outfielder Sam Rice — and the league's Most Valuable Player — shortstop Roger Peckinpaugh — clocked in at 34. The Pirates had a graybeard here and there but, for the most part, were driven by the explosive young talent of men such as Cuyler, Traynor and Wright.

McKechnie owned the experience edge over his counterpart in the Senators dugout. Ironically, all those grizzled veterans were led by 28-year-old

Bucky Harris, in his second year as player-manager. Like McKechnie, he won recognition as managerial material from an early age. Both grew up in Pennsylvania coal country, too, though only Harris worked the mines. Baseball became their escape and now they sat atop it. For the "boy manager," it was a dream-come-true that he never saw coming. Two years earlier, he'd completed his fourth season as a so-so second baseman on a poor team. The Senators had gone through four managers in four years, so it came as no surprise when a fifth became necessary. Eddie Collins' name emerged as a likely replacement, but the great White Sox infielder stayed put at Comiskey Park and soon got a chance to manage there. He had no previous experience but owned a wealth of player's know-how, gleaned from 16 seasons and six World Series.

Harris had barely been around the block, so he blinked in disbelief after opening a special delivery letter from team president Clark Griffith.[8] The job was his if he wanted it. When the curtain rose on the 1924 season, Harris became boss of a major league baseball team and began issuing orders to his players, most of whom were older than him. If there were reservations about him, they evaporated with success. Experience seemed overrated when a stripling could take a perennial loser and turn it into a champion overnight. The kid had an innate understanding of the game.

Ownership rewarded him with a fat, three-year contract that made him one of the highest-paid men in baseball. It was good to be Bucky Harris in 1925. His legend grew even bigger when the Senators made it two straight pennants. This wasn't like winning in New York, Chicago, Boston or Philadelphia, where fan memories were imprinted by past glory. This was Washington, D.C.—first in war, first in peace and last in the American League. Harris took the team places it had never been, or even come close to. He could've run for mayor of the city and might've even got D.C.'s electoral votes in the presidential election.

Farther west, McKechnie had his own army of admirers, and some arranged a testimonial banquet in his hometown. The support, however, was not unanimous at Forbes Field. "Through the curious twist of human nature which rules that men cannot become well liked by many, without becoming an enemy to others, he has been forced to run his team under a stream of constant heckling," complained the *Wilkinsburg Progress*. "His ill-wishers were for the most part made up of those who could not see that a quiet determined air would carry one further than an openly aggressive mein."[9] Pittsburgh fans could be tough on managers and players; even beloved Honus Wagner heard the occasional catcall during his storied career. It was one big love-fest on September 23, however, when the Pirates clinched the pennant and supporters swarmed the field in celebration. A happy clubhouse saw McKechnie surrounded by giddy players, who praised their manager, then danced about and hugged each other. The wildness continued until National League president John Heydler arrived to offer formal congratulations. He also complimented the men on the sportsmanship they displayed throughout the season, on and off the field: "There never was a team that showed such fine deportment at all times. Now I want you to go out and win the world's series."[10]

Standing in the middle of that joyous scene was Fred Clarke, the living Pirates legend who'd amassed 2,675 hits and 1,602 victories during his long tenure as player-manager. He was there in 1903 when Boston upset Pittsburgh in the first World Series, and in 1909 when his team won the Series from Detroit. The following year, he put a young McKechnie on his roster. Now nine years into retirement, he answered Dreyfuss' call to return to the bench in 1925. It was a mid-season acquisition, designed to put fire into a squad struggling to keep pace with the Giants.

Clarke certainly didn't need the money; his financial profile put him in the same class with owners, not employees. Over time, he'd built a lucrative portfolio that included holdings in land, oil and patented baseball products. It all started, however, with a talent for leadership in the national pastime. The boss loved McKechnie's brain but wondered about his ability to inspire players. Could a calm, cool-headed tactician push his team to the very top? Dreyfuss had his doubts. He knew Clarke as a master motivator who encouraged toughness, instilled confidence with optimistic words and shot harsh comments towards those who made mental errors. Clarke was fire, McKechnie was ice, and Dreyfuss wanted both. So "fire" took a hard-to-define executive position that encompassed roles of vice-president, assistant manager and personal assistant to the owner.

The team prospered under two masters, and Clarke got as much credit as the official manager, if not more. Like McKechnie, he heard congratulations from president Heydler and praise from Pirates players during the pennant celebration. It wasn't like sharing the spotlight with a well-known coach; as a front-office suit and on-field officer, Clarke outranked McKechnie. Everybody seemed satisfied in the fall of 1925, but a rift was bound to develop.

10

The 1925 World Series

Unless all signs fail, it will be as close a struggle as was the sensational championship series last fall, with Washington's great defensive club, led by Bucky Harris and Walter Johnson, pitting its experience and steadiness against the youthfully inspired and brilliant attack of Billy McKechnie's Pirate crew. — Washington Post[1]

Most of the baseball world expected a second straight World Series title for the Washington Senators, but few thought they outclassed their opponent. The two teams seemed evenly matched for the most part. Pittsburgh had no Walter Johnsons on its pitching staff and that, more than anything, tipped public opinion toward the defending champs. It mattered little that the Pirates did have an older and more successful postseason hurler; Babe Adams won three games in the 1909 Series but the 43-year-old wasn't the pitcher he used to be. McKechnie felt no fear of the Senators legend or his 397 career victories. "The Giants slapped Johnson last fall, and there's no reason why we can't hit him," he told his players. "All we have to do is play our game and we'll win."[2]

Pittsburgh certainly seemed to believe in its team, and so did faithful fans from outlying areas; ticket requests poured in from western Pennsylvania, West Virginia and eastern Ohio. Demand far exceeded supply so team officials had to return thousands of dollars. A day before the opener, die-hard fans began arriving to stand in ticket lines at Forbes Field. They remained through the night and into the morning, protecting their spots outside the gates to the bleacher sections.

Most customers did not resort to such extremes, and a good night's sleep was possible for those lucky enough to secure advance spots in reserved seating. Some of the earliest arrivals were famous gate-crashers, known for sneaking into various venues and then announcing it to the world, via the press box. Among the ticket-less publicity hounds were One-Eyed Connelly and Pitts Blackman, intruders of note and renown.

Cash customers started filing in before noon, when the main gates

When the 1925 World Series shifted to Washington, D.C., President Calvin Coolidge arrived to throw out the first pitch. McKechnie is shown at the left and Washington Senators manager Bucky Harris stands to the right while Commissioner Kenesaw Landis peers over his shoulder (Library of Congress, Prints and Photography Division).

opened, and it wasn't long until the open seating areas were packed. The reserved sections saw many early arrivals as well; they were too excited to wait. Besides, these events always featured some kind of pre-game entertainment. Brass bands belted out snappy turns from an early hour and a couple of baseball comedians kept folks laughing with their slapstick show. Nick Altrock and Al Schacht were former major league pitchers who built second careers as pantomime clowns of the ball diamond. Easily accessible today on Youtube, there's a video clip of them performing at the 1925 series, with both sitting in a straight line and pretending to row a boat.

The stadium continued to fill until every seat was occupied by an eager face and open spaces were occupied by armies of standing-room customers. When the final numbers were tallied, officials released an attendance figure of 41,723. About 20,000 more milled around outside the stadium, unable to gain admittance but still wanting to stay close. It was a cool, crisp afternoon with clear, sunny skies, a great day for a World Series. Men showed up in formal dress, wearing coats, ties and warm overcoats. And the women? Good luck finding one in the old pictures or archival film footage.

As game time approached, some notable stragglers rushed in. The *Washington Post* described the scene as "a few moments before the game, when dignitaries of the State and nation pushed and shoved with the rest of the seat holders to get into the park in time for the throwing of the first ball." Delivering that ceremonial opening pitch was Pennsylvania governor Gifford Pinchot. In other pre-game fun, McKechnie accepted a floral gift, Kiki Cuyler admirers presented a golden bat and baseball to their hero, and the crowd went crazy when 1909 World Series opponents Honus Wagner and Ty Cobb took their bows at home plate. Baseball was big on ceremony.

When game time finally arrived, near-sighted Lee Meadows took the mound for Pittsburgh. One of the few major leaguers ever to wear glasses, he also wore the obligatory sobriquet of "Specs." With Walter Johnson starting for Washington, it was a nickname mismatch of epic proportions — "Big Train" versus "Specs." History says the mismatch extended to their right arms, too, as one finished his career with over 400 wins and the other with under 200. But McKechnie liked his chances at this stage of their careers. Finishing the regular season at 19–10, Meadows was the Pirates' ace and one of the National League's best hurlers. The bespectacled look did not inspire fear in opponents but, at six feet tall and 190 pounds, he projected a strong physical presence and threw very hard. Johnson was slightly bigger and considerably older.

The tale of the statistical tape gave Johnson a small edge in wins and shutouts, and a fairly big advantage in earned run average. Meadows got the nod in complete games and innings pitched, and surrendered fewer walks. Of course, Senators fans believed their guy was clearly better and they probably had a point, but the better regular-season man doesn't always prevail in October. Did age and fatigue catch up with Johnson in the previous year's World Series, when he twice got outpitched? McKechnie believed his hard-hitting boys could certainly beat that guy.

After Meadows held Washington scoreless in the top of the first, the Pirates quickly discovered they would face Johnson at his best. With the old fastball cutting through the strike zone like a lightning flash, he struck out the first two Pittsburgh batters. This was the Big Train, not the Rusty Choo-Choo of 1924. Dominating from start to finish, he held an explosive offense to five hits and struck out ten batters while leading the visitors to a 4–1 victory. Pittsburgh's lone score came on a Traynor home run in the bottom of the fifth. By then, the Senators already had three runs on the board, more than enough when Johnson was in peak form.

Washington broke on top in the second inning, thanks to a solo homer from an unlikely hero named Joe Harris. His rags-to-riches story was sliding back toward rags before he found redemption at the Fall Classic. After an impressive rookie season as first baseman for Cleveland in 1917, Harris was drafted into the Army during World War I and suffered serious injuries in a truck crash. He recovered well enough to return to big-league baseball in 1919 but was banned the following year for playing on an industrial team in an outlaw league. Harris applied for reinstatement, and Commissioner Landis showed mercy on him, a miracle in itself. He landed with the Boston Red Sox in 1922 and hit well for three seasons, then got traded to the Senators. Platooning at first base and in the outfield, Harris batted .323 — the sixth straight .300 season of a six-year career.

In Washington he became known mostly as a part-timer who hit like a starter but didn't play defense like one. His reputation got a major upgrade during the World Series, and it all started with that Game 1 solo shot. Not long afterward, Max Carey took a shot to the body courtesy of an errant Johnson fastball. Fans gasped in horror as their veteran star collapsed on the ground; only five years earlier, Cleveland shortstop Ray Chapman was killed by a Carl Mays pitch that struck his head, and Johnson threw a lot harder than Mays. Carey quickly popped back to his feet.

Johnson had a reputation as a nice guy who was careful with that dangerous heater; he would never intentionally throw at somebody. So Carey felt particularly unlucky when another pitch hit him later. "I thought in the American League you could stand in the batter's box all season without that big guy ever hitting any one," he said to teammate Stuffy McInnis, a former American Leaguer. "I'm up there four times and he hits me twice. Don't you think he likes me?"[3]

Holding the Senators to six hits through eight innings, Meadows showed he belonged in the spotlight. His downfall came in the fifth when he courted danger, rejected it, then married it. Three singles loaded the bases with no outs, but he bore down and struck out the next two batters. With the home crowd roaring its approval, he reached the edge of escape by firing two strikes past Sam Rice, but then the veteran batter sent a single up the middle that scored two. Now the crowd went silent, knowing a three-run lead was nigh insurmountable when Mr. Johnson had his good stuff.

Many important issues were addressed on the editorial page of the next day's *Washington Post*. Poland faced danger from Russia and Germany, aerial photography seemed a great tool for military strategists, and donations were needed to fund the erection of a memorial to former president Warren Harding. But the lead editorial focused entirely on the World Series, which would undoubtedly be won by the Senators; Game 1 proved it. So much pastime praise poured out on that page that much spilled onto the Pirates:

If the Washingtons were not in existence, the Pirates would stand out as perhaps the most perfectly proportioned team ever hammered together. But the Washington players are more experienced men, who have gone through terrific campaigns in which the mettle of every man has been thoroughly tested and coordinated play developed to the finest point. The team functions as though it were directed by a single brain, operating upon a single hand.[4]

Though a winner had already been declared in the nation's capital, the two teams agreed to play out the Series. Game 2 saw somber pre-game ceremonies in honor of Christy Mathewson, who had died the previous day at Saranac Lake, New York. His long battle with tuberculosis was finally over. The entire baseball world grieved over the loss of the sport's first white knight, though New Yorkers felt it worst. His pitching skill and personal character had long been a source of enormous pride to the Big Apple residents. A year earlier, he had seemed relatively healthy while watching his Giants in the World Series, but he'd never been well since inhaling mustard gas in a World War I training exercise. Most historians say it damaged his lungs and dealt a slow-moving death sentence, while some believe his disease was in the genes and had no connection to that overseas experience.

Wearing black bands around their arms, both teams lined up at home plate and slowly marched to center field, where flags would be brought down to half-mast. John McGraw joined the walk, as did Barney Dreyfuss and Commissioner Landis, and a band played "Nearer My God to Thee." McKechnie, of course, had a personal connection to the departed, having played with him as a Giant and for him as a Red.

The Senators put another old guy on the mound for the second game, this one better known for spitballs than fastballs. Stan Coveleski had better stats than Johnson that year, so Pirates batters faced their second tough challenge in as many days. Yet another product of coal country, "Covey" was born Stanislaus Anthony Kowalewski in Shamokin, Pennsylvania. The youngest of five brothers, he went into the mines at age 12, working 11-hour shifts for $3.75 a week. In his spare time, he liked to tie a can to a tree and throw rocks at it. In time, the rocks became baseballs, the cans home plate, and the child laborer an adult athlete. The national pastime had rescued another one — two, counting his brother Harry, a southpaw hurler who paved the family path to the majors. Both Anglicized their Polish last name a bit, changing Kowalewski to Coveleskie and later dropping the last "e."

Harry spent nine years in the bigs, highlighted by three consecutive 20-win seasons for the Detroit Tigers from 1914 to 1916. Stan crafted the far better career, baffling AL batters with that world-class spitball for ten years. He did most of his damage in Cleveland, winning 20 games four times and posting some of the league's lowest ERAs. Tops on a long list of impressive feats was his dominance of the 1920 World Series, when he went 3–0 with an 0.67 ERA in Cleveland's lopsided triumph over Brooklyn. If he pitched like that in the current Series, Pittsburgh didn't have a chance.

Spitballs had been illegal for five years but some, like Coveleski, were still allowed to throw them. He fell into a small group of old-timers who'd built their careers on saliva and probably couldn't compete without it. A grandfather clause permitted them to continue their wet ways. Opposing Coveleski on this day was Pittsburgh right-hander Vic Aldridge, former school teacher and future state senator of Indiana. Owner of a 15–7 record and team-low 3.63 ERA, he matched Washington's veteran pitch for pitch. One of those pitches landed behind the ear of Senators third baseman Ossie Bluege, who left the game after that sixth-inning mishap and handed the hot-corner reins to a raw rookie. It was a seasoned teammate, however, who made a pivotal fielding mishap at crunch time. With the score tied 1–1 through seven-and-a-half innings, reliable Roger Peckinpaugh fumbled a grounder at shortstop, allowing Eddie Moore to reach first. One out later, Kiki Cuyler blasted a two-run homer.

Aldridge faltered in the ninth, issuing two walks and a single that loaded the bases with no outs. Next up was pinch-hitter Bobby Veach, longtime Detroit Tigers star whose career was winding down. He lifted a sacrifice fly that plated a runner and cut the lead to 3–2. Dutch Ruether batted for Coveleski and went down on strikes for out number two. A pitcher himself, Ruether wielded a strong bat; back in 1919, he had helped his own cause with some timely World Series hits for the Cincinnati Reds. Against Aldridge, he could do nothing. That left it up to Rice, the same guy who'd broken open the previous day's contest. This time, he made a meek third out that ended the contest and tied the Series at one game apiece.

The battle shifted to Washington, D.C., where hard rains caused postponement of the first scheduled contest there. Most agreed that delays were good for the Senators, bad for the Pirates. One Washington player explained the rationale in a syndicated column for the *Post*: "Walter Johnson and Stanley Coveleski both have turned in well-pitched games and are our mainstays in the box," Peckinpaugh wrote. "They have reached the age, however, when they can not be worked too often and the off day may fix it so that if the full seven games are needed, Johnson may come back for a third try."[5]

With low temperatures and high winds, it wasn't exactly baseball weather the following day either, but at least it was dry. A capacity crowd of 36,495 braved the conditions and another hardy group of thousands crowded in front of tall newspaper buildings to watch updates on large, overhead scoreboards. Fans also had a third option — listen to Graham McNamee inventing the art of the baseball radio broadcast. At the Seventh Street entrance to Griffith Stadium, some ticket-holders probably wished they were sitting in front of a radio instead; thousands got caught in a pedestrian traffic jam and missed a chunk of the big game. A few dignitaries found themselves trapped in that crowd, too, though the big boys gained entrance without trouble. President Calvin Coolidge took a seat of honor and posed for a photo with McKechnie and Bucky Harris. Commissioner Landis was visible, too, though he seemed an afterthought. Standing in the presidential box, Coolidge held a baseball aloft, ready to throw out the ceremonial first pitch. McKechnie stood smiling next to the throwing arm of the nation's most powerful man; they must've been proud back in Wilkinsburg — again. Included in the president's entourage were the Secretary of State, Attorney General and, of course, his wife; in the nation's capital, heavy hitters strode both sides of the backstop.

Game 3 would best be remembered for a controversial catch that might've cost the Pirates a victory. It happened in the eighth inning, with Washington nursing a 4–3 lead of a tight game and right fielder Sam Rice sprinting after a long drive by Pittsburgh catcher Earl Smith. Making a leaping effort for the catch, he fell into the temporary bleacher area in right field and emerged with the ball. Umpire Cy Rigler made the out call, a decision that angered Pirates folks, who firmly believed he did not come down with the ball, but plucked it from a patron. Why else would it take him several seconds to return to the field? McKechnie shot out of the dugout to make his point, and a few Pirates accompanied him. The umps remained unmoved and so did Commissioner Landis when McKechnie filed a protest. Both sides agreed that Rice robbed the Pirates of a home run but disagreed on the method. Years later, author Fred Lieb ran into Rice at a golf outing and asked him if he really caught that ball in 1925. "Well, Cy Rigler said I did; you wouldn't want me to make a liar out of him at this late date," he laughed.[6]

The game didn't end with that play; Pittsburgh came back in the ninth and loaded the bases with one out. Clyde Barnhart popped up to the catcher, and Traynor came up with two outs and worked the count to 3–0, one inaccurate pitch away from walking in the tying run. Firpo Marberry threw two strikes under extreme pressure and Traynor swung at the next one, flying out to center. The 4–3 final gave Washington a two-games-to-one Series lead.

A pioneer in the realm of relief pitching, hard-throwing Marberry gave the Senators a unique weapon. He had played a key role in the championship season, then came back to save 15 games in 1925. For the record, his name was Fred, not Firpo; the unwanted nickname compared him to a well-known boxer, Luis Firpo, of Argentina. There was a facial resemblance and both were large men. The pugilist earned eternal fame by knocking Jack Dempsey through the ropes and out of the ring during their heavyweight championship fight of 1923. Dempsey dominated the rest of the fight, recording a second-round knockout at the Polo Grounds. Pittsburgh batters came close but could not do the same to Washington's Firpo.

The bigger story was Senators starter Alex Ferguson, a late-season acquisition who had led the league in losses a year earlier and then bounced between different cities before arriving in Washington. He'd pitched only seven times in his new home but compiled an impressive 5–1 record that convinced manager Harris to go with the hot hand. After playing such a pivotal role in Washington's regular-season success, 18-game winner Dutch Ruether seemed a more logical choice, but the Dutchman was a lefty and Pittsburgh was murder on southpaws. Swinging from the right side, all those future Hall of Fame hitters got good, long looks at balls arriving from the portside. Ferguson rode his screwball-tossing right arm to seven strong innings of work, surrendering six hits and three runs before giving way to Marberry. Harris' gamble paid off and now, with Johnson slated to pitch Game 4, the Senators had a good chance to put a stranglehold on the Series.

McKechnie selected Emil Yde, the young southpaw who'd burst into the majors with a magnificent freshman campaign in 1924. He wasn't nearly that good as a sophomore but still compiled a strong 17–9 record. It looked like a mismatch on paper; Johnson had a far better season, much more experience and was gradually becoming a postseason veteran too. Yde's only possible advantage was a fresh arm that might outlast one that had already been used. As things turned out, the opposite proved true; Yde couldn't make it through the third inning, and Johnson crafted a complete-game, six-hit shutout.

Pittsburgh's best chance came in the second inning, with runners on second and third and two outs. With the pitcher at bat, it wasn't a great opportunity, but things never got that promising again, as Johnson mowed 'em down the rest of the way. Scoring all its runs in the third inning, Washington triumphed, 4–0. Johnson led off that inning with a blast that looked good for a double, but he was thrown out after injuring his leg on the base paths. His legend grew even larger when he kept pitching on a painful peg. Yde endured a different kind of pain, inflicted by Senators bats. After Johnson limped to his dugout, the next two batters reached base on an infield hit and an error, and Goose Goslin drove everybody home with a shot over the left-center wall. A crowd of nearly 39,000 roared its approval, then roared again as Joe Harris made it back-to-back homers.

When Yde walked the next batter, McKechnie had finally seen enough and yanked his starter. Fellow 17-game winner Johnny Morrison took over and held the Senators scoreless for the next five innings. His performance must've set tongues of second-guessers wagging in Pittsburgh; Morrison had more experience and a lower ERA, so why didn't McKechnie start him instead of Yde? With their team trailing, three games to one, they'd soon have an entire off-season to ponder that and other questions. At least Babe Adams provided a few feel-good moments in defeat; 16 years after winning three games in the 1909 Series, he came in for the final inning, worked around two singles and kept the home team from scoring.

Senators fans were giddy with anticipation of the inevitable, and players seemed equally confident. "It puts us on easy street, as all we have to do is to win one of our next three," Goslin wrote in a *Post* column. "For my part, I think that [the Pirates] are shot and that Coveleski will end things today."[7] Goslin almost hated to see it end so quickly. With three round-trippers in the last Series and two in the present one, he broke the all-time home run record and wanted to break it some more. At this point in history Babe Ruth had only four, young Lou Gehrig hadn't yet played in a Series, and Mickey Mantle wasn't born. Those three Yankees would set the standard one day but for now, Goose was the man, and he told readers he may have a few more

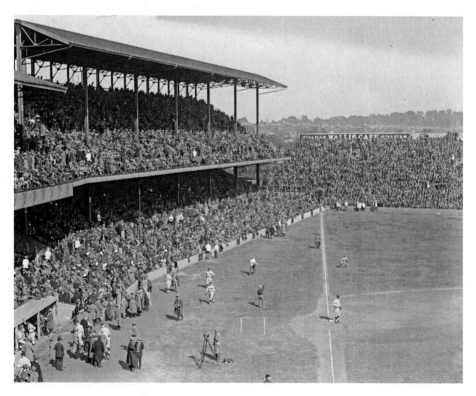

Scene from Griffith Stadium during the 1925 World Series in Washington, D.C. The Senators came in as defending champions (Library of Congress, Prints and Photography Division).

homers in his bat. It was good to be Goose Goslin; at 25 years of age, he'd already established himself as one of the best in a stacked field of AL outfielders. Named Leon by his parents, the New Jersey native became "Goose" soon after joining the Senators. He had a long neck, a large nose and a birdlike tendency for arm flapping while camping under fly balls. Thus the ornithological nickname.

No team had ever rallied from a 3–1 World Series deficit since the very first one, when Boston did the trick against Pittsburgh in a best-of-nine format. Fred Clarke was around for that one and now sat on the bench for a Pirates team that needed to do the same with a smaller, best-of-seven margin of error. Remaining upbeat, McKechnie told reporters, "We ought to get out of the hole tomorrow and get going in earnest. We are anything but beaten and will fight it out all the way."[8]

Behind the scenes, he accepted some grumpy advice from John McGraw, who hated to see any American League team take the Series. "Why don't you get that Grantham out of there? He's not doing you any good. Why not play Stuffy McInnis on first? He's been in a lot of World Series, and knows what this is all about."[9] Indeed, the 17-year veteran had played in three for the Philadelphia Athletics and one for the Boston Red Sox. He never hit worth a hoot in any of them but his teams usually won. At the age of 35, McInnis brought championship experience to the Pirates dugout, a proven glove to the field and a timeless bat to the plate. With nothing to lose, McKechnie placed McInnis in the starting lineup. He also moved Aldridge ahead of sore-armed Meadows in the pitching rotation to match up against Coveleski. It had worked out pretty well in Game 2 and the Pirates hoped history would repeat itself.

The Senators had better-rested hurlers to pick from for Game 5 but, with his opponent reeling on the ropes, Bucky Harris went for the knockout. One mediocre World Series outing did not change the fact that Coveleski was baseball's best pitcher in 1925, and it couldn't erase the memory of his utter dominance in the 1920 Series. He was born for this moment at Griffith Stadium. After escaping a bases-loaded jam in the top of the first, Coveleski was staked to a 1–0 lead in the bottom half. He cruised through the second but got wild in the third and walked two batters who both came around to score, one on an RBI single, the other via sacrifice fly.

Joe Harris tied things up with a leadoff homer in the fourth and the game stayed knotted at 2–2 until the seventh, when Coveleski issued a one-out walk, then surrendered three consecutive singles that plated two runs. That prompted a call to the bullpen, and he never threw another pitch in that or any other World Series. Dormant for so long, the Pirates offense finished with 13 hits in a 6–3 victory. Coveleski's stat line read: 6⅓ innings, nine hits (all singles), four runs (all earned).

With the Senators' lead cut to three games to two, the Series moved back to Pittsburgh. Undecided on which Senators pitcher would start Game 6, manager Harris had plenty to ponder on the long train ride to the Steel City. He'd been so confident of a title-clinching victory that he really hadn't given the issue any forethought. Dutch Ruether was still waiting for his chance and still incurably left-handed, as was fellow starter Tom Zachary, who'd been knocked around in relief during the latest defeat. Alex Ferguson eventually got the call, and the Pirates went with Ray Kremer — a familiar matchup, since both started Game 3. "I'm depending on you, Ray," McKechnie said on the train trip back. "Pitch as well as you did in the third game, and you can win." Kremer responded confidently, "I'll win for you."[10]

Goose Goslin and Roger Peckinpaugh wasted no time in trying to make a liar out of him, the former blasting a first-inning homer and the latter launching an RBI double in the second. Kremer settled down after that, however, and retired 12 of the next 14 batters. The Pirates manufactured two tying runs in the third inning, moving around the bases on a walk, a sacrifice, an RBI groundout and a run-scoring single. Peckinpaugh complained of a bad call during that sequence and continued complaining in his syndicated column that ran the next day. The controversy arose after he fumbled Max Carey's grounder, recovered the ball and tried to make an unassisted force out. Umpire George Moriarity ruled Eddie Moore safe at second, though Peckinpaugh swore he beat the runner by a foot. Right or wrong, it was a pivotal call that put Pittsburgh runners on first and second with no outs.

Moore left no room for second-guessing in the bottom of the fifth, when he put the home team ahead with a leadoff home run to deep left-center. Rabbit Maranville's replacement had just become Pennsylvania's newest favorite second baseman. In Kremer's hands, a one-run lead never looked so large; he allowed only four men to reach base after the second inning and picked off one of them. There were nervous moments at the end, as Washington put a runner on second with no outs in the eighth and another on second with one out in the ninth. Both times, Kremer put out the fire by inducing harmless pop flies and grounders. Nearly 43,000 frenzied fans cheered the final out of a 3–2 victory that tied the Series at three games apiece. Momentum belonged to their Pirates now but, unfortunately, Walter Johnson still belonged to the Senators. Working on three days' rest, he would shoot for his third win in the deciding Game 7 and, as the saying goes, momentum is the next day's starting pitcher. Washington fans liked their chances.

Not to be outdone by Senators player-scribes, Stuffy McInnis championed a Pirates perspective in his own newspaper column. He predicted bad things for the Washington legend: "Johnson will hardly have had enough rest to go in there. The pace was beginning to tell on him Sunday and brilliant fielding and the breaks of the game cost us the sweets of victory. We've got them on the run after they thought they had us licked to a frazzle."[11]

Questions remained about Johnson's gimpy leg, too, but who else could the team put on the mound? Not Ferguson or Coveleski, and management still didn't trust the lefties. Besides, as Bucky Harris put it, "he doesn't pitch with his leg, does he?" Suffering from a nasty spike wound to the hand, Harris would soldier on too.

Outside Pirates country, almost everybody wanted to see Johnson get that magical third win. Only four pitchers had ever done it — two of whom sat in opposite dugouts of the present Series — and the Big Train would've made a fine addition to the club. The baseball gods believed it too; why else would they have sent rain to cancel the October 14 game and give him another day of badly needed rest? Almost lost in the affectionate rooting was Vic Aldridge's bid to accomplish the same thing with even less rest. After posting his second victory in Game 5, he needed the extra day off more than Johnson. Without it, McKechnie probably would've picked somebody else, although his options were limited; Meadows still had a sore arm, Kremer was all used up, Yde looked bad in his lone appearance, and Adams looked his age. Before the postponement, newspaper men believed the Pirates would go with Red Old-ham, a seldom-used southpaw who threw 51 innings in the regular season.

Another postponement seemed likely when folks looked out their windows on the morning of Thursday, October 15. After the previous day's gulley washer, Forbes Field needed to dry out under clear, sunny skies but instead got fog and intermittent showers. It was a sloppy mess. Judge Landis wanted to finish off the Series, however, and ordered the teams to play on. Despite the miserable conditions, a crowd of 42,856 hunkered down to support their team. A few innings into the game, their resolve was tested further when a cold drizzle turned into a relentless downpour. Groundskeepers carried buckets of sawdust onto the field, spreading it over the baselines and pitcher's mound, and towels were furnished to hurlers for drying off baseballs. Visibility became an issue, too, with the field enveloped by a haze that made it hard to follow the ball over long distances.

This was the backdrop for the deciding game of a World Series. Aldridge was just as bad as the weather, if not worse; he couldn't even make it out of the first inning. Slipping and sliding off a slick pitching rubber, he surrendered three walks, two wild pitches and two singles. Two runs crossed the plate and more damage seemed imminent when McKechnie yanked his starter with one out and the bases loaded. Next to jump into the pool was Johnny Morrison, who seemed much better suited to the task. The Senators didn't make good contact on his pitches but bad luck hit him hard, as two more runs scored on a catcher's interference and an infield error.

With the great Walter Johnson leading the way, the Washington Senators were favored to win their second straight World Series title in 1925. Most fans rooted for the gentleman superstar (Library of Congress, Prints and Photography Division).

A stunned crowd sat in soggy disbelief at Forbes Field, while thousands cheered the radio broadcast outside the *Washington Post*. The game seemed all but over; mighty Walter Johnson had given up only one run in his previous 18 innings and now he'd been staked to a 4–0 lead. How would a train handle the rain? He rode right through it, striking out two batters in a scoreless bottom of the first. After putting out that fire in the top half, Morrison kept his team in the game by keeping the Senators off the scoreboard for a while. It was a whole new game when Pittsburgh batters finally got to Johnson in the third inning and scored three runs on four hits. The Senators padded their lead to 6–3 in the fourth, chasing Morrison out of the game when that persistent irritant, Joe Harris, smacked a two-run double. Kremer came in next and held Washington scoreless while his teammates chipped away and eventually tied things up on Traynor's RBI triple with two outs in the seventh. Trying to turn his three-bagger into an inside-the-park homer, Traynor was tagged out at the plate as he slid through thick mud.

For pure back-and-forth excitement, it was turning into a Game 7 for the ages and, throughout it all, the Senators seemed doggedly determined to make Johnson a three-game winner. His manager refused to take him out, even as Pittsburgh's offense racked up hits and runs. When Peckinpaugh homered in the top of the eighth, Sir Walter stood six outs away from hat-trick glory. The number soon decreased to four, as he retired his next two enemies without incident, but the Pirates launched a two-out rally that tied the game on back-to-back doubles. The drama grew when two more batters reached, loading the bases, but Bucky Harris still refused to summon a reliever. His offense had been scoring runs all day and could do it again in the ninth; one more out and the dream remained alive.

Up came Cuyler, the regular-season ripper who had hit just .240 for the Series and was 1-for-4 on the day. By the end of his at-bat, his average jumped to .269. After fouling off a few fastballs, he slammed one deep into the dusky mist, down the right field line. Lacking luminosity, the ball was hard to follow but every Pirate believed it cleared the fence for a grand slam and celebrated accordingly. While four men took turns crossing home plate, the umpires huddled and agreed on a partial-proof theory that the pill had landed in fair territory, then bounced into foul ground amongst relief pitchers. They pronounced it a ground-rule double, allowed two runners to score and ordered two back to the base paths. Needless to say, Pittsburghers disagreed with the verdict and screamed for a new trial. McKechnie's voice could be heard above the others, yelling, "It was a homer! It was a homer!" Maybe they should've been happy with the double; Goose Goslin swore the ball landed foul.

The Pirates took their two-run lead into the ninth, where McKechnie selected Oldham to get the final three outs. It was his fourth pitcher of the game, a rare stratagem for those days when starters expected to finish. Facing the meat of Washington's lineup, Oldham struck out Rice and Goslin, then retired manager Harris on an easy fly. For the first time in 16 years, the Pittsburgh Pirates were champions of the baseball world.

Already assaulted by Mother Nature, the playing field was finished off by man when rejoicing fans spilled onto the diamond and tramped around long after their heroes headed indoors. It didn't matter, for the season was finished and groundskeepers had all the time in the world to restore the Forbes Field landscape. It also didn't matter that the celebrants were soaked and muddy; in their minds, they'd gone to a happy place of warmth and sunshine. So had the Pirates, who soon took the celebration indoors to the clubhouse.

Barney Dreyfuss joined the party, yelling, "You did it, Bill! You did it!" The owner placed a kiss on his manager and the manager did the same to his co-manager, Fred Clarke. When Commissioner Landis arrived on the scene, the Pittsburgh brain trust finally had its long-delayed meeting with his majesty. John McGraw was there, too, pleased that his recommendation helped produce this result. After taking over first base in the fifth game, Stuffy McInnis hit .286 —153 points higher than the guy he replaced at McGraw's suggestion. Also included in the parade of power brokers was NL president John Heydler, beaming with pride that the AL had been conquered: "You are the gamest ball team I have seen in my 20 years in baseball," he proclaimed.[12] Never a great quote for newspaper writers, McKechnie did his best to satisfy questioners: "What can I say? We're overjoyed at the victory after coming back from Washington one behind. But after we started hitting Monday, didn't I predict that we would take 'em? Well, we did and there's not much to say."[13]

The mood matched the weather in the losers' clubhouse, where Senators dwelled on opportunities lost. They'd failed to hold a Series lead of three games to one, and squandered leads of 4–0 and 6–3 in Game 7. A franchise formerly known for futility had come so close to winning two consecutive World Series. For the team and the city, it was a tough pill to swallow. Above all else, however, folks mourned for their beloved pitching icon. According to the poetic Post, Mother Nature showed her disappointment too: "Pittsburgh skies wept in sympathy for the lost hopes of Walter Johnson and Washington."[14]

Pirates fans became respectfully quiet when Johnson left the visitor's dugout and walked through the grandstand toward his waiting car. Many shook his hand and said they were sorry it had to be him that Pittsburgh beat. Johnson was all class after the defeat, refusing to place blame on weather conditions or injury. The mound was just as wet for Pirates pitchers and his bandaged leg felt good enough. "They beat us and I guess that's all there is to it," he said.

For American League President Ban Johnson, it wasn't that simple; he blamed management for the Game 7 loss and wasn't alone in that assessment. Surrendering a whopping 15 hits, Walter Johnson obviously wasn't himself and needed bullpen help. If he couldn't win three games, so be it; it was more important that Washington win four. Ban summed it up succinctly in a telegram to Bucky Harris: "You sacrificed a World Championship for our league to mawkish sentiment."[15] Harris stood by his strategy, saying he would do the same thing all over again if placed in a similar situation. It wasn't entirely about a Big Train trifecta; with awful field and weather conditions, he believed an awfully special pitcher was needed, someone with the mental toughness to endure overwhelming difficulties. Walter Johnson was his man till the end. "It's only one of those things," Harris said. "We have a new champion, although we do not concede that they are any better than we are any more than we thought we were better than the Giants because we won [last year]. I am confident that had we played the Pirates in Washington today we would have won again."[16]

Eight years passed before the Senators won another pennant, after which they disappeared from the postseason radar forever. The 1925 campaign was Johnson's last hurrah; he followed with two losing seasons and retired. Arriving in the majors around the same time that the Model T Ford was born, he departed in the same year its final versions rolled off the assembly line. A new era was in full swing, one where Ford's newer and better Model A competed against sleek autos like the Packard, Studebaker and La Salle. Nobody will ever know how many were parked outside speakeasies while tipsy flappers danced the Charleston inside. In baseball, the Pirates looked poised to put their own stamp on the Roaring 20s and beyond. Young and accomplished, this talented group figured to get even better with age. Bill McKechnie could've run for mayor of Pittsburgh, but then again, so could've Fred Clarke.

11

Trouble in Horsehide Paradise

Young Bill McKechnie, who handles the reins on the champion Pirates, is a much maligned young man. Bill has been called everything from a numbskull to a moron—even by the good citizens of Pittsburgh, who are about as tough losers as you'll find this side of the Hindenburg line.[1]— Port Arthur News

Not that the defending world champs needed any help but, with the arrival of rookie sensation Paul Waner, they got a big dose of it anyhow. Making an immediate impact, he became part of an outfield for the ages, one with three future Hall of Famers. It soon became apparent that Waner was the best of them. Born in Oklahoma territory a few years before it became a state, he grew up on his father's farm where corncobs and sticks were plentiful. From those humble conditions sprang a makeshift game that sparked a great baseball career. It was a country version of stickball, with corncobs broken in half and each half serving as a ball. Waner became an expert cob buster, and it seemed to prepare him well for what lay ahead; hitting baseballs with a bat was easy compared to that countrified version of the same skill. Groomed as a pitcher in his early minor league days, his stick skills went unappreciated until the San Francisco Seals gave him a chance. Waner proceeded to blast Pacific Coast League pitching, even eclipsing the .400 mark one year. He wasn't a big man, but impeccable timing and technique caused the ball to jump off his bat. It kept jumping in the majors too.

After winning 95 games without Waner in 1925, how far could the Pirates go with him? Maybe they'd eclipse the century mark and coast to the pennant. The 1926 campaign did go down as one of the most memorable in team history, but for all the wrong reasons. It's famous for an attempted mutiny, followed by quick reprisals and an eventual leadership change.

Pittsburgh opened the season with McKechnie and Clarke still sharing the bench; why wouldn't they, after sailing to a championship on a ship with two helms? The arrangement tasted bitter, however, when it wasn't slathered in sweet victory, and the defending champs did not start well. Troubles continued into summer where, at the end of June, they trailed league-leading Cincinnati by six games.

July brought quick recovery, with the Pirates eventually taking over first place and staying there through much of August. Somebody was always breathing down their necks, though, and that had rarely happened the previous year. Despite lofty expectations, the current team just wasn't as good.

Though the lineup still had many .300 hitters, the team average dropped several points, power numbers fell and, most importantly, run-scoring decreased significantly from 1925. The most dramatic decline came from aging center fielder Max Carey, who'd posted magnificent numbers in 1925 and now hit in the .220s. Off the field, things got even worse for him when he became the focal point of controversy.

It all started during an early August trip to Boston, with Carey mired in a slump and the Pirates struggling to generate offense. Clarke implored McKechnie to replace him, but McKechnie replied that there were no strong replacements on the roster. When asked whom they should use, Clarke came back with a biting response. According to author Fred Lieb, the comment was, "Anybody. Put in the batboy; he can't do any worse than the fellow you are playing."[2] A contemporaneous account from *The Sporting News* has him saying, "Put somebody out there even if it is a pitcher." Whatever was said, Carey did not hear it; another player did, however, and repeated the story to him. Carey felt betrayed; he'd played so long and so well for the Pirates, plus served the vital role of team captain. Now, one slump made him fodder for disparagement and demotion by a man who shouldn't even occupy the dugout. Carey talked it over with some teammates and asked Babe Adams what he thought about the situation. The old pitcher gave an old school answer: managers should manage and nobody else should interfere — not even Clarke. Believing he had enough support to hold the curmudgeon accountable, Carey called a team meeting and conducted a secret-ballot vote on whether Clarke should be asked to stay off the bench. Proving that the salty old skipper still had admirers in the trenches, the proposition failed by a lopsided 18–6 margin. Not satisfied with his victory, Clarke demanded that the mutineers face severe consequences for their actions.

All this occurred with the owner away on a European vacation that included a visit to his father's homeland in Germany. Dreyfuss' son, Sam, would handle the situation stateside, using his executive axe to make heads roll. Adams was released unconditionally, as was Carson Bigbee, who had lit the uprising fuse by reporting Clarke's unkind comment. Carey got placed on waivers, then sold to the Brooklyn Dodgers. When Stuffy McInnis was released a month later, it seemed part of the same house-cleaning; he had supposedly leaked the vote to the press.

The controversy became known as the ABC affair, each letter corresponding to a key conspirator. "A" certainly didn't think he'd done anything wrong. "I am 18 years in baseball without ever opening my mouth, and then when I answer a question, I find myself chucked off the club," Adams complained.[4] Bigbee had been around a decade and Carey for 15 full seasons. All three were Pirates pillars, and each found himself discarded like yesterday's trash; management was sending a strong message about underlings knowing their place.

Saying they'd been railroaded, the dismissed trio appealed to NL president John Heydler, who seemed to side with them. Placing partial blame on the confusing bench boss situation, he exonerated them from the charge of willful insubordination but refused to order reinstatement. He felt the league had no authority to interfere with a team's roster moves. McKechnie found himself in a no-win situation; though agreeing with the mutineers on most points, he belonged to management and could not support a proletariat uprising. Instead, he criticized it, though not soon enough for some people. *The Sporting News* said, "Why McKechnie ever let the matter get beyond his control is a mystery. A manager should have stepped in and knocked that kind of agitation out before criticism of his players had come to a vote and no vote ever should have been undertaken."[5]

The press generally supported absolute front office authority but, at the same time, some writers took the franchise to task for putting two managers in one dugout. If it became a house divided, then Barney Dreyfuss bore the blame. "Dual control is anathema in all business," wrote noted sports journalist John Sheridan. "In no business is dual control quite so deadly as in managing a baseball team. That so capable a businessman as Dreyfuss could make such an amazing mistake was a considerable shock to me. Nor was it, in my opinion, warranted."[6]

A one-manager movement didn't necessarily champion McKechnie's cause; some said to give him the job and get out of his way, but others believed him too soft to be the "one." Why else would Clarke have been brought in? Even as he criticized Dreyfuss, Sheridan said McKechnie should've quit when presented with that untenable arrangement in 1925. The writer figured that McKechnie swallowed his pride to keep a five-figure salary, just as most tight-fisted Scotsmen would do. "I give Bill credit for a hard Scotch head. Evidently the prevailing influence with McKechnie was his job. Oh, for the good old days of the wild Irish, when, 'Take your job and to — — with it,' was the word in baseball. The Irish have their faults. Lack of intestinal fortitude and love of money are not among them."

Folks underestimated McKechnie's fortitude; it's easy to walk away but he stuck around, rolled up his sleeves and tried to make a bad situation better. When the Pirates won the World Series, it seemed two managers played a big, interactive role in making it happen; now it looked more and more like a barrier to ultimate success. Would the house-cleaning improve their chances or make them worse? The lineup didn't lose much on the stat sheet but lost plenty when it came to veteran leadership. Twenty-six-year-old Pie Traynor replaced Carey as team captain.

The Pirates had to battle two teams down the stretch, neither of which resided in New York. Their old nemesis, the Giants, were non-factors for a change and though they became competitive in coming years, would never win another pennant under John McGraw. Now setting the NL pace were non-traditional powers from Cincinnati and St. Louis. Led by Edd Roush and a typically strong pitching staff, the Reds set their sights on the second pennant in franchise history, while Rogers Hornsby and the Cardinals looked for their first. Trying to spoil both coming-out parties, Pittsburgh leaned heavily on a great one-two pitching punch at the top of the rotation. Ray Kremer and Lee Meadows both posted 20 wins and finished in a four-way tie for the league lead. With the NL's lowest ERA and highest winning percentage, Kremer was a stopper who could do serious postseason damage but would never get the chance.

Leading the NL by a few percentage points on August 30, the Pirates were struck by a mystifying slump that dropped them to second, then third, then out of serious contention. When Cincinnati and St. Louis both struggled in the final week, Pittsburgh couldn't take advantage and finished 4½ games out of first. The Cardinals backed into the pennant by splitting their last eight games for a final 89–65 record, two games better than the Reds.

Hornsby's boys proved themselves worthy NL representatives, however, upsetting the Yankees in a seven-game World Series. The Clarke controversy resurfaced while New York and St. Louis fought it out; with nothing to lose now, the ABC boys communicated openly about misery in Piratesville. Clarke's harshly-worded order to remove Carey from the lineup was just the tip of the iceberg. They said his methods created dissension long before, all the way back to the previous season. When players gathered to divvy up the World Series shares, they reportedly voted to give Clarke nothing. Readdressing the issue, they decided to make it $1,000, far less than a typical player's share.

The Clarke affair had a polarizing effect on the press and public, with aftershocks that continued rumbling long after the gang of three was sent packing. Beyond the broad themes of respect and authority, there was the simplicity of a talented team that underachieved. Convinced that off-field discord cost Pittsburgh another World Series appearance, Pittsburghers continued grumbling. To feed the beast, more heads had to roll.

On October 18, Dreyfuss fired Bill McKechnie. Praising his ex-employee

McKechnie still had the title of manager but things got uncomfortable when Fred Clarke joined him on the Pirates bench as an honored adviser. A legendary Pirates manager in his day, Clarke stepped on toes upon his return to the dugout, and it led to a clubhouse civil war (National Baseball Hall of Fame Library, Cooperstown, New York).

up and down, he said the decision was actually made by John Q. Public. "Many fans have been expressing the opinion that a change should be made and they are fully entitled to have something to say on occasions of this kind. The fact must not be overlooked that the public is the big factor in supporting a baseball club and accordingly it would be poor policy not to give this same public all the consideration deserved."[7] Thus ended the Pirates career of a hometown boy who got his dream job, then watched it slip through his fingers. With even more talent on the way, the 1925 title could've been just the beginning.

Clarke stepped down that winter, making the exodus complete; he didn't need the grief or the paycheck. Even some of his supporters had expressed reservations about a team executive doing double duty in the dugout. A line had been crossed there that bothered baseball insiders more than the one he crossed with Wilkinsburg Bill. The name of Fred Clarke continued to resonate amongst the people of Pittsburgh folk but it would never be considered fit for discussion in the McKechnie household, and not just because of Daddy. Momma felt bitter because they'd just built a home and now her husband couldn't live in it during the season.

That household now included three children, two parents and zero jobs. Such were the fickle winds of baseball — a champion one year and unemployed the next. For Rogers Hornsby, only two months passed between title time and rejection. Already regarded as the greatest right-handed hitter in baseball history, he looked like the next big thing in managing after guiding St. Louis to its first World Series crown. But his second year as Cardinals player-manager would be his last; when an impasse developed at contract negotiations, St. Louis quickly traded him to the Giants for Frankie Frisch. The two sides had argued over salary but the trade wasn't entirely driven by money issues. Hornsby's off-putting personality annoyed players and executives alike, so it came as a relief to be rid of him.

Frisch filled the hole at second base, left by Hornsby, but the Cards still needed a field boss. Promoting from within, they gave the job to veteran catcher Bob O'Farrell, the reigning NL Most Valuable Player. Arriving in a trade the previous year, he'd spent most of his career with the Cubs but fans didn't hold that against him. One of the few players to call Hornsby friend, O'Farrell sought his blessing and got it. Hornsby praised him to the press, saying, "O'Farrell is a good man, a smart baseball player, and I wish him and his players all the luck in the world."[8]

One of his smartest moves came early, with the selection of a coach to assist him. His choice: Bill McKechnie. Brand new to the managing game, O'Farrell now had a right-hand man with six years' experience. McKechnie landed in a good situation, too, jumping from one champion to another.

After leading the National League in almost every offensive category, the Cardinals didn't need much batting advice from the new brain trust. Losing Hornsby was a blow that fans resented, but Frisch eventually played his way into their hearts. Another drama played out in the pitching corps, where the supremely talented and fatally flawed Grover Cleveland Alexander stood in position to make or break pennant hopes.

Owner of 327 career victories, the 39-year-old was no longer that overwhelming performer who once dominated the NL, but he could still paint those corners when right. As always, his greatest opponent was alcohol. He seemed to have it under control while crafting a sublime, seven-year stretch in Philadelphia, but then the draft board came calling and he ended up on European front lines of World War I. Alexander returned shell-shocked, hard of hearing, epileptic and a prisoner of booze. At his worst, he was a staggering drunk who couldn't be counted on by bosses or teammates — at his best, a high-functioning alcoholic.

Alexander spent most of his post-war career with the Cubs, always winning more than he lost and twice eclipsing the 20-victory mark. He looked like his old self in 1920, recording a league-high 27 wins while also leading in ERA, innings, complete games and strikeouts. Never again did he post the best mark in any category. By June of 1926 it seemed the headaches outweighed the rewards, so Chicago released Alexander. Hornsby convinced Cardinals general manager Branch Rickey to claim him off waivers. "Even though Alex ... had been in a sanitarium at Dwight, Illinois, the winter before to try to quit drinking, I knew he still had a fastball," Hornsby remembered years later. "Even if it was only half as good as it once was, it was still good. He had the greatest control I've ever seen."[9] It seemed a brilliant decision when Alexander contributed to the title run with a 9–7 regular-season record, two World Series wins and a famous relief appearance in Game 7. Trailing, 3–2, in the seventh inning, the Yankees had loaded the bases with two outs when Hornsby signaled for Alexander. Legend says he was asleep in the bullpen at the time, perhaps nursing a hangover. Regardless, he retired Tony Lazzeri for the final out, then sealed victory with two more scoreless innings. For the first time in his amazing career, Alexander was the star of a World Series.

Cardinals fans hoped he could carry his momentum into 1927, and they were not disappointed. Squeezing one more wonderful season out of those weary bones, Alexander went 21–10 and posted a 2.52 ERA. With 33-year-old Jesse Haines winning 24 games, St. Louis rode its savvy hurlers to another pennant chase. Standing squarely in the way of a potential repeat were McKechnie's former students, the Pittsburgh Pirates. They'd deepened their talent pool again with the arrival of Paul Waner's brother, Lloyd. Also a hard-hitting outfielder, the younger sibling put together a remarkable rookie season, batting .355 and scoring a league-high 133 runs. Not to be outdone, Paul led the NL in batting average (.380) and RBI (131).

The Giants rebounded strongly from a season of mediocrity and made it a three-team race for the 1927 flag. McKechnie's buddy, Edd Roush, played for them now, filling a decade-old void in center field. John McGraw wasn't the only one beefing up his roster; an American League dream took shape in Philadelphia, with Connie Mack opening the dusty club coffers to buy Ty Cobb, Zack Wheat and Eddie Collins. The Athletics already fielded three legends in Lefty Grove, Al Simmons and Mickey Cochrane, not to mention a promising 19-year-old named Jimmie Foxx. Throw them all together and the 1927 A's owned more Hall of Fame talent than Heaven and Hell combined. The latest additions were way past their primes, however, with Cobb the only starter.

On July 18, the Cardinals hosted New York in a game that became entirely overshadowed by a world-famous visitor. Sitting in a special box seat near the home team's dugout was Charles Lindbergh, fresh off his historic transatlantic solo flight to Paris. Lindy's nation-wide, victory-lap tour included a stop in St. Louis on this day and, upon arrival at Sportsman's Park, he was greeted with a deafening roar of approval from 40,000 hero worshippers. "Voices that tried to express honor, admiration, awe and worship in one breath-taking scream," said the *New York Times*. The Cardinals also commemorated their World Series title that day, raising a championship pennant and presenting diamond rings to the players. Ironically, Hornsby stood first in line for jewelry. After leading a pre-game mini-parade across the playing field, Lindbergh returned to his seat of honor, watched the first three innings, and then departed to another ear-splitting salute. Focus returned to the diamond and home fans aimed all cheers toward their Cardinals, who gave them a 6–4 victory.

While the National League showcased a close pennant race, the American League proved downright dull by comparison. Fielding a team that still merits consideration as the best of all time, the Yankees went 110–44 and finished 19 games ahead of second-place Philadelphia. Whoever faced them in the World Series would undoubtedly get crushed, and that dubious distinction went to Pittsburgh and its new manager, Donie Bush. The Cardinals made a strong late push but wound up second by 1½ games, and New York finished two back.

Close wasn't good enough for Cardinals fans and questions arose about management. Though guiding his team to more regular season wins (92) than the title team had (88), O'Farrell still sat on the hot seat. Nicked up by nagging injuries, he suffered a terrible season in the field, playing only 53 games and batting .264. If he'd been the same guy he was in 1926, maybe the 1927 team would've won it all too. Some blamed his troubles on the weighty responsibilities of management. "Spoiling a great catcher, the best in the business, is an expensive way of having a leader," owner Sam Breadon said. "It is easy to get a manager. There are plenty of them. But it is difficult, almost impossible, to get a star player to replace one who is lost. For that reason I am uncertain as to whether I want O'Farrell to again have the worries of a manager."[10]

And with that comment from the man in charge, O'Farrell's Cardinals managing career unofficially ended at one season. The only question was who should replace him. A few days later, the announcement came down; on the same November 7 day that Russians celebrated the tenth anniversary of their Soviet revolution, Bill McKechnie was named manager of the St. Louis Cardinals. O'Farrell acted perfectly content with the situation, so there seemed small chance of the kind of dissension that once tore apart the Pirates clubhouse. He never really wanted the job in the first place. Nevertheless, his bosses praised him for a job well done, then gently dismissed him with a lovely parting gift — a fat pay raise for the upcoming season. Despite all the tributes to O'Farrell's value as a full-time player, he lasted exactly 16 games before getting traded to the Giants for an outfielder.

McKechnie's work hours didn't change much; even as a coach, he was known for coming in early and leaving late. But now, he walked into Sportsman's Park as the guy in charge. With several top-flight players on the roster, it was a good time to be manager of the St. Louis Cardinals. They had a great slugging first baseman in Sunny Jim Bottomley, an elite infielder in Frisch, a formidable outfield and a balanced pitching rotation, anchored by the reborn Grover Alexander. If fragile Chick Hafey could only return to form, it might push the Redbirds over the top. Plagued by health problems and deteriorating eyesight, the talented young outfielder missed a big chunk of the 1927 season. After going under the knife for sinus surgery, he hoped to reclaim his acclaim as golden boy of the future.

Born in Berkeley, California, Hafey grew up to play town ball and eventually signed with the Cardinals as a pitching prospect. That lasted until general manager Branch Rickey saw him swinging a bat at spring training. He drilled pitches so hard and far that it seemed obvious this was his true calling. That pitching arm never went to waste, however, as Hafey became famous for his rocket throws from the outfield. The kid was a unique baseball specimen who could do it all but, at the same time, was fatally flawed by unusual ailments. Management crossed its fingers and hoped he'd make a full recovery.

New to the starting lineup was 36-year-old Rabbit Maranville, who took over at shortstop after playing nine games for St. Louis the previous season. The old hell-raiser had apparently mellowed enough to warrant a second chance with McKechnie, who couldn't control him in Pittsburgh. Traded by the Philadelphia Phillies, Jimmie Wilson arrived to play catcher and started a lifelong friendship with his new manager.

Six NL teams posted winning records in 1928, with three of them serious contenders. The defending champion Pirates never made much impact and finished nine games out, in fourth place. Meanwhile, McKechnie's crew put a stranglehold on first place for most of the season. His great players played great, and the question mark kids turned into exclamation points. At the age of 25, Hafey fully met his potential, hitting .337 with 101 runs and 111 RBI, and fellow outfielder Taylor Douthit enjoyed the most productive season of his young career.

Often leading the field by four or five games, the Cardinals looked like the class of the league but could never put that final nail in the coffin. Meanwhile, the mighty Yankees went through a similar situation in the American League. Exploding out of the gates with 39 wins in their first 47 games, they looked every bit as dominant as the team that steamrolled to the 1927 title. By the end of June, they owned a 50–16 record and an 11½-game lead over the second-place Philadelphia Athletics. Babe Ruth and company looked indestructible. Connie Mack's crew gradually pulled closer, however, as the sizzling Yanks cooled off. Beset by injuries, the New Yorkers saw their lead shrink to 5½ games at the end of July and two games on the evening of August 31.

Both leagues were in for an exciting finish. Sweeping a doubleheader from the Boston Red Sox on September 8, Philly moved into first by a half-game. At the same time, Chicago's Cubs pulled within 2½ games of St. Louis. The following day, New York took two from the Athletics in a crucial twin-bill and recaptured the AL lead. The Yankees never trailed again, clinging to a small lead for the final two weeks. Determined to make it a New York sweep, the Giants got red-hot in September and pulled within one game of St. Louis on the 22nd. Four days later, the lead shrank to a half-game. The Cardinals pulled it out in the end, winning three straight from the lowly Boston Braves, while McGraw's boys dropped three of four to the Cubs at the Polo Grounds.

For the second time in three years, Bill McKechnie was taking a team to the World Series, and this time he was favored to win. At full strength, the Yankees would've been prohibitive favorites but several players were either sidelined by injury or playing hurt. Pitching depth took a hit with the unavailability of Herb Pennock and Wilcy Moore, and defense suffered when a banged-up wrist knocked Earle Combs out of center field. Tony Lazzeri planned to play but a sore arm limited his effectiveness, and even the Bambino limped around on a badly sprained ankle. Taking all that into consideration, some predicted a cakewalk for the National Leaguers. Two years earlier, they beat this same team when it was at full strength for the 1926 Series. Pennock won two games for the Yankees back then while Combs hit .357, so no St. Louis fans mourned their absence from the present showdown.

Also posting a 2–0 mark in the last Series was Cardinals pitcher Jesse Haines, an accomplished veteran who recorded his second straight 20-win season in 1928. Joining him at the top of the rotation was Bill Sherdel, a happy-go-lucky southpaw who went 21–10 with a 2.86 ERA. It was a career year for the 11-year veteran, and some folks were crediting his manager for getting the most out of him. This early example was a sign of things to come for McKechnie, who was known throughout his career as a great molder of pitchers. Of course, the mold had already hardened for Grover Alexander — probably in a 120-proof mixture of some sort. He crafted a strong regular season, going 16–9 between drinks, but could his teammates count on him? Columnist Westbrook Pegler thought so:

> Mr. Grover Alexander's idea of pleasure has received so much publicity ... that one might picture him as being in a speechless condition most of the time. However, I am advised that this is an exaggerated conception of the elderly gentleman who won three games from the Yankees in the World Series of 1926 and will endeavor to do something on the same order in this one. I hear that Mr. Alexander is conscious and capable of coherent speech much of the time.[11]

The Series began in New York on a warm October 4 day, with a mammoth crowd of 75,000 squeezing into Yankee Stadium. Thanks to Waite Hoyt, they did not go home disappointed. Appearing in his sixth Fall Classic, the veteran pitcher held St. Louis batters to three hits in a 4–1 victory. Bottomley had two of them, including a solo homer in the seventh inning, while the rest of the team went 1-for-26 against Mr. Hoyt. Bill Sherdel pitched well, too, surrendering four hits in seven innings' work. Each hit went for extra bases, though, as Ruth slugged a couple of doubles, Gehrig hit one, and Bob Meusel launched a two-run homer. There would be no Cardinals sweep.

McKechnie picked Alexander for the next start and quickly regretted it. Lacking his usual accuracy, the old master didn't even make it through three innings before getting the hook. Gehrig set the tone with a three-run homer in the first inning, and New York added five more runs over the next two stanzas before coasting to the finish line with a 9–3 triumph. The Yankees had early moments of pitching crisis, too, when George Pipgras surrendered three runs in the top of the second. He escaped the inning without further damage, then found his groove and dominated with a sharp-breaking curveball.

Staring into a two-games-to-none hole, Cardinals fans seemed stunned. This was supposed to be easy but the Yankees weren't cooperating at all. Even wounded, they still played like a team that expected to win its third title of the decade. It wasn't too late for the National Leaguers, however; with the Series shifting to St. Louis, they'd enjoy a home field advantage and wouldn't have to face Hoyt or Pipgras for a while. Throw in injured Herb Pennock and that made three elite pitchers who couldn't answer a call for Game 3.

There was no rest for the weary when the Cardinals arrived home after a 24-hour train trip from New York. As cheering fans greeted them at Union Station, they were whisked away to waiting cars for a parade through the streets of downtown St. Louis. It wasn't a tribute to the first two games but a delayed celebration for winning the pennant. That same day, the most rabid fans began a long vigil in ticket lines at Sportsman's Park. By nightfall, about 160 of them stood or sat near the bleacher gate, many passing the time by playing poker, rummy, pinochle or bridge. Those cards would see a lot of use before ticket sales began the next morning. Some were willing to sell their spots in line and said so to passersby. At the pavilion gate, a smaller and quieter group sat on boxes or camp stools. The masses would begin arriving in both areas on game day.

Scraping the bottom of their bullpen barrel, the Yankees surprisingly went with 32-year-old Tom Zachary, a so-so southpaw claimed off waivers in August. He'd recorded four straight losing seasons and went 3–3 in limited action for New York. Making the third game an official mismatch, McKechnie went with Jesse Haines, who had recorded a 1.08 ERA against the 1926 Yankees. Zachary had World Series experience, too, winning two games for the Senators in 1924, and that probably played a big role in his selection. Manager Huggins sounded confident when he wrote about "Zach" in his newspaper column. "Zach is the type of pitcher who ought to bother the Cardinals a lot. He has an assortment of slow stuff that should be twice as effective since they have been looking at fast balls from Hoyt and Pipgras."[12]

Finally showing signs of emerging from their hitting slump, the Cardinals jumped on Zachary for two runs in the bottom of the first but scored only once more over the next eight innings. Though St. Louis batters amassed nine hits against him, his "slow stuff" did indeed prove effective. Haines fell victim to shoddy defense and long-ball offense, as New York rolled to a 7–3 victory. Gehrig belted two home runs, one deep over the outfield wall and the second an inside-the-park job, after center fielder Douthit failed to make a shoestring catch. Three untimely errors also helped the Yankees cause. "For the first time, we outhit the Yanks nine to seven and for the first time, proceeded to be generous in the matter of giving away runs," McKechnie wrote in a column for the *St. Louis Post-Dispatch*. "The Yanks made seven runs, and the way I look at it, we gave them six of the seven."[13]

In a must-win situation, the Cardinals did not bring their "A" game. Now leading the Series by a commanding 3–0 margin, the Yankees felt supremely confident that they would close it out in four straight. Manager Huggins remained tight-lipped but some of his biggest stars were providing bulletin-board material for the opposition. Lazzeri delivered the following gem to reporters: "I'll be doggoned if they looked like a pennant-winning club to me. I can't understand how the Cardinals managed to win out. They must have played better ball than they have shown us. Didn't they look terrible today?" Babe Ruth went even further in his own by-lined column, saying the Cardinals lost their spirit. "When the Yankees beat Haines yesterday, they beat the last of the Cardinal aces. And what is more important than all, they cracked the St. Louis morale wide open. It showed when the Cardinal players went all to pieces in the sixth and we scored three runs on two hits."

With a rainout the following day, all of St. Louis had plenty time to digest those words and rally against them. Unfortunately, they had the ring of truth and the city did not "get up" for Game 4 like it had for Game 3. The stadium filled slowly on October 9, with no long lines or big rush to get in. Throughout the morning, people walked right up to ticket windows, laid down their money and casually strolled in. Scalper business was not brisk.

Seats did eventually fill and a large standing room crowd took positions in the grandstand at $3 a pop. Official attendance figures registered in the 37,000-plus range, about 2,000 fewer than two days earlier. It was actually a lot of bodies for so little hope. As if the 3–0 game deficit wasn't depressing enough, the Yankees went for the kill with Hoyt, the same hard-throwing ace who made Redbird batters look feeble in the opener. He would not come close to repeating that performance, however, as the St. Louis offense knocked him around for 11 base hits. With a few more reaching on walks, the base paths were crowded with Cardinals. If only they could've gotten a few more of them to step on home plate.

After pitching well in defeat during Game 1, Sherdel battled through several tight spots and held the Yankees to one run through six innings of Game 4. His good work allowed St. Louis to take a 2–1 lead into the top of the seventh. Everything unraveled there, however, and it all started with one of the most controversial calls (or non-calls) in Series history. After retiring the first batter, Sherdel got two strikes past Ruth and quick-pitched a third one across the plate. (They called it the "quick return" back then.) Umpire Cy Pfirman disallowed the apparent strikeout, saying he had called time out for the batter. McKechnie argued the point but to no avail. The quick return was legal in the National League, but not so in the American or the World Series. Since Sherdel took a windup, however, McKechnie insisted all conditions were met for a legal pitch.

Given a second chance, Ruth blasted a game-tying homer, his second of the day. That opened the floodgates, with the New Yorkers putting three more runs on the board before the third out was recorded. The Babe launched a third bomb in the eighth, tying his own record for most home runs in one Series game. Eighty-four years later, nobody has surpassed the feat and only two have matched it: Reggie Jackson in 1977 and Albert Pujols in 2011. By game's end, a jeering crowd had become Bambino fans. The big lug had won them over with excellence and a running exchange of words and gestures with left-field bleacherites. Returning to the field after his first home run, he faced the crowd and used a sweep of the hand to pantomime the trajectory of that shot over the pavilion roof. He did it over and over, smiling all the way.

In the bottom of the ninth, Ruth ended the game with a great running catch of a foul pop fly behind third base. New York's 7–3 victory gave it a second straight World Series sweep. There were many hitting heroes in 1927 but only two in 1928, as Ruth and Gehrig carried the Yankees on their broad backs. The banged-up Babe hit a phenomenal .625 and scored more runs than anybody else. Gehrig batted .545 while producing more home runs and RBI than anybody else. Baseball clown Nick Altrock wrote, "I will go to my grave wondering why Huggins pays seven other baseball players to get in Ruth's and Gehrig's way when they is winning baseball games. Some day Ruth will step on a Yankee infielder and Huggins will learn his lesson. Give me the Babe and Lou and I will not only win the serum but I will also capture Berlin and chase them Chinese bandits back into their laundries."[14]

The Yankees celebrated deep into the night on their way back to New York. A midnight parade found players walking through the train and demanding that everyone hand over their shirt or pajama top. Those who refused ran the risk of having it torn off.[15] It would be a long, strange and fun trip. The mood was somber in St. Louis, where few folks seemed consoled by the honor of being National League champions. Losing a World Series was one thing, but to lose it so decisively when their team had been favored ... that was quite another. Questions immediately arose about whether roster changes were needed. Cornered by newspapermen, owner Breadon said he just wanted to get away from baseball for a while. Yes, he was upset about what just transpired but any corrective measures should be calmly deliberated over time. "But how about McKechnie?" persisted one questioner. "Well, what about him?" Breadon answered. "He won a pennant, didn't he? And where would you get a better man?"[16]

It was a nice endorsement by the big boss but questions persisted, and it seemed telling that he never gave guarantees of McKechnie's return. Mixed in with the reasonable criticism that he wasn't aggressive enough to inspire rowdy men, were whispers about strategic shortcomings. Some said he'd done a poor job directing base-runner traffic when serving as third-base coach. A few players joined in the whispers, though they prefaced criticism by first saying what a great guy their manager was. Roy Stockton, of the *Post-Dispatch*, summed it up this way: "Bill is a gentleman, a diplomat, and in councils of war he is shrewd. He makes a fine impression in any discussion of the plans of battle. There has never been a discordant tone at conference between McKechnie and Breadon. But the public has the idea that McKechnie is a rotten manager and that the Cardinals won a pennant in spite of him, rather than because of his leadership."

Public opinion was blamed for his firing in Pittsburgh, and now it threatened his career again. Saint Louis was a tough baseball town, too, or maybe they all were. McKechnie put it all behind him, returned home and embarked on a hunting trip to a remote region of Pennsylvania. He wasn't there long when a local came to his shack and relayed a message that Sam Breadon had been in contact and wanted a return call from his wayward manager. Traveling several miles to find the nearest phone, McKechnie did as instructed and was told to come to St. Louis immediately. This couldn't be good.

Ushered into the owner's office at Sportsman's Park, he was told that he'd lost control of his players during the second half of the season. For that, and other reasons, the club had decided to make a managerial change. "Do you mean to say you interrupted my hunting trip to tell me that I am fired?" roared McKechnie. "Why the hell didn't you fire me when we talked on the phone? As for me losing control of my players, look up our record and you'll find out we won 15 of our last 18 road games."[17]

McKechnie did not get fired outright but he did get demoted, changing places with Rochester (NY) minor league boss Billy Southworth. Once teammates with the Pirates, they were now managers heading in different directions. Architect of a powerhouse International League team, Southworth became a hot property in the Cardinals chain when his Red Wings won the 1928 pennant. They played in the "Little World Series," losing to American Association champion Indianapolis, five games to one. A similar postseason failure cost McKechnie his job, but Southworth got a pass and a promotion. Maybe it also had something to do with Southworth's clutch performance with St. Louis in the big World Series of 1926, when he hit .345 in a winning cause.

Located a little south of Lake Ontario in western New York state, Rochester was centrally located in International League territory. To the north lay Canadian entries Toronto and Montreal; to the west Buffalo; to the south Reading (PA) and Baltimore (MD); to the southeast New Jersey cities Newark and Jersey City. Once again, McKechnie would take over a good team when moving to new environs, but he had a big hole to fill. As player-manager, Southworth had hit .361 for the champs. Rochester kept right on winning without him, though, showing no ill effects from the leadership or roster change.

Like most high-level minors throughout history, it was a league of fallen stars and promising prospects. After his great major league career sputtered to an inglorious end the previous year, Tris Speaker took over as player-manager in Newark and proceeded to light up opposing pitchers. He had several former major leaguers — most notably, Wally Pipp — but couldn't mold them into a contender. Meanwhile, McKechnie's roster included Specs Toporcer, the first major leaguer to wear glasses in modern times, and a young pitching prospect named Paul Derringer, who had greatness in his future. There really weren't many big names in Rochester. A year earlier, the Red Wings far exceeded expectations while winning the IL title by the slimmest of margins. Under Wilkinsburg Will, they threatened to run away with the pennant.

Back at St. Louis, the Cardinals were doing quite well under Southworth. They led the league at the end of May and clung to a 1½-game advantage in mid–June. The wheels came off shortly thereafter, however, and a month later they sat in fourth place, 14 games behind the Pirates. Behind the scenes, there had been trouble all along. A teammate and friend to these same players just two years ago, Southworth now came across as a hard-ass. He ran a tough spring training in Avon Park, Florida, and his newly obstinate personality grated on the men. A trip to Miami turned into confrontation when Southworth forbade players from traveling by car with family or friends. Even if it was only a minor spring excursion, his team would travel together as a team by train. Catcher Jimmy Wilson argued that his wife was looking forward to the drive and he wouldn't let her down. Southworth threatened to fine him.

In the end, everybody fell in line and rode the train, but it was a Pyrrhic victory for the rookie skipper because he lost respect in the process. Before they even had a chance to bond, there were already significant signs of erosion in the player-manager relationship. His reputation diminished further during the season when he conducted an unwarranted curfew check that woke two star players from a sound sleep. Behind his back, the Cardinals called Southworth "Billy the Heel."

It's uncertain whether ownership cared if players liked their field boss or not, but that horrible losing streak meant the hard-discipline approach was not working. Maybe the previous manager knew what he was doing when he treated his men with respect. On July 23, Breadon admitted his mistake by sending Southworth back to Rochester and recalling McKechnie to St. Louis. "I think [Southworth's] case is just like that of a minor league ball player who comes up about two years too early," the owner said. "He did not have the experience necessary to cope with such veteran managers as John McGraw, Joe McCarthy, Donie Bush and others."[18] Southworth coped quite well back in the minor leagues, winning a string of pennants for Rochester over the next few years. He would eventually return to the majors and manage for 13 years.

Breadon had nothing but praise for the guy he'd humbled last November. "This year [McKechnie] had the Rochester 'farm' in first place in the International League race with a lead of five games over the Toronto team. You can't get away from that record and now I realize that I took the World Series last fall too much to heart." He went on to predict that the Cardinals would rejoin the pennant race with the old master back at the helm. In the span of eight months, McKechnie had gone from scapegoat to miracle worker. Thirteen games out of first with a little over two months remaining, the Cardinals weren't going anywhere. They did play better under kinder leadership, however, improving from one game under .500 to three over by season's end.

If Breadon thought his latest move made everybody forgive and forget, he was wrong. Though never lodging specific complaints in public, McKechnie resented the treatment he'd received the previous season and hated that his employment situation could change drastically on a whim. He saw greener pastures in politics and filed to run for the office of Wilkinsburg tax collector. If elected to the four-year post, he would quit baseball. The Cardinals offered him a contract for the 1930 season, but McKechnie refused to consider signing until he knew his electoral fate.

Beryl McKechnie worked hard to do drum up support for her husband and reportedly convinced many women to cast their vote for him. Sounding like a campaign manager, she told an Associated Press reporter that "Mr. McKechnie" had as good a chance for the Republican nomination as anybody else. If he could pull it out, victory in the general election was virtually assured because the Democrat party had few followers in Western Pennsylvania. Beryl admitted to an ulterior motive for working so diligently on behalf of Bill. "Of course we want him to win. Then we can have him home all the time. He has not had a bed of roses in baseball and his worries have been plenty."[19]

Grover Alexander kept plugging away in 1929, winning nine games at the age of 42 and recording a decent ERA along the way. He remained a hopeless alcoholic, becoming so irresponsible that his long-suffering and faithfully supportive wife finally divorced him. Headed toward a predictably sad end, Alexander the Great still had one sublime moment left in the game, and it happened on August 10 in Philadelphia, when he broke the career record for National League victories. Making a late relief appearance, he threw four scoreless innings in an 11–9, extra-inning victory that gave him 373 wins — one better than the late Christy Mathewson.

Afterward, Alexander asked permission to socialize with some Philadelphia friends that night; he'd spent the best years of his career in Philly, so he knew a lot of people. With no game scheduled for the following day, McKechnie gave his blessing but with one important condition: he had to return fresh-faced on Monday morning. In hindsight it looked like a bad decision, but Alexander had recently undergone treatment for his addiction and the early results seemed promising. Thirty-two years later, McKechnie recalled, "We had sent Alexander away for the Keely Cure in 1929, and he reported to me in Pittsburgh, clear-eyed and ready to work. I worked him against the Pirates and he turned in a shutout."[20]

Born way ahead of its time, the "Keely Cure" was an early version of rehab that put alcoholics in treatment centers and counteracted their addiction with an injected drug cocktail. Since the late 1800s, proponents swore by its cure rate. The famous pitcher looked like one of the success stories at first but then came the record-setter, celebration and two-day test of willpower. He did show up Monday — red-faced, bleary-eyed and in no condition to pitch. McKechnie suspended the fallen hero and sent him back to St. Louis, where Breadon banned him for the rest of the season. Newspapers explained the situation with words like "out of condition" and "broke training"— code for drunken bender. Alexander never pitched for the Cardinals again and fizzled out the following season, going 0–3 for the Phillies.

Many years later, researchers found an error in Mathewson's totals and credited him with 373 wins too. McKechnie always regretted that his executive decision probably cost Alexander the title of National League victory king. Without the suspension, they surely could've come up with a workable plan to pad the total. It would've sent a bad message to the team, however. After exiting baseball for good, Alexander fell into poverty, drinking away his wages from odd jobs. He died a shell of a man in 1950.

McKechnie did not leave the game, his fate secured by a lopsided beating in the political arena. On September 17, the Wilkinsburg electorate sided with his opponent in the Republican primary race for tax collector. With 26 of 33 districts reporting, Walter Elder owned an insurmountable 3,150–1,276 lead. It had been a long shot from day one; though McKechnie had the community's respect, he was out of his element in an election against a highly popular incumbent. He had about as much chance against Elder in politics as Elder had against him in baseball. The defeat made Cardinals folks smile because it meant they wouldn't have to break in another manager, an annual rite that was getting old. Wilkinsburg Bill had just become St. Louis Bill, or so they thought.

In truth, McKechnie still sought job security, and these one-year Cardinals contracts didn't inspire confidence. Nor did the memory of that abrupt demotion of a pennant-winning pilot, or his similar situation in Pittsburgh. He grew sick of dating flashy, fickle suitors so from now on, he would insist on a commitment. Famous for avoiding the "C" word, Breadon told McKechnie to shop around for something better if he could get it. He went to Chicago for the opening of the World Series and met up with Boston

Braves owner Emil Fuchs, who promptly offered a multi-year deal to take over his hapless cellar-dwellers. On the same day that newspapers ran previews about the pennant-winning Cubs and Philadelphia Athletics, a separate story appeared about Bill McKechnie signing a four-year contract with the Braves. No salary figures were released. He secured his future just in time, as the stock market crashed a few weeks later, setting the stage for the Great Depression. McKechnie continued to easily furnish all his family's needs, including that of a live-in maid. Also living in the house was his widowed mother-in-law who, like her son-in-law, was a first-generation American whose parents emigrated from Europe. Sophilda Bien's roots grew in German soil and she learned the mother tongue from a mother who spoke no English.

Back in St. Louis, *Post-Dispatch* columnist Ed Wray lamented another departure on the managing merry-go-round. He believed the franchise would never keep good leaders as long as the front office reserved ultimate power for itself and stuck its nose into every aspect of operations. The field boss needed authority too. "Time alone can tell whether the front office system of development is adequate to provide a club with championship material, irrespective of leadership. One doubts it. Looking back into history, we note many instances where great teams were led into ignominious defeat for want [of] inspiring leadership. And a great leader can not be hired on the same basis as a factory superintendent."[21]

McKechnie became a dim memory when the Cardinals won the 1930 pennant.

12

The Braves and the Babe

[McKechnie is] one of the finest guys in the game. Baseball has been good to Ruth. He's made enough money. Why come over to the National League and knock a fellow like McKechnie out of a job? ... I resent Ruth coming to the National and I think practically every player in the league will feel the same way about it.[1]—Dizzy Dean

You know, a change in scenery can be a big help in baseball. I'll hustle and work my head off this season for Bill McKechnie. There won't be any misunderstandings so far as I am concerned. All I ask is that they let Bill and me alone. I'm satisfied to let next year take care of itself.[2]—Babe Ruth

Five years down the road, ownership would have to choose between the game's greatest legend and its finest gentleman. In 1930, however, nobody would've dreamed that Babe Ruth and Bill McKechnie were on a collision course. They lived on parallel lines that couldn't intersect, one tearing up American League pitching and the other managing a National League bottom-feeder.

McKechnie went to work for Emil Fuchs, known better as "Judge" Fuchs because of his short stint as a New York City magistrate. He bought the Braves in 1922, intent on getting his friend Christy Mathewson back into the game with a front office position. Matty served as club president when able but poor health limited him.

A husky man who loved cigars, contract bridge and baseball, Fuchs introduced Ladies Days, arranged a radio broadcasting agreement, spearheaded a successful movement to allow Sunday baseball in Boston and dabbled in the practice of profit-sharing with players. Still, he was probably better known as the owner who booted Rogers Hornsby from leadership and made himself manager in 1929. Few believed he had the know-how to run a team on the field but he seemed at least partially vindicated when his Braves occupied first place in the opening couple of weeks. Their success proved short-lived, how-

McKechnie, left, sits next to his boss, Boston Braves owner Emil Fuchs. Most called him "Judge" Fuchs because of his short stint as a New York City magistrate (courtesy Boston Public Library, Leslie Jones Collection).

ever, and they soon tumbled toward the abyss. At season's end, the Braves ranked dead last, 43 games out of first place with a record of 56–98.

Granted, Fuchs didn't have much to work with and Hornsby hadn't fared any better the previous year, but many thought the owner/manager a comically inept figure who proved he didn't belong anywhere near the bench. Agreeing with his detractors on some points, Fuchs fired himself and brought in the proven skipper, McKechnie. Here was a blank canvas where McKechnie could truly show his artistry. Free from stratospheric expectations and quick finger-pointing, he had time to mold pieces into a greater whole.

Though his options were limited, the cupboard was not entirely bare at Braves Park. The great George Sisler played in Boston now, and the years had not conquered his batting eye. Rabbit Maranville was there, too, playing adequately for a man of his age. Coming off a 17–7 season in Pittsburgh, spitballer Burleigh Grimes went to the Braves in an early April transaction but didn't stay long. McKechnie sent him to the Cardinals in June and got two younger pitchers in the exchange. At the age of 36, Grimes could not be part of the Braves' future.

On May 12, McKechnie added additional depth to his staff by grabbing Tom Zachary off the waiver wire. The veteran lefty started his career in 1918, pitching a couple of games for the Athletics under a fake name because he wanted to retain his amateur status in college. A long career awaited him in professional baseball, though, and he became known throughout the game as the pitcher who surrendered Babe Ruth's 60th home run in 1927. Two years earlier he was on the mound when Tris Speaker rapped his 3,000th career hit. Beyond those dubious milestones Zachary had his own moments of personal glory, and chief among them was a leading role in the Washington Senators' World Series championship of 1924. Pushed down the depth chart by new arrivals, he threw only a couple innings against McKechnie's Pirates in the 1925 Series. Zachary bounced around between different teams, eventually landing with the Yankees, where he posted a perfect 12–0 mark in 1929. His 2.47 earned run average was best in the league, though a low innings pitched total prevented him from claiming the ERA crown.

Going from prince to pauper in record time, Zachary made three appearances the following season and then got cut loose. The Braves swooped in to sign him, and he repaid the franchise by winning 11 of 16 decisions. His ERA soared but that was typical among major league hurlers in 1930, the year of the hitter. Trying to keep the turnstiles spinning in hard times, big league magnates supposedly conspired to increase crowd-pleasing offense by juicing up the baseball. Final NL statistics seem to prove something was amiss: Chuck Klein drove in 170 runs and placed a distant second to Hack Wilson's 191; 24-year-old Woody English scored 152 runs but finished six behind Klein; Lefty O'Doul's .383 average ranked only fourth among league leaders; and Bill Terry eclipsed .400, a feat that no National Leaguer has repeated in the past 80-plus years.

Nine teams cracked the .300 mark compared to three the previous season. Boston was not one of the nine, its .281 average tying for last in the NL, but one Brave took his place among the best. Rookie outfielder Wally Berger exploded into the majors with 38 home runs (fourth best in the league), 98 runs, 119 RBI and a .310 average. Here was a sturdy building block for the new manager. Squeezing all he could from a balanced but unremarkable pitching staff, McKechnie guided his team to sixth place and a 70–84 record. Under his leadership, the Braves improved by 14 games over their 1929 victory output.

A 64-win season followed in 1931 as the team adjusted to life without Sisler, who retired after hitting .309 in 1930. Missing several games with various ailments, he'd felt the clock ticking, and a low .300 average was no cause for celebration to a man who twice surpassed .400. League statistics returned to mortal levels, as zero teams hit over .300 and Berger's home run total dropped in half, though his batting average jumped 13 points. McKechnie's reclamation project wouldn't happen overnight but, regardless of final records, he had a plan and was slowly developing it.

In his personal life, something wonderfully unplanned arrived that winter. At the age of 45, old Bill McKechnie became a new father when Beryl gave birth to a daughter. They named her Carol and, with siblings who were far older, she always felt like she had multiple sets of parents. Only two years younger than her husband, Beryl often said they felt more like grandparents. Carol grew up around baseball and probably became a bit spoiled by all those nice athletes. One of her earliest memories was playing hide and seek with Rabbit Maranville during spring training at St. Petersburg, Florida. Another player took her to the beach.

It wasn't always easy being the daughter of Bill McKechnie; in the eyes of her blue-collar schoolmates in Wilkinsburg, she was a child of privilege, and nobody likes the rich kid. She wore nice clothes, lived in a nice house with the live-in maid and, unlike most kids, rode to school in a car. Life was good at home, though, where Carol basked in the love of her large family. She grew into a strikingly photogenic young girl — so much so that, according to family legend, *Life* magazine almost put her on its cover.

A lifetime later, she wrote a book about her life as *The Deacon's Daughter* and also shared memories and photographs with the author of *this* biography. Residing in Florida for the past six decades, Carol still lives in a nice home and owns nice things, which seems entirely fitting for such a kind, engaging person. Birth-certificate math says she's a new octogenarian but the lady looks much younger, carrying herself with straight-posture grace that must've first surfaced in her child self. She's a treasure and a treasure-trove of information.

A few months after Carol came into the world, her father pursued his next miracle — turning the Braves into a winner. He nearly pulled it off in 1932, guiding his team to a 77–77 record. With an anemic offense and a pitching staff of nondescript journeymen, it was a mystery how they could win as many games as they lost. Baseball insiders knew the answer, though, giving credit to the man in charge. Without berating or belittling, McKechnie drove those pitchers to the second-best team ERA in baseball. National headlines focused on the kidnapping of Charles Lindbergh's son, John McGraw's resignation, Franklin Roosevelt's election and Amelia Earhart flying across the Atlantic Ocean. The aviation empress even stopped by Braves Field in July, posing for a picture with Fuchs and heavyweight champ Jack Sharkey. Beneath the radar, Bill McKechnie was building something special in Boston.

It all came together in 1933, with the Braves recording their first winning season since 1921 and just the second in 17 years. At the end of August they were 15 games over .500 and occupied second place, five games behind the

Giants. A slump followed but they finished strong for a final mark of 83–71 and took fourth in a field of eight teams, a "first division finish," as people used to say back then. The Deacon Development program reached its pinnacle with pitcher Ben Cantwell, who came into the season with a 38–52 record and went 20–10 with a 2.62 ERA. He recorded the best winning percentage in the entire league.

The year was best known for the end of Prohibition and the beginning of the All-Star Game, both seminal moments in American history. Most insiders thought McKechnie should take charge of the National League but fans pushed for recently retired John McGraw. If it truly was a team of stars, then who better to lead it than a man who shined so bright for three decades? The fans got their way. A separate movement emerged to select coaches from the ranks of lovable legends such as Honus Wagner. Sentimentality may have put McGraw in the manager's chair but he showed little himself and shot down the idea. Insisting on taking the best men available, he selected McKechnie and Brooklyn Dodgers manager Max Carey.

Though he nearly got the top job, McKechnie had no hard feelings about the demotion and always felt honored by his selection as coach. It gave him a chance to be part of history. For the first time ever, baseball's greatest players would share the same field on the same day. It happened July 6 in Chicago, during the height of the Depression. National unemployment stood at an eye-popping 25 percent, and many of the employed took pay cuts or were reduced to part-time status. Meanwhile, home foreclosures and bank closings continued to swallow up working men. Though still thriving at the start of the decade, baseball had seen attendance drop precipitously since then. Over the span of a couple of years, all the "lively ball" gains were wiped out by a dead economy. In the midst of all that, 49,000 enthusiastic fans filled every seat at Comiskey Park for the inaugural All-Star Game.

Walking through the National League dugout, McKechnie rubbed shoulders with former pupils from his Pittsburgh and St. Louis days, and reassured Wally Berger, who struck a solitary pose as the Braves' only all-star. On the American League side, Connie Mack filled out a lineup card loaded with Yankees; he took the showdown pretty seriously, feeling no obligation to get everybody in the game. Tony Lazzeri didn't play, nor did his Yankees teammate Bill Dickey or Philadelphia slugger Jimmie Foxx. McGraw used all his position players.

Surrounded by younger stars, Babe Ruth still managed to stand out, and not just because of his protruding belly. The great one blasted a two-run homer that was the pivotal blow in a 4–2 victory for the American Leaguers. McKechnie would get many more shots at the AL in the future, beginning with the next year. After McGraw died of uremia in the off-season, McKechnie seemed the obvious choice for NL skipper in 1934 but once again had to settle for first mate. Though he was, by far, the most experienced candidate, major league executives decided to select the pennant-winning managers of 1933. So the senior circuit job went to Bill Terry of the Giants, while Washington's Joe Cronin took over the AL reins. McKechnie got a coaching job again and that made him an up-close eyewitness to Carl Hubbell's legendary strikeout string at the Polo Grounds. The Giants ace used his unfathomable screwball to notch consecutive strikeouts against five of the world's greatest hitters — Ruth, Gehrig, Foxx, Al Simmons and Cronin. Law enforcement put together a similar streak the following year, killing Bonnie and Clyde, John Dillinger, Pretty Boy Floyd and Baby Face Nelson. It took multiple agencies to do it, however, whereas Hubbell put five notches on one belt. After his early dominance, it became a hitters' game that saw the American League prevail, 9–7.

The season resumed with the Braves two games over .500, in fifth place. They crossed the finish line in fourth with a 78–73 record that looked ordinary but actually marked a significant milestone. McKechnie had just delivered two consecutive winning seasons, an extreme rarity for that franchise in the 20th century. Over at Fenway Park, the Red Sox finally showed a pulse after a dozen years of horrible baseball and finished at .500. To take the next step to serious contention, both Boston teams needed to upgrade their hitting attack next season.

October optimism turned to winter despair when news surfaced of the Braves' dire financial straits. Hit hard by the Depression, Judge Fuchs appealed to the community for help and talked about renting out Braves Field for dog racing. He emphasized that nobody was asking for charity; fans just needed to buy lots of tickets for next season's opener and to buy them soon. Home attendance dropped greatly in 1934, something Fuchs attributed mostly to bad weather and competition from horse racing. Money was in such short supply that 1935 spring training sat on the chopping block until a citizens' committee raised $28,000. The National League office soon provided help on another front, signing a lease renewal that guaranteed rental payment for the next 11 years at Braves Field. Rent was in arrears and it wouldn't reflect well on the league if one of its teams got evicted like a sharecropper in Dustbowl country. The Braves would sub-lease their stadium from the NL on "highly favorable terms." The move also gave league magnates power to veto dog racing, a low-grade form of entertainment that nobody wanted to see connected to baseball.

Fuchs optimistically told the press he expected to get out of debt within a couple of weeks. He also had a semi-secret plan to boost future profits by signing Babe Ruth. Desperate to become a major league manager, the Babe couldn't get a commitment in New York and would go anywhere that gave him an opportunity. Worn down by two decades in baseball and bars, the 40-year-old was coming off a bad season by his standards — .288 average, 22 home runs, 84 RBI. If he produced similar numbers as player-manager in Boston, attendance could go through the roof, and no franchise needed a boost more than the Braves. It was common knowledge that the Bambino's chubby body was breaking down, but even if he only appeared sporadically in the starting lineup, it would surely create a buzz in Beantown.

The Braves already had a manager, however, and that was no small stumbling block. Yet it didn't stop Fuchs from dangling the managing carrot in front of Ruth, not for 1935 but probably the following year and beyond. Though usually drawing denials or no-comments, it was the worst-kept secret of winter, and McKechnie resented the judge for never confiding in him. He had to read about it in the newspapers.

Ruth was still a Yankee when he returned from a Japanese barnstorming tour on February 20. He wanted to manage full-time but would consider playing, too, if it helped him meet the ultimate goal. One rumor had the Yankees signing Ruth, then trading him to Chicago, where he would manage the White Sox. Another said Ruth would get the Yankees job if Joe McCarthy failed to win the pennant for a third straight year.

On February 27, front page headlines shouted the news: Babe Ruth was returning to Boston. He'd started his career there, winning three World Series with the Red Sox, while earning acclaim as a phenomenal pitcher and surprisingly talented slugger. The city hadn't won a title since the Yankees bought him in 1920, and now he was back. McKechnie remained manager while Ruth wore three hats — vice president, assistant manager and player. It was like Pittsburgh all over again, only worse. At least McKechnie didn't have to find a spot for Fred Clarke in his Pirates lineup. Ruth revisited the situation in his 1948 autobiography: "The whole thing got off to a bad start. Bill McKechnie was not consulted before I was signed as his assistant manager. Fuchs then intimated that someday I would be the manager. It put both Bill and me in awkward positions."[3] Speaking from spring training in St. Petersburg, Florida, McKechnie told the press, "As far as the question of manager is concerned, there never has been a ball club that could stand two managers and there never will be. I'm manager until such a time as the club sees fit to ask me to step down or I think it right to step down myself. The judge and I understand each other on those matters as well as on all others."[4]

He offered words of praise, too, saying Ruth could still hit the ball and would be a gate attraction for the entire league, not just the Braves. While fellow managers dreamily contemplated the attendance bumps when Ruth came to town, one NL star aimed a scathing rebuke at him. Fresh off a World

Series championship with the 1934 Gashouse Gang, Cardinals pitcher Dizzy Dean told reporters that the Bambino had no business coming after McKechnie's job. Let the American League find a place for him, he said. Dean considered the Deacon one of his best friends and never forgot the time some fatherly advice saved him from big trouble. As a disciplinary meeting with Judge Landis loomed in 1934, Dean planned on giving the Commissioner a tongue-lashing and said so during a visit to Braves Field. McKechnie got wind of it, convinced him to take a more civil approach, and the meeting went quite well. That event and others made Dean feel protective of his pal, so he came out swinging on the Babe Ruth affair. His stance softened when he heard that McKechnie would be bumped up to a front office position if relieved of managing duties.

Fuchs invested a lot of money in Ruth, giving him a three-year contract and a percentage of the profits. At the time, his pay was reported at anywhere from $20,000 to $40,000 a year. Biographers usually put the figure at $25,000, though Ruth said $35,000 in his autobiography. Whatever the total, it was certainly a lot more than McKechnie's unannounced salary, and most followers agreed that ownership wouldn't dish out that kind of cash for a part-time player with bad legs. Management had to be in the long-range plan. Ruth soon stated it definitively, telling a New York reporter it was all settled that he'd take charge next year. Asked for a response in St. Petersburg, McKechnie came back with, "It's all news to me. I certainly have received no official notification of the change.... As far as my present status is concerned I'm going to work right along as if the Babe never even made that statement."[5]

A certain statement from Fuchs was harder to ignore. He made it in a letter to Ruth that was published for all to see: "If it was determined after your affiliation with the club in 1935 that it was for the mutual interest for you to take up the active management on the field there would be absolutely no handicap in having you so appointed."[6] When asked by reporters to explain the situation, Fuchs referred them to the letter and said it was very explicit, frank and unmistakable. In reality, it was none of the three and left room for interpretation. Which might have been his plan all along.

Everybody could agree on at least one thing: McKechnie was manager for the present season and Ruth was not. One of the first tough decisions was where to put Ruth on defense. First base seemed a logical spot for a slow-moving man but the Braves already had a good, young player there. Ruth owned tons of right field experience but didn't yet have a feel for National League outfields. He had to play somewhere, though, and no other positions suited him any better. If only they had the designated hitter back in those days.

The Babe's shortcomings didn't bother Fuchs much. Where pessimists saw a round belly, he saw an island of financial security in an ocean of the Great Depression. McKechnie was the guy who had to make it work. If Fuchs wasn't entirely straightforward with him, he had a straight-shooting supporter in Charles Adams, a leading stockholder and the judge's silent partner. Ending his silence during the management fiasco, Adams publicly and privately supported his incumbent. He sent a letter of encouragement to McKechnie at the West Coast Inn in St. Petersburg, telling him, "It is difficult to criticize Judge Fuchs in his emergency. I might have under the same conditions yielded. You have been far too loyal and considerate of the Braves organization and its upper executive staff for me to feel happy or satisfied to have you in any way humiliated or discredited. You do not deserve it."[7]

He also said McKechnie should remain with the club, manager or no manager. If Ruth took over as field boss, he had a job waiting as Adams' right-hand man. With Fuchs impossible to read, the offer had to come as a huge relief. Six months later, President Roosevelt signed the Social Security Act, but at least one Wilkinsburg constituent already felt pretty secure. Regardless of what happened on the management front, the formerly silent partner anticipated a bright future, with Bambino-worshipping fans bringing in big money and the franchise using those greenbacks to buy better players. It would be a good time to work for the Braves.

McKechnie sent a letter back, saying he'd gladly work for Adams. He sounded a cautionary note about the future, however, painting an alternate version where disappointed fans stay home when worn-down Ruth sits out because of injury, fatigue or strategic reasons. "I am doubtful if Ruth is not able to play, whether the Braves are going to realize their investment as they hope. I am looking now beyond the first flush of enthusiasm and the temporary gate receipts to the time when Ruth will, of necessity or his own choice, be on the sidelines."[8]

The Babe arrived to a hero's welcome at Boston's Back Bay Train Station on February 28. A police detail escorted him though the packed platform and took him to the Copley Plaza Hotel, where he signed contracts that night. A banquet followed later. It was a similar scene four days later, when 3,000 excited supporters greeted him at the St. Petersburg train station. The Babe was his vintage, effervescent self, charming the crowd with his broad smile, booming voice and waves of the cap. "Where's Bill McKechnie? I want to see Bill McKechnie," he roared. The boss was there but preferred to stay in the background for the time being, while the city mayor and Chamber of Commerce officials conducted an official greeting ceremony.

McKechnie eventually worked his way through the crowd and shook hands with the big guy while newspaper photographers snapped pictures. Accompanied by his wife, Claire, Babe then began the long walk to his awaiting car — not long in distance but in duration. He stopped frequently to shake hands or pose for a photo. Along the way, he bellowed his typical greeting over and over: "Hello, kid. How'r ya?" For Braves secretary Ed Cunningham, he offered a "Hello, Bill!" The Babe was always bad with names. When the Ruths finally began the drive to their spring residence, several photographers tagged along and convinced McKechnie to come too.

Never at a loss for words, Babe kept up the banter while posing for another photo with his new manager. "What time do you practice in the morning, Bill?" he bellowed. "10:45. Whoa. I'll have to get an alarm clock, I guess." When the shutters stopped clicking for the day, interviews began with newspaper reporters, who barely noticed when McKechnie left for his hotel. The next morning, Ruth arrived at Waterfront Park for his debut in a Boston Braves uniform. He felt blessed to reunite with his old friend and fellow hedonist Rabbit Maranville, who was struggling to come back from a career-threatening leg injury. Before Ruth arrived, Maranville wore the crowd-pleaser crown in Boston. Local sportswriters practically drooled over the inevitable bounty of colorful quotes with those two in the same clubhouse.

Maranville quickly christened Ruth with a new nickname of "Exec," as in executive. "Say, exec, what's the idea of trying to trade my roomie, Bobby Brown?" he yelled out in the clubhouse. "Don't forget I'm captain of this club." Ruth shouted back, "Whaddya mean, ya little runt. I'll fine you in my capacity as vice president." Then they walked onto the playing field, where their mere appearance induced thunderous cheers from 5,000 throats, the biggest crowd in Waterfront Park history. McKechnie asked Ruth if he wanted to say anything to the boys before practice commenced, and he did. "Fellows, I want every one of you to know that I am 100 percent with this club. We're all going to stick together and hustle and we'll get some place. I can't promise you all pennant winners but we'll have that old fight and make the rest of the guys in this league know we are in it."[9]

A hard workout followed under a broiling sun, and Ruth sweated profusely. When he called it quits after hitting a home run in batting practice, half the crowd quit too. Several days later, a bunch of St. Louis Cardinals traveled up from Bradenton to watch a meaningless early exhibition game between the Braves and Cincinnati Reds. Such was the drawing power of Babe Ruth. In the fourth inning, Dizzy Dean entered McKechnie's dugout to smooth things over with the big guy. Shaking hands in front of a battery of photographers, they had a pleasant exchange. "I hope you don't believe all you read in the newspapers, Babe," said Dean, to which Ruth responded, "Aw, I don't pay any attention to all that stuff, Diz." Trailing 3–1 at the time, Boston went on to lose a 12–1 blowout.

It was big news when the Braves faced Ruth's former teammates, and they performed well in those exhibitions against the Yankees. Three Boston hitters led the way to a 9–4 victory on St. Patrick's Day, though only the Babe received mention in *Globe* headlines. Delivering one little single in four at-bats, he was praised for sparking an all-important, early uprising. If it seemed Ruth was getting too much credit in the Grapefruit League, one had only to look at the franchise financial report to realize he wasn't getting enough. Teams usually ran at a deficit during spring training, with expenses far outweighing income; it was just part of business in major league baseball. Ruth changed all that in a heartbeat, with an undiminished popularity that made major events out of mere exhibition contests.

Eight games into their preseason, the Braves had already taken in more gate money than they did in the entire 1934 Florida sojourn. At that rate they'd return to Boston with a substantial profit that could cover all training expenses AND Ruth's salary. When Babe went up against Dean and the Cardinals, the showdown drew a crowd of 6,500—a Florida record for major league exhibitions. With everything going smoothly down south, Charles Adams focused complete attention on professional hockey, where his other "baby" was trying to make some postseason noise. He was the founding father of Boston hockey, bringing the Bruins to town in 1924. Like the Braves, they had one championship to their credit, but unlike them, would win another before the decade was finished. It didn't happen in 1935, though, as the Toronto Maple Leafs knocked them out of the playoffs.

On the whistle-stop tour home, Ruth hit his first home run in Savannah, Georgia. It came against dubious competition, however, during a 15–1 victory over Southern Georgia Teachers' College. A day later, the team stopped at the North Carolina city of Fayetteville, where Babe once trained as a member of the minor league Baltimore Orioles. He hit his first professional home run there, and a record-setting horde of fans hoped he could repeat the feat against North Carolina State University on April 5. Paid admission registered at 5,000 but many more jumped a fence at the adjacent fair grounds.

The Braves won, 6–2, in a game that stopped in the sixth inning when they ran out of baseballs. With an overflow crowd encroaching close to the playing field, foul balls would disappear into the masses and be kept as souvenirs. When it happened for the 40th time everybody had to quit, which was just as well for Ruth, who had a bad day at the plate. In Newark he clubbed two homers, the second earning distinction as the longest ever launched at the Bears' field. Maranville played five innings, marking his first appearance in a game since breaking his leg a year earlier.

Back in Boston, the Braves prepared for an exhibition showdown with their cross-city rival, the Red Sox. The series drew such attention that a retiree drove down from Maine through a pounding rainstorm to see it. His name was Bill Carrigan, and he laid claim to a distinct honor as Babe Ruth's first major league manager. They'd slayed many a dragon together in the old Fenway Park days and still held each other in great esteem. When the game was cancelled because of bad weather, Ruth gladly joined his old mentor for a trip down memory lane and they talked baseball for hours in Carrigan's hotel room.

With the regular season opener just days away, pundits made their annual predictions about who would contend for pennants. Nobody picked the Braves to take first but they'd earned respect for steady improvement over the past few years. It certainly wouldn't shock the baseball world if they finished in the middle of the pack or moved into the top three. McKechnie believed his current team was stronger than the one that took fourth place in 1934. He predicted a return to form by former ace Ben Cantwell, who'd supposedly conquered his injury demons. With "Big Ben" renewed, a deep pitching staff

In an on-field welcoming ceremony, Babe Ruth accepts a gift from Boston Braves owner Emil Fuchs while McKechnie watches from the background. Braves outfielder Tommy Thompson is standing behind McKechnie's left shoulder (courtesy Boston Public Library, Leslie Jones Collection).

corps might carry the Braves far. In a perfect world, Ruth could stay healthy enough to inject some pop into an offense that needed it.

Opening day saw the New York Giants come to town with Carl Hubbell ready to throw. Bill Terry said it was the best team he'd ever managed. About 22,000 fans came out on a cold day at Braves Field and that was a great number, regardless of weather. Though many franchises would scoff at such a turnout, it ranked as an Opening Day record-breaker for the Braves. Among the crowd were governors from five northeastern states, and the Massachusetts one threw out the first pitch. Also attending was National League president Ford Frick, who had a vested interest in seeing Ruth succeed. What was good for the Braves should be good for the entire circuit.

As he'd done so many times before, Ruth rose to the occasion and sent everybody home with a smile — everybody but the Giants, that is. Knocking in three runs and scoring once, he had a hand in every Boston score during a 4–2 victory. The transcendent moment came in the fifth inning when Ruth tore into a Hubbell screwball for home run number 709. Right fielder Mel Ott took one look at the soaring sphere and gave up, becoming just one more spectator who watched it land deep up a runway between bleacher and pavilion. Pandemonium reigned while Ruth trotted around the bags and McKechnie came out of the third base coaching box to shake hands when he passed by. After crossing home plate, he doffed his cap to the crowd and disappeared into the dugout.

That two-run bomb put Boston up, 4–0, though the score was less important that what it represented: Babe Ruth was back, in all his clutch-hitting glory. Ed Brandt pitched brilliantly for Boston and that bode well for the future, too, but this day belonged to the Bambino. After the last out, Fuchs took a victory lap of sorts, expressing feelings of vindication and optimism. President Frick predicted that NL attendance would increase by about 500,000 over the course of the season — not entirely because of Ruth, but he was a major factor. Meanwhile, Carrigan gushed over his former student's fairy-tale performance: "You'd think it was part of a story. Babe never hit the ball any harder during the height of his career than he did today."[10] Just for good measure, Ruth also made a sparkling catch of a pop fly in shallow left field.

After the game, Bruins hockey star Eddie Shore dropped by the clubhouse, offering congratulations to all. He had a second motive for the visit, which became transparent when he quickly sidled up to the hot stove. An hour and 45 minutes was a long time to watch a baseball game in the cold. "I thought hockey players liked cold weather," Wally Berger told him. Shore replied, "They sure do, when they have a hot stove to keep warm."[11] In the losers' locker room, manager Terry made a prediction that the Braves would make a lot of trouble for NL teams in the coming months.

The Babe hit his second homer in the team's fifth game, an 8–1 loss to Brooklyn, and stayed stuck on that number for a while. On May 6, the *Boston Globe* carried a story about Ruth reuniting with a Massachusetts boy he had visited in a hospital 15 years ago. Though crippled by infantile paralysis, Joe Chmieliewicz took inspiration from his baseball hero and began playing baseball after returning home. He couldn't run but moved at the pace of a brisk walk and eventually became a high school pitcher. He met with Ruth before a game, sharing a warm handshake and kind words. Fuchs had to love it; you couldn't buy that kind of publicity.

A week later, the country breathed a sigh of relief when the president declared the Depression over — not president Roosevelt, of course, but National League president Frick. His economic indicators focused narrowly on increased attendance at baseball games. Though it was a premature projection, the sporting industry did endure hard times better than most businesses. When Suffolk Downs began its horse racing schedule in July, the track set opening day records for attendance and betting. A pessimist might say it siphoned potential customers away from Braves Field, but Charles Adams didn't care. He owned the horse track too.

After a solid start, the Braves had fallen on hard times and Ruth's batting average dropped all the way to .171. Still stuck on two homers, he had all the strikeouts of a power hitter but very little of the power. When his team sank to 6–14, Judge Fuchs threatened personnel changes. "I am going to have a talk with those boys — with all of them, including manager McKechnie and Babe Ruth — I have quite a lot to say to them."[12] The honeymoon was over.

Missing more and more time because of illness or sore limbs Ruth was looking his age, if not older. He blamed a simple cold for his batting problems, saying the watery-eyes symptom made it tough to see a baseball. For nearly two decades, Ruth was a superhuman figure who dominated without sleep, nutrition or penicillin. Now he couldn't overcome the common cold. This wasn't working out.

On May 25, the struggling Braves arrived at Pittsburgh's Forbes Field for the third of a three-game set. They'd already lost the first two. Back when he was playing for, then managing the Pirates, McKechnie never could've dreamed he'd return one day with a shell of Babe Ruth in tow. National League fans still wanted to take a look at him, however, so McKechnie put him in right field that day and batted him third. As things turned out, it was fitting that the game fell on a Sunday because Babe looked as though he'd been touched by God. He smashed three home runs, the last one supposedly traveling farther than any he'd launched in the previous decade. Disappearing over the right field wall, the ball bounced around rooftops in the distance before returning earthward. One source estimated the distance between home plate and rooftop at about 600 feet.

The home fans gradually became Ruth rooters, with the defection rate leaping exponentially every time another ball soared over the fence. He went 4-for-4 on the day, then exited the game to a huge ovation in the seventh inning. For all his heroics, the Babe could not prevent an 11–7 defeat. Not terribly far away in Michigan, an Ohio State University track and field star was having a remarkable day too. In one of the greatest performances in the sport's history, Jesse Owens shattered three world records and tied another at the Western Conference Meet. It was a sign of things to come for him, unlike Ruth's feat, which served as a grand finale.

The Babe did not walk off into the sunset after that day, as some believe. He was still around on May 29, when the Philadelphia Phillies honored him with a "Babe Ruth Day" at the Baker Bowl. Berger stole the show with a grand-slam homer in Boston's 8–6 victory, while the guest of honor walked twice and struck out twice. He played a few innings the following day, then exited the game with a charley horse. Four days later, Ruth and the Braves parted ways. Prior to a contest against the visiting Giants, the Babe called his teammates together and told them he was getting out. An awkward silence followed, then came a rush for autographs. McKechnie even joined the crowd and secured two signed baseballs. Watching yet another game from the bench, Ruth bided his time until he could tell the whole world that he was through. Ownership came to that conclusion some time ago, and when the moment finally arrived, it wasn't entirely clear whether Ruth resigned or got fired. After the game he met with reporters to announce his decision, but Judge Fuchs had already told them the franchise was cutting ties.

Perhaps it didn't matter who jumped first, but Ruth complicated matters by suggesting that he could possibly return to the Braves at some point. Putting himself on the "voluntary retired" list meant he remained on the roster and would be ineligible for two months. In theory, he could rejoin the team after 60 days. Fuchs did not subscribe to the theory and announced the unconditional release of Ruth. It was not an amicable parting, and the Babe said he'd never return to the Braves as long as the judge was still there.

The two men had butted heads over Ruth's invitation to a gala welcoming celebration aboard the *Normandie*, a French ocean liner en route to New York City. Nursing a sore knee, Babe saw no harm in leaving the team for a day and representing baseball at the social event of the season. Especially when the Braves were only playing an exhibition game that day. Fuchs insisted that he had better be on the bench, in uniform. That was the last straw for Ruth, who made a quick exit one day before the exhibition. "Judge Fuchs has double-crossed me too many times for me to continue the way things are," he told reporters.

Ruth got his salary for the year but nothing else that had been implied in his contract. He obviously would not become manager, and a percentage of profits meant little on a cellar-dwelling team that didn't make money. Ruth said Fuchs wanted him to invest $50,000 of his own money in the franchise. Aside for his affection toward teammates and fans, the Babe's Boston experience was an unqualified disaster. If he'd known what lay ahead, he never would've come. In his autobiography, he said, "[Fuchs] expected to cash in on me as a player and at first people did come out to see me, as a curiosity. But my batting average had fallen to .181 for 28 games, and people wouldn't have come out to see St. Peter himself hit .181."[14]

The judge said his manager complained frequently about Ruth, and pitchers protested that he was a defensive liability. McKechnie confirmed the comment, saying he told Fuchs that the team couldn't function properly with the Bambino in the outfield. There were apparently off-field issues too. "I frankly stated that certain actions of Ruth ... which I would absolutely forbid with any other member of the club, were responsible for the lack of discipline and that unless Judge Fuchs could convince Babe Ruth to retire I was unable to get any real baseball discipline or proper spirit."[15]

"Somebody must have forced McKechnie to say that," Ruth countered. "Why Bill was almost in tears the other day when he told the club that I was leaving. I never worked with a better bunch of fellows than those boys up there. Bill and I got along good. Of course, Judge Fuchs is someone else again."[16] Indeed, McKechnie often insisted there was no friction with Babe and issued denials about demanding his ouster. Maybe he did get pressured into taking responsibility for discharging the most popular figure in baseball history. Sportswriter Victor O. Jones smelled conspiracy and said so in his *Boston Evening Globe* column of June 4: "The statement rapping the Babe, issued over McKechnie's signature, doesn't sound like Bill, either in point of content or in literary style. On the other hand, it has all the characteristics of a typical Fuchs statement."

Wasting no time after bidding adieu, Ruth left for New York the following morning with his wife, daughter and mother-in-law. They would travel by car, with the lead-footed Babe behind the wheel. His June 3 departure stood in stark, glum contrast to the memory of his grand entrance last winter. There were no cheering hordes or city officials to pay tribute. Everybody wanted a piece of Ruth when he arrived with high hopes, and few desired to comfort him when he left as a failure. Only a handful of people showed up to see him off outside his hotel. Thank goodness for the wedding party that moved through the lobby and recognized George Herman Ruth. They added an element of festiveness and celebrity worship to an otherwise melancholy scene. Some threw confetti and rice at Ruth, and he seemed to appreciate the gesture.

Though packed, loaded and ready to leave, the traveling party stayed grounded for about ten minutes while waiting for a certain person to show. When Bill McKechnie made his dramatic appearance, Ruth immediately perked up and proudly proclaimed, "I guess that should answer Judge Fuchs' charges. If I had actually done what I was charged by Fuchs with doing, I don't think McKechnie would have come down here to say goodby."[17] It was a sweet slice of vindication pie to take on the trip. Dressed in a suit and tie, McKechnie walked up to Ruth and shook his hand as they stood near his car. They looked each other directly in the eye and exchanged brief, sincere words of parting.

"I'm sorry to see you go, Babe, but I guess it had to come. I wish you all the luck in the world."

"I know you do."

Ruth climbed into the car with his women and drove away. He never played another game, nor did he ever manage one. Judge Fuchs was forced out a couple of months later, with Adams taking over and giving his manager a second job as temporary general manager. Deacon Bill McKechnie had weathered a storm that brought legends to their knees and emerged stronger than ever.

Now what to do about his horrible baseball team. Sure, Ruth hit a paltry .181 with six homers and 24 strikeouts, but it seemed hard to believe that one player could sabotage a club so badly. It became nigh impossible to accept when the Braves continued their hapless ways long after he left. Their offense was the worst in baseball, by a long shot, and the pitching staff finished with the National League's worst ERA. After two straight winning seasons, the Boston boys fell apart with essentially the same cast that had once created such optimism. The only significant difference between then and 1935 was Babe Ruth and the executive power struggle.

The Braves completed their misery at 38–115, a win-loss figure that still ranks as one of the worst ever. It was back to the drawing board for McKechnie but he had at least one mighty building block. Though surrounded by weak hitters, Wally Berger led the league in home runs (34) and RBI (130) — the latter stat particularly impressive since so few teammates reached base. He received far more support in 1936, as McKechnie rebuilt his team. Perhaps trying to distance itself from unpleasant memories, the franchise tried on a new nickname — the "Bees." [To avoid confusion, your author will still refer to them as Braves.]

Most players returned from the debacle squad but a few newcomers spiced up things. A winter trade brought in Tony Cuccinello, a Long Island native and Brooklyn Dodgers second baseman. He hit over .300 in his first tour at Braves Field. Arriving in that same trade was catcher Al Lopez, a future

Hall of Fame manager. In his second year on the roster, former Red Sox Danny MacFayden broke out with the league's second-best ERA (2.87) while going 17–13. A nine-year veteran who'd never accomplished much, his success made McKechnie look like a pitching guru again.

The Braves improved their win total by 33 games in 1936, going 71–83 and placing sixth. After a one-year hiatus, they were on the way up again. Offense remained a weak spot, however, so the front office loosened its purse strings and bought a good Pacific Coast League player by the name of DiMaggio. The older brother of Joltin' Joe, Vince hoped to match his sibling's recent rookie-year success with the Yankees. He looked bad at spring training, however, and team president Bob Quinn talked about cutting him. Vince could play third base well enough but he seemed overmatched against major league pitching.

In the boxing world, former heavyweight champion Jack Johnson drew attention that spring by criticizing current contender Joe Louis. His stance was all wrong and he was a sucker for a right-hand counter. Johnson didn't enjoy seeing the kid get knocked out by Max Schmeling last year but knew it was coming. Some said old Jack was just jealous that the black community had a new hero. "Jealous? I was heavyweight champion of the world," Johnson told the famous sports scribe, Grantland Rice. "I've had my day. Why should I begrudge the boy his? ... Envious of his skill as a boxer? He hasn't any."[18] The sagacious Rice had his own opinion about the topic: "The truth is that when a fighter goes to Louis in a straight line, he will get his brains knocked out, but if he employs any artifice Louis becomes bewildered and doesn't know what to do with him."[19]

The "Brown Bomber" won the crown a couple of months later and wore it for 12 years. A smaller honor went to the Boston Red Sox, who earned city bragging rights with two preseason wins over the Braves. It was a franchise on the rise, destined to recapture the passions of New England. The glory days of Smoky Joe Wood and Tris Speaker were long since buried, with new standouts carving a niche in modern times. Jimmie Foxx, Joe Cronin, Bobby Doerr — these men were guiding the team toward a brighter future, and more help was on the way. McKechnie sent a friend to check out a West Coast wunderkind by the name of Ted Williams and heard rave reviews. The Red Sox got to him first, however, and the skinny prodigy would join them after another year of seasoning.

It wouldn't be long before the Braves struggled to keep up with their city brothers. In April of 1937, however, they seemed evenly matched, as both preseason games went down to the wire. It came as no great surprise that Wally Berger smacked a home run in game two, but hearts soared when much-maligned Vince DiMaggio launched one too. The "slender, swarthy" rookie also doubled to the wall in a ninth-inning rally that fell short. Looking more and more like his little brother, Vince provided an optimism-injection to fans of the National Leaguers.

Their positivity was put to the test on opening day, when the Braves dropped a doubleheader to the lowly Phillies and Wally Berger broke a finger. It was an odd day, with the city's attention divided between baseball, the Boston Marathon and Patriot's Day festivities. Dressed in 1770s garb, a horseman reenacted Paul Revere's famous ride, and the less famous ride of William Dawes received tribute too. Adding a dose of dramatic realism to the pantomime, a police officer rushed forward to save a small boy from the thundering hooves of Mr. Revere's cavalry escort.

The city held a parade, of course, and surrounding communities arranged events too. It was an all-day affair at Lexington and Concord. The British got their revenge in the marathon — sort of — when a young Canadian upset the hometown favorite to win in a time of two hours, 33 minutes and 20 seconds.

Kind-hearted McKechnie had his fiery side too. Here, he argues a call with the home plate umpire at Braves Field while catcher Al Lopez supports his position (courtesy Boston Public Library, Leslie Jones Collection).

After watching the race, thousands rushed to Braves Field for the second baseball game and boosted attendance to about 25,000. They saw the home team fall, 1–0.

In some ways it was a sign of things to come, as the Braves fell quickly to the back of the pack and never contended. But the 1937 campaign greatly enhanced respect for McKechnie, who somehow squeezed out a winning record by season's end. Nobody hit over .300 for him, DiMaggio led the league in strikeouts and Gerber was traded away in June for a promising young pitcher who never panned out. Yet the Braves still flirted with .500. In a July 27 column for the *New York World Telegram*, Dan Daniel called the "Bees" a "truly sorry aggregation" that overachieved to the very edge of a first division berth. "Not the least vital factor in the strange achievements of these latter-day Hitless Wonders is the managerial acumen of McKechnie. He is one of the greatest field leaders of the last twenty years and deserves better material for his skilled effort."[20]

Pitching was the key, with McKechnie molding two rookies into 20-game winners. Jim Turner went 20–11 with a league-leading 2.38 ERA, while Lou Fette was 20–10 with a 2.88 ERA. Meanwhile, last year's golden boy — Danny MacFayden — saw fewer wins but maintained an impressive earned run average. Paced by those three thoroughbreds, the Braves staff led all of baseball in team ERA.

Called home to his youngest daughter's sickbed, McKechnie missed the final two games of the season. At the vulnerable age of five, Carol had pneumonia, a frightening condition in an age without antibiotics. Her condition remained serious after McKechnie's arrival, and doctors predicted the coming of a "pneumonia crisis," whatever that meant. Seventy-four years afterward, she reflected on that time: "I remember being sick. We'd been downtown and it was cold. That night I got real sick and, of course, Mother felt terrible. She felt like she had caused it." They used oxygen therapy on Carol at the McKechnie home in Wilkinsburg. Her treatment also included aspirin, some kind of powder and a teaspoon of whiskey every three or four hours. While taking a break from his bedside vigil, Bill told the Associated Press, "All the ball games in the world aren't worth as much as my little girl."[21] The stoic Scot gave folks a rare peek at his emotions that day and probably did more of the same privately when Carol made a full recovery.

Joe McCarthy managed the Yankees to 102 wins and a World Series title in 1937, while Bill Terry guided his Giants to 95 wins and the National League pennant. When it came time to pick a Manager of the Year, however, *The Sporting News* bestowed that honor on Bill McKechnie. Anybody could succeed with studs like Gehrig, Joe DiMaggio, Bill Dickey, Lefty Gomez, Mel Ott, and Carl Hubbell, but try winning with the likes of Gene Moore, Elbie

Dressed in civilian clothing, McKechnie strikes a friendly pose with Brooklyn Dodgers manager Casey Stengel. Stengel would one day become the dean of major league managers, but at the time of this photograph in 1935, he was still a kid compared to McKechnie (courtesy Boston Public Library, Leslie Jones Collection).

Fletcher and Debs Garms. McKechnie led them to a 79–73 record, an act of prestidigitation that had legions of experts and magicians wondering how he did it. In a *Sporting News* profile of McKechnie's career, Fred Lieb wrote what most baseball men were thinking: "It truthfully can be said that Bill McKechnie can do more with less than any other manager in the majors."

The Cincinnati Reds needed a manager like that. Capping a decade-long stretch of ineptitude, they stumbled through the 1937 season at 56–98, 40 games out of first. There was a time when you could barely tell the Reds and Braves apart, such was the mirror-image incompetence of both franchises. That all changed with the arrival of McKechnie, and eight years later, his stock was at an all-time high. The Braves and Reds weren't the only suitors trying to capture the Deacon's hand. For the first time in his career, he found himself in position to leave a job on his own terms, without boot prints on his backside.

13

Resurrecting the Reds

[McKechnie] was the real fatherly type. You liked to play for him. He was very understanding, sympathetic. And yet I'll tell you one thing—when he put his hand across his chest and looked at you over his bifocals, he was mad. And as fine a gentleman as he was, he could be rough as a corncob when he thought you hadn't done the right thing.[1]—Frank McCormick, Reds first baseman

Cincinnati won the bidding war, signing McKechnie to a two-year deal for $25,000 per season that made him one of the highest-paid managers in baseball. It was big-market money in the major leagues' smallest city; that's how much owner Powel Crosley wanted the Deacon. One of the most innovative industrialists of his time, Crosley amassed a large fortune from producing radios, household appliances and auto accessories. He bought the Reds franchise in 1934, saving it from financial ruin and paying for much-needed renovations to Redland Field. Folks were so grateful that they renamed the ballpark after their generous owner.

Crosley was accustomed to successful business ventures but his baseball team continued to fail. At the end of the decade, he sent word to his underlings to spare no expense in landing the manager who could help turn things around. As extra incentive, they offered potential bonus pay for significant attendance increases and a top-four finish. If McKechnie worked his typical magic he might pull down 30–35 grand, a figure that dwarfed his rumored $18,000 salary in Boston. The Braves could pay that to Babe Ruth but not to a manager who wasn't named John McGraw.

"I knew that four or five clubs were after McKechnie," said Braves president Quinn. "But I was in hopes that we could keep him in Boston, where we looked upon him as the best manager in baseball. When he informed me he had a chance to get considerably more money in Cincinnati, I wouldn't stand in his way."[2]

The announcement came on the eve of another World Series clincher for the Yankees. Cincinnati hadn't been to a Fall Classic since 1919, though it fielded strong teams through most of the 1920s. During the 1930s, Reds fans didn't even dream of marching into the postseason. Now they had a guy in charge who gave people hope again. Optimism radiated from the top down, beginning with general manager Warren Giles: "There's no question in my mind that McKechnie is the smartest manager in baseball today. He knows the game, and above all, how to handle men. Our next step is to get some players for Bill."[3]

The previous manager probably would've liked some better players, too, but who knows what he could've accomplished with them. Under McKechnie's leadership, a talent investment seemed sure to produce results. Back in Boston, the rumor mill had Tony Lazzeri as a practical shoo-in for new Braves manager, and his release from the Yankees seemed to remove the last obstacle. Next came stories about the club making offers to Donie Bush and Gabby Hartnett. The job eventually went to McKechnie's good friend, colorful Casey Stengel, who didn't seem to mind that he was neither the first nor second choice of President Quinn. He'd only managed a few years and didn't do it at all in 1937. In his autobiography, Stengel explained that the opportunity came just in the nick of time. "I was possibly going to give up baseball and stay in the oil business but in 1938 I was invited back to the major leagues by Mr. Bob Quinn."[4] McKechnie owned a piece of those oil fields too.

In 1937 the Reds scored the second-fewest runs in the National League, outdone in futility by only one team — McKechnie's Braves. Their lone .300 hitter was lead-footed catcher Ernie Lombardi, but the pitching staff had enormous potential, and that gave McKechnie his favorite building block. Maybe he could develop their greenhorn southpaw, Johnny Vander Meer. It was not a strong defensive team, however, and McKechnie always built success through pitching and defense. Changes would have to be made.

Everybody knew McKechnie as a pitcher's manager but he never felt inadequate in discussions about offense. He said Honus Wagner taught him valuable batting lessons that were never forgotten, even though he didn't become a good hitter himself. McKechnie passed along plenty of tips about the art of hitting. Still, it obviously wasn't his strongest suit and, when it came time to select a coaching staff, he reserved a spot for an expert on the subject: his old buddy, Edd Roush. They'd been teammates on the Reds of 1916 and 1917 before McKechnie left town. Enjoying his retirement and considering the $3,600 coach's pay a joke, Roush was reluctant to take the job. "Why, good God almighty, it cost me more money being on the ball club than it did at home," he remembered four decades later. "Thunder! Why, I always figured it cost me five or six thousand dollars to be with the club."[5] Of course, the club paid for major expenses like travel and lodgings, but the out-of-pocket stuff could add up. Old ball players find themselves drawn to ballparks, however, and Roush got an extra nudge from his wife, who thought her beloved needed something to do.

It was quite a coup for McKechnie. In Roush he had a man of gravitas, who'd won two batting titles and recorded a career batting average of .323. A great center fielder in his day, he also qualified as an expert instructor on outfield defense. The Hoosier country boy had his best years in Cincinnati and remained a popular figure among fans and players alike. Roush was a candidate for the manager's job at one point. Coming to Cincinnati shortly after the last skipper was fired, he supposedly analyzed the roster and promoted himself as the best choice. Roush did outclass McKechnie on the charisma scale but McKechnie had all the managing experience. For Reds executives, the decision was a no-brainer.

Signing in early March, Roush soon traveled south to Tampa, Florida, for spring training. There, he joined his manager and fellow coach Hank Gowdy, a former weak-hitting catcher whose expertise leaned toward pitch and catch. Gowdy had assisted McKechnie in Boston and did such a bang-up job that he got an invitation to perform similar duties in Cincinnati. Across the nation, many remembered him as the first major leaguer to enlist for duty in World War I.

After watching the Reds practice awhile, Roush came to the quick conclusion that they could not hit, run or throw. Speaking with characteristic bluntness, he called his students together and delivered a dose of verbal tough love. "All bad hitters take the first pitch, wave at the curve and get themselves so far behind there's no way out ... and you all do this. You're all bad hitters and it's no wonder you're a last-place ball club."[6]

A new directive required every Red to leave the bench swinging. As their coach liked to say, "Take three swings and you might hit one." Roush taught the old-fashioned method of scientific place-hitting and scoffed at the reckless power swing that Babe Ruth popularized. Not that they stopped thinking about home runs entirely, but the Reds listened and learned. With the Roush technique giving them another weapon in the eternal battle between hitter and hurler, they showed considerable improvement during spring training games.

The Reds got younger in 1938, with rookie Frank McCormick taking over as starting first baseman and two aging outfielders exiting the stage. Gone were Chick Hafey and Kiki Cuyler, who brought famous names and little else to the franchise. Beyond that, there weren't many changes to a roster that flirted with the 100-loss mark in 1937. On paper, the lineup looked no better and perhaps a little worse; on grass and dirt, a fresh generation was itching to change the culture of losing. Even before Roush performed his magic,

McKechnie predicted that his team would not finish last again. From the clubhouse to the front office, this franchise far surpassed his previous one. As the *Cincinnati Enquirer* put it, "You could see the hopes of a gold rush reflected in McKechnie's sharp face — just as it might have been reflected in the countenances of pioneers who had moved Westward in the old days. At last Wilkinsburg Will was moving into a baseball enterprise where he would not feel the pinch of poverty from above — where he might have money to spend on players and things."

In the season opener, Cincinnati bats delivered 14 hits and seven runs in a narrow loss to the Cubs at Crosley Field. Despite the defeat, it counted as an encouraging beginning, played out in front of a capacity crowd of 35,000 on a hot, cloudless April day. Typical pre-game festivities found the home manager presented with flowers and the owner with an American flag. Hope is a tangible thing on opening day, free with the purchase of any ticket and redeemable throughout April. Reds fans still had it at the end of the contest; their offense was off and running, and everybody just knew that McKechnie would get the pitchers on track. Less certain was the situation at catcher, where Lombardi had only lukewarm support, at best, from his manager. McKechnie didn't like his defense, handling of pitchers or monumentally slow feet. The big guy sure could hit, though. Nicknamed "Schnozz" because of his large nose, Ernesto Natali Lombardi was the son of an Italian immigrant who became a California grocer. Tipping the scales at 6'3" and 230 pounds, he hit the baseball as hard as anybody who ever played the game. When he came to the plate, third basemen and shortstops often backed toward the safety of the outfield. Unlike most power hitters, Lombardi rarely struck out, and that made it extra dangerous on opposing fielders.

Any grounder meant an out for the ponderous one, even if it traveled well beyond the infield, yet Schnozz usually ranked among the league's top batters. McKechnie once said if infielders played him straight up, at normal distance, Lombardi could break baseball's all-time, single-season record for batting average. That's how consistently hard Lombardi scorched baseballs. He was a human log jam on the base paths, however, and hit into lots of double plays.

Lombardi grew enormously popular among fans and surprisingly so with women, who were drawn to his relaxed, yet engaging personality. He had a presence about him, but beneath it all, seemed like a regular guy comfortable in his own skin and his own nose. McKechnie considered trading him but dared not pull the trigger on a move that surely would've ignited a firestorm. Beyond the popularity factor, he was the only good batter on a poor-hitting team. Then again, one player couldn't generate much offense without help from teammates. Maybe the Reds could've received multiple players in return for a guy like Lombardi. McKechnie liked his back-up catcher, former Newark Bears star Willard Hershberger, who had more tools than the current starter. As things turned out, it was best that Lombardi stuck around; he won the batting crown and MVP award in 1938, hitting .342 with 19 homers, 95 RBI, 40 walks and only 14 strikeouts. If he'd posted those numbers for a different team, McKechnie might've faced a full-scale uprising in Cincinnati.

Roush's job got a little easier when cavernous Crosley Field became smaller. Or maybe it would actually make things more difficult if batters ignored his teachings and swung for those shorter fences. The big change came about with minimum effort, as officials simply moved home plate up by 20 feet and bumped the bases forward by an equal distance. Left field's fence now stood 328 feet away, down from 339; right field shrunk from 377 to 366 and dead center went from 395 to 387. The reduced dimensions certainly made things more challenging for pitchers, but it still took a good jolt to hit one out.

Starting slowly in 1938, the Reds recovered by the end of May. A June 6 trade brought outfielder Wally Berger to the Reds, reuniting McKechnie with the greatest hitter of his Braves teams. He wasn't that guy any more but still had enough left to strengthen the offense. The Reds sat three games over .500 and 5½ games out of first place when young Johnny Vander Meer took the mound for a home game against Boston on June 11. Winner of four straight decisions, the 23-year-old southpaw faced his manager's former players from Boston. Now known as "Bees," they had little sting in their offense; Casey Stengel couldn't cure that in six months. They hit well enough to produce a winning record, however, and trailed second-place Cincinnati by only 1½ games.

Gilbert English pounded a Vander Meer pitch to deep center in the second inning but Harry Craft chased it down and made a great catch. The defense rose for another big play in the fifth, when third baseman Lew Riggs knocked down Vince DiMaggio's hot smash and made a quick throw that barely beat the runner. Beyond those two moments, Vander Meer faced little challenge on his way to a no-hitter. He issued three walks, but nobody got any farther than first base during Cincinnati's 3–0 victory.

McKechnie suddenly saw big possibilities for his team. He already had a strong staff ace in big Paul Derringer, a pitcher with pinpoint control, and now Vander Meer was winning every time out. If they could land one more front-line starter, the Reds might make a run at the pennant. Of course, no team wanted to part with an accomplished starter, so they'd have to find a diamond in the rough. Fitting the bill almost perfectly was Philadelphia Phillies pitcher Bucky Walters, a former infielder who got a couple of cups of coffee from the Deacon during the Braves days. At a post-season meeting of major league brass, word got out that Phillies owner Jerry Nugent had a big bank note coming due and couldn't pay it. McKechnie ran into him on an elevator and offered to cover the cost of the note, plus throw in a couple players, if he would part with Walters. A wave of relief fell across Nugent's face as he quickly accepted the deal.

Walters was a reluctant pitcher at first, preferring the path of an everyday infielder. He'd performed quite well with the bat and glove during his minor league tour, but never showed enough hitting consistency at the next level. Walters began his professional career as a pitcher and infielder for a North Carolina team in the Piedmont League, so everybody knew the guy could pitch when he reached the majors, and some encouraged him to give it a try. It certainly didn't look like he would make it as a third baseman. With manager Jimmie Wilson urging him on, Walters became a Phillies mound man and, over a three-year span, went 34–45 with an earned run average of about 4.40. A trained eye could see big potential, however. He'd pitched for a bad team in a hitter's ball park, so the numbers couldn't be taken at face value. McKechnie knew what the kid was capable of and snatched him up when the opportunity arose. He came with a heavy price tag: $50,000 and two players in return.

Walters joined the team in New York, just in time to witness history. On June 15, the Brooklyn Dodgers hosted Cincinnati in the first night game at Ebbets Field. A capacity crowd of nearly 39,000 showed up to see baseball under the lights and a pitcher who'd thrown a no-hitter in his last start. Babe Ruth made an appearance, paying visits to both benches before the game. A few days later he took a coaching job with the Dodgers, earning $15,000 for the rest of the season. Even the Babe couldn't match spotlights with the Reds rookie hurler at this point in history. A native of New Jersey, Vander Meer was cheered like a hometown boy by the Brooklyn faithful. How many more no-hit innings could he record before surrendering to the inevitable?

Vandy had even better stuff than he displayed a few days earlier against Boston; his fastball traveled much quicker and the curve broke sharper, leaving Dodgers batters with a helpless feeling. Nobody was even coming close to a base hit. Then again, a lot of pitches weren't even coming close to home plate. The only thing that could conceivably stop Vander Meer was his erratic control. It reached its low point in the bottom of the ninth inning, with a one-out meltdown that produced three consecutive walks. Two outs away from a feat unprecedented in major league history, the young hurler was letting it all slip away.

Walters began warming up in the bullpen and McKechnie went to the mound, where he was joined by the entire infield. It was a sight nobody wanted to see, not even the home fans, who had long since jumped on the Vander

Meer bandwagon and cheered for history at the expense of their Dodgers. Many yelled, "Don't take him out!" at the Deacon. With the Reds leading, 6–0, there seemed little danger of that but Vander Meer needed to start throwing strikes before long. McKechnie was just there for comfort and reassurance. Patting his pitcher on the shoulder, he told him to relax and take his time. McKechnie returned to the bench and Vander Meer's control returned soon after. He retired the next batter on a force-out at home, then Leo Durocher skied to center where Harry Craft squeezed it for the final out.

Fans spilled onto the field in celebration and encircled the newly minted legend before he could exit. With the help of teammates and police, he made it to the clubhouse, where another celebration soon ensued. Vander Meer staggered in and collapsed on a bench, smiling and saying nothing. McKechnie congratulated him, then Lombardi kissed him on the ear. Because they call the pitches, catchers feel more ownership on such occasions than any other position players. Wally Berger reportedly threw his hat in the air and exclaimed, "Whew! At last I'm with a real ball club!"[7]

Vander Meer stuck around the clubhouse for a long time, not to soak in accolades from teammates but to avoid the crowd outside. Finally he sneaked off to his parents' house in Midland, New Jersey, where he slept until 5 A.M., then rose for a fishing trip. The Reds were off that day. Back in Ohio, the no-hit double-dip took the club to new heights of popularity. They'd already generated goodwill with their unlikely pennant contention, but now *everybody* was talking about Cincinnati baseball. For Vander Meer, the attention went nationwide. One no-hitter made him *a* star but that second one made him *the* star.

A week later, more than 70,000 people turned out at Yankee Stadium to watch the birth of an even bigger icon. This one didn't play baseball; his name was Joe Louis and he knocked out Max Schmeling in the first round off their much-ballyhooed heavyweight boxing bout. It washed away the memory of Schmeling's KO of Louis two years earlier and, more importantly, gave Hitler a black eye when his master-race specimen caught that fierce beating from a Negro. With the Third Reich poised to overrun Europe, the bout took on fairytale symbolism of American good versus German evil. Never mind that Louis was excluded from much of white America and Schmeling had no love for the Nazis who'd taken over his homeland. It made for good copy, and Schmeling's masters really *were* far worse than segregationists.

Vander Meer captured more attention when he started the All-Star Game in July. Held at Crosley Field, the contest saw the host franchise well-represented with four starters and McKechnie on the coaching lines. Vander Meer threw three innings of scoreless, one-hit ball and got the win in a 4–1 National League triumph. A boisterous scene followed in the dressing room, with players yelling words of encouragement at each other and recounting the battles of war.

Vander Meer remained quiet, dressed quickly, and moved amongst his teammates, asking for autographs. Halfway through his second major league season, he still seemed like a kid among men when off the field. On the mound, it was an entirely different story. With so much incredible success coming so quickly, he found himself besieged by national media, and advertisers came calling with product endorsement deals. Barely out of his teens, the Dutch immigrants' son was the toast of baseball.

Further exciting the home base, McKechnie's crew pulled within 1½ games of the first-place Giants on June 28. When a six-game losing streak followed, it looked like the underdogs were all done, but they launched a late-summer charge that brought them to second place, four games behind Pittsburgh, on September 5. Regardless of what happened afterward, the Reds had proven themselves serious contenders. Bucky Walters helped fuel the surge by going 11–6 while giving the pitching staff that third quality starter that McKechnie craved. But Edd Roush's offense deserved just as much of the credit and probably more. One short year earlier, it could've been called Ernie Lombardi and the seven dwarves, but now it was a fearsome unit. Lombardi had an MVP season and Frank McCormick turned in one of the greatest rookie campaigns of all time, churning out a league-high 209 hits while batting .327 and driving in 106 runs. After hitting 12 home runs the previous year, outfielder Ival Goodman belted 30 in 1938. With every returnee improving, the team batting average increased by 23 points, home runs went up and strikeouts declined.

The Cubs took the pennant in thrilling fashion, erasing a late, seven-game deficit to the Pirates by going 21–5 in September. New York edged Cincinnati for third place but that 82–68 Reds record still shined like a beacon compared to the hopelessness of 1937. Posting their first winning season in ten years, they'd made a gallant bid for a worst-to-first campaign and reinvigorated their fan base in the process. The future looked bright for McKechnie and his hitting coach.

The Damn Yankees won the World Series yet again, sweeping Chicago with relative ease. Their future looked shaky a few weeks later, however, when a Halloween radio broadcast reported an imminent Martian invasion. The alien force landed in New Jersey first, annihilated the state militia, then moved its strange craft into the Hudson River on a trek toward New York City. Some erstwhile listeners took up arms to protect home, family and cherished institutions like baseball, but what chance did they have if the army couldn't make a dent? It seemed just a matter of time until Yankee Stadium and the Polo Grounds were reduced to rubble like every other landmark.

The news-bulletin radio reports were, of course, part of a creative spin on H.G. Wells' novel, *War of the Worlds*. Directed by Orson Welles, the finely-crafted drama was a Mercury Theatre production that aired over the Columbia Broadcasting System. Those who tuned in from the start knew it wasn't real because they heard the occasional disclaimer. Many joined it in progress, however, and pockets of panic broke out across the northeast United States and Canada. A day later, Lombardi was named National League MVP.

Reds fans couldn't wait for the 1939 season to roll around. With continued improvement, there seemed no limit on how far their team could go. One important piece declined to return, however, and he'd done more for the offense than any two players combined. Edd Roush refused to work another year at slave wages, and the money men offered only a $400 increase from the previous year. That made a total of $4,000—an insult to a man who'd spent his entire playing career fighting for every cent he could get. Meanwhile, he heard McKechnie was pulling in $35,000, including bonuses.

The wound still seemed fresh for Roush's wife in 1964, when author Lawrence Ritter came to their west-central Florida home to conduct an interview for his book, *The Glory of Their Times*. Pulling no punches, Essie Mae Roush told him, "Well, it was disgusting, that was all. Edd only went back because he liked Bill and he wanted to [coach] for him there. I thought that was the raw treatment."[8] McKechnie did not control the franchise purse strings but Essie thought he held enough influence to get her husband a better deal. So did Edd, for that matter.

"But you're still friends," Ritter said.

"Oh well, what are you gonna do about it?" Essie responded. "Sure, we're friends. Bill comes over here and eats with us and we go over there and we're together."

The Roushes never asked for an explanation about that ticklish topic, and the McKechnies never offered one. Some things are better left unsaid. Their friendship survived and they ended up retiring to the same neighborhood down south. Unlike so many other Depression-era Americans, Roush wasn't hurting for money in 1939. His old contract wars had produced a nice nest egg, and he'd invested wisely too. Returning to his hometown in Southern Indiana, he lived perfectly content without baseball and never took another major league job. Replacing him on the Cincinnati staff was former Phillies manager Jimmie Wilson.

In 1938, Roush told McKechnie that the Reds were one good third baseman away from a pennant. No offense to incumbent Lew Riggs, but he was ordinary. An extraordinary talent fell into their laps in the off-season when a contract impasse put Athletics third baseman Bill Werber on the market. The 31-year-old hadn't reported for spring training by mid–March, so cash-strapped Connie Mack gladly sold him to the Reds for a reported $25,000.

Werber haggled with the Cincinnati front office, too, and eventually got his price.[9] It was quite possibly the best money Warren Giles ever spent, as the career American Leaguer became a sparkplug that propelled the Reds atop the senior circuit.

Werber's success came as no surprise to those familiar with his past. In his sophomore season, he burst into prominence with the Red Sox, scoring 129 runs and stealing a league-high 40 bases while posting a .321 batting average. Though he never duplicated those numbers again, he remained a proven run-scorer and often reached double figures in home runs. During his farewell season with Philadelphia, Werber hit only .259 but still crossed home plate 92 times. Fortune surely smiled on the Reds when this top-level infielder unexpectedly became available.

Big numbers were just one part of his appeal, however. Werber also brought a big personality to the clubhouse, with an energy that became infectious. He liked to dole out nicknames to teammates, and they usually liked getting them. Some might've considered him overbearing but most admired his style, especially when the team was winning. Scoring a league-best 115 runs, Werber put his new team in position for lots of wins.

McKechnie knew the Reds could be something special but remained humble when asked for a prediction on the upcoming season. He said they were a top-four team with a chance to take first, but ultimate success hinged on pitching depth. They needed good starts out of every member of the rotation, and that was a tall order. "Right now I can't see my club finishing any better than third," McKechnie told the *Cincinnati Enquirer*. "The Cubs and Giants both appear stronger." Lou Holtz did not invent "poor-mouthing" while coaching Notre Dame football in the 1980s and 1990s. He stood on the shoulders of masters like Bill McKechnie. (Holtz was two years old when McKechnie downplayed Cincinnati's deep talent pool.)

The Reds won 12 straight games in May, moved into first and stayed there the rest of the season. By the end of July, they owned a 60–30 record and led their nearest competition by 12 games. When a challenger finally emerged, it was the Cardinals and not the Cubs or Giants. Most of the old "Gas House Gang" boys were gone by then, though Ducky Medwick still swung a mean bat and Pepper Martin remained as an effective part-time starter. Planting their flag as the new generation of stars were slugging first baseman Johnny Mize and outfielder Enos Slaughter. Going 20–9 in August, the Cards pulled within 5½ games of slumping Cincinnati.

It was an inconvenient time to make television history but the Reds did so anyhow, playing in the first televised baseball game on August 26. While Red Barber did the play-by-play for NBC's two-camera experiment at Ebbets Field, McKechnie's boys took a 5–2 victory over the Dodgers. Few people owned TV sets back then, so it was more a triumph of technology than a unifying moment for the nation. A few thousand people probably tuned in. Since it was a doubleheader, the two teams also took part in the *second* game ever televised, with that one going to the home squad, 6–1. Baseball's first postgame show included an interview with McKechnie.

Staying red-hot, the Cardinals came within three games of first on September 10 and 2½ by the 20th but Cincy had a good month and held them off. Posting an impressive final record of 97–57, the Reds finished 4½ up on St. Louis and led everybody else by double digits — tremendous numbers for a tremendous season. Off the field and beyond oceans, the world was at war and the bad guys were winning. While managers ran drills at spring training, Germany invaded Czechoslovakia; when the baseball season entered its final month, Nazis entered Poland. France and Great Britain declared war on Germany, but could do little to slow the blitzkrieg that toppled one nation after another.

Say what you want about the human carnage, but the war did plant seeds for America's economic recovery. Many people were drafted into full-time jobs with free room, board and rifles. It also put people to work on the home front, manufacturing the tools of combat. For the time being, America was separated by neutrality, but Cincinnati had a huge population of residents with German ancestry. They wore it as a badge of honor, much as they had before World War One created a climate of anti–Germany sentiment. That blew over eventually but things were about to get uncomfortable again. For now, though, the city was united in support of its resurgent baseball team.

As McKechnie predicted, pitching was the key, though he never would've expected such success without much help from Vander Meer. After going 15–10 with a 3.12 ERA the year before, he fell to 5–9 and 4.67. People barely noticed, though, thanks to Bucky Walters and the National League's best staff. His bosses always thought he'd make a pretty good pitcher but in 1939 Walters became the greatest in the game, leading all of baseball in wins (27), ERA (2.29) and strikeouts (137). Also hitting .325 at the plate, he was the runaway winner of the Most Valuable Player Award.

The Reds had a strong candidate for second-greatest pitcher, too, with Paul Derringer winning 25 games and slipping in under the 3.00 mark in earned run average. He placed third in MVP voting and started in the All-Star Game, throwing three scoreless innings. Cincinnati's riches continued with 22-year-old rookie Junior Thompson, who won 13 of 18 decisions, recorded more shutouts than Walters and had a better ERA than Derringer.

On offense, many players saw their numbers fall after the explosion of 1938 but still contributed with solid, if uninspiring, bats. Lombardi's average dropped all the way to .287. McCormick lost no ground, cranking out another

The 1939 Cincinnati Reds took a quantum leap under Bill McKechnie's leadership, winning their first pennant in 20 years. He is shown in the front row, fifth from the left and fifth from the right. The team improved immediately when he took charge in 1938, then reached another level the following year (National Baseball Hall of Fame Library, Cooperstown, New York).

209 hits and leading the league in RBI, while Goodman remained strong in all departments except home runs. One of five Reds to start the All-Star Game at Yankee Stadium, Goodman entered as Cincinnati's hottest hitter and left on the disabled list. He injured his shoulder while diving for a catch in the outfield, missed the next five weeks and never fully recovered his power stroke. Hence the dramatic decline in homers from 30 in 1938 to seven in 1939.

If there was a weakness on the Reds roster it rested in the outfield, where Harry Craft and Wally Berger owned batting averages in the .250s. Their World Series opponents sported an outfield that hit well over .300 and averaged about 100 runs and 100 RBI. Then again, the Yankees were loaded at nearly every position. Never challenged in the American League race, they won 106 games and finished 17 games ahead of second-place Boston.

A large hole existed at first base, however, where Lou Gehrig used to be. He wore down in 1938 and felt even weaker at the start of the current season. Could his consecutive games record be winding down to a finish? Not any time soon, according to retired shortstop Everett Scott, who used to hold the record before Gehrig shattered it. "Gehrig always starts slow but he should be able to keep his streak intact this season. And he will still be playing ball three or four years from now.... I think for Gehrig's own good that he should end his streak, though. I think the right manager would take him out of there and give him a midseason rest."[10]

Gehrig resigned in May, ending a record consecutive game streak of 2,130, and made a very famous goodbye speech at Yankee Stadium on July 4 after learning he had a fatal disease, amyotrophic lateral sclerosis. He took a place on the Yankees bench during the World Series, offering moral support because his body wouldn't let him offer more. Babe Dahlgren did his best at first base that year but had impossibly large cleats to fill.

The Yankees were big favorites to win the World Series, so big that there really wasn't a lot of buzz in New York for Game 1. They'd won the last three championships and number four seemed a foregone conclusion. The old "Murderers' Row" Yankees of Ruth and Gehrig had nothing on the present dynasty of DiMaggio, Dickey, Rolfe, Keller, Ruffing and Gomez. By large margins, they led the AL in runs scored, RBI, home runs and earned run average. Doing his best to squash the mismatch talk, McKechnie told reporters, "The Yankees are a long way from being a super-team. Every club

The McKechnie family sifts through letters and telegrams that congratulate Bill for winning the 1939 pennant. An artist's portrait of the youngest member is partially visible above the couch. Seated, from left, are Bill Jr. and his wife Margaret, Beatrice, Bill and his wife Beryl, Carol and Jim (International News photograph provided by Wilkinsburg Historical Society).

in their league has beat them this year and I think I have a lot better team than most of them in that league."[11]

His players talked like they had a good chance, whether they truly believed it or not. Thinking them sincere, *Cincinnati Enquirer* sportswriter Gayle Talbot wrote, "The players, themselves, think they are going to take the Yankees. At least they are a different tribe from the Chicago Cubs of last year who knew they were licked before they started." With that dynamite one-two pitching punch, they had reason to believe. At the very least, they seemed unlikely candidates to get swept like the Cubs.

Derringer pitched a whale of game for Cincinnati in the opener at Yankee Stadium, holding New York's explosive lineup to four hits and one run through eight innings of a 1–1 tie. Charlie Keller slammed a pitch to deep right-center in the bottom of the ninth and Goodman couldn't quite haul it in. Keller went to third and later scored the game-winner on a single by Bill Dickey. An argument broke out in the losers' clubhouse, with Derringer and Goodman nearly coming to blows or actually coming to blows, depending on the source. The pitcher told his outfielder he should've made the catch, and the outfielder didn't appreciate it.

This loss was a narrow one and proved that the Reds could compete against the mighty New Yorkers on their own field. They didn't hit well but neither did the Yankees, and Cincinnati's best pitcher would throw next. This Series seemed a long way from over but, as things turned out, that opener was as good as it would get for the Reds. Monte Pearson shut them out on two hits in Game 2, while Walters surrendered three quick runs in a 4–0 loss.

The action shifted to Cincinnati next, with McKechnie saying all the right things about defending home turf and getting back into the Series. It even seemed plausible in the second inning, when Yankees starter Lefty Gomez injured himself on the base paths and the Reds scored twice on his replacement to build a 3–2 lead. Held to six total hits in the first two games, Cincinnati's offense produced ten on this day while three pitchers held the visitors to five. Four of those Yankees hits went for home runs, however, while the Reds knocked nothing but singles in a 7–3 defeat. New York now led the Fall Classic, three games to none and, like the title of that new Clark Gable movie, Cincinnati's title hopes were *Gone with the Wind*.

Even incurable optimists conceded that McKechnie's boys were doomed, but one win would give them something to cheer about. Just one, then maybe two, and send the Series back to New York without the Yankees celebrating on Crosley Field. Derringer took the mound for Game 4 and threw six innings of shutout ball. After two solo homers put New York up in the seventh, the Reds rallied for three runs in the bottom half and took a 3–2 lead. Lombardi later delivered a clutch RBI single in the eighth, pushing the advantage to two runs. The Reds stood three outs away from a pride-saving victory.

Walters came in to pitch the ninth inning and surrendered two quick singles. Dickey followed with a perfect double play ball to second base but Lonny Frey threw high to the covering shortstop and everybody was safe. With help from the error, New York scored twice to tie the game at 4–4. In the tenth inning, another error gave the Yankees runners on first and third with one out. Then the wheels fell off, as Goodman misplayed DiMaggio's drive to left-center and two runs scored. As Goodman's throw arrived at the plate, the second runner — Keller — slammed into Lombardi and knocked him head over heels. Lying stunned on the ground with the ball sitting nearby, Lombardi remained motionless while DiMaggio rounded third and headed for home. Teammates yelled at the catcher to get up and tag the latest runner, but he reacted a tad too late and "Joltin' Joe" crossed the plate safely with a textbook hook slide.

Cincinnati lost the game, 7–4, and the World Series, 4–0. For the rest of his career, Lombardi would never live down that play at the end of Game 4. It soon earned the nickname "Lombardi's Snooze" and variations thereof. Never mind that he'd been knocked senseless or that DiMaggio's run meant very little. The frustration of the sweep and that specific sequence overrode all loyalty and compassion. The "snooze" was usually referred to in derogatory fashion, not as good-natured ribbing.

In the winners' clubhouse, Yankees players celebrated as if the whole thing was *not* a foregone conclusion. They'd swept a very good team. Manager Joe McCarthy threw his arm around DiMaggio's shoulders and announced, "The old dago is OK. We'll have plenty of spaghetti in San Francisco this winter."[12] The old dago was actually 24 years old and had barely begun his legendary journey, though he would never hit for a higher average than his league-leading .381 in 1939. Lou Gehrig stood near the celebration, grinning widely, but took no part. He quietly changed out of uniform and into street clothes, preparing for the team train ride back to New York. He died two years later, just short of his 38th birthday.

A cloud of somber silence hung over the Reds locker room, with few words necessary for the losers. McKechnie went into his office and sat in a swivel chair, with his feet propped on the window sill. After staring out the window awhile, he got up and mingled amongst his players, shaking hands with one after another. "Be sure and stop in Wilkinsburg, Pennsylvania, if you're going through," he told them. "And don't figure on just staying a minute because you're staying overnight at least."[13] The room went somberly quiet again, until an unseen mouth voiced the battle cry of every team that ever failed but came close: "We'll be back next year."

Yes, they would.

14

Triumph and Tragedy

He is a quiet, kindly, lovable man with a friendly smile, iron gray hair and brown eyes that can be as soft as a woman's or hard as a gunman's, and a disposition that can change as rapidly as a chameleon's color.[1]— Newspaper Enterprise Association

Out of the dugout walked the Cincinnati manager, Bill McKechnie. The way he always did, with his arms crossed and walking real slow, as if it pained him deeply to have to be doing this.... He wore glasses, and he had a mild reasonable way about him that allowed him to get away with murder.[2]— Leo Durocher

Angry over the World Series rout, General Manager Warren Giles supposedly blew off some steam during a closed-door meeting with his manager. But nobody was going to run Bill McKechnie out of town after *this* World Series sweep, and he departed for a Canadian hunting trip with a clear mind. When he lost four straight to the walking-wounded Yankees in 1928, his St. Louis bosses had expected to win. Eleven years and two cities later, the Deacon jumped into battle with decided underdogs. Not that his strategies went entirely unchallenged — some wondered why he left Berger in the lineup when the guy couldn't buy a hit. Why not go with Al Simmons, the former Athletics star who came to the Reds in a late-season transaction? True, old Al batted poorly during his month with Cincy but he couldn't have done any worse than Berger's 0-for-15. Finally given a chance in Game 4, Simmons went 1-for-4 with a double and scored once.

That said, too many good things had transpired for Reds fans to focus on negative minutiae. In the space of two short years, the franchise had gone from last place to the World Series. Not content to rest on those laurels, Cincinnati players looked to complete the rags-to-riches transformation with a championship in 1940. The front office did its part to improve their chances, making two winter trades that would pay huge dividends in the pitching department. Joe Beggs came over from the Yankees and took a starring role as one of the game's first relief specialists, while 36-year-old Jim Turner revived his once-promising career after hitting the skids with the Boston Braves.

Cincy's roster returned intact from 1939 except for a couple of pieces of trade bait and Wally Berger, who got released and wound up with the Phillies for the final 20 games of his career. Bill Werber set off alarms by hinting at retirement but signed before the new year arrived. The team looked good and so did its manager, who had lost lots of weight to stress last season and saw his hair turn gray almost overnight. He appeared much healthier and more energetic after getting away from the job for some rest and relaxation. At spring training, McKechnie managed in an all-star benefit game for the Finnish Relief Fund. Losing a heroic fight against Soviet Union invasion, Finland earned the respect of America and would soon have some of her money. As the year progressed, things only got worse in Europe, and grim front-page headlines steered escapists toward the sports section. Hitler had no place there, nor did Mussolini or Hirohito.

It seemed a good omen when the Reds won on opening day for the first time in eight years. The usual suspects led the way to a 2–1 victory over the visiting Cubs; Derringer tossed a six-hitter, while McCormick and Goodman launched solo home runs. Spring flooding soon complicated things, with the Ohio River rising above 60 feet and spilling into a creek near Crosley Field. Slow-rising waters went knee-deep in the dugouts and eventually lapped at the playing field on April 22, but the Reds and Cards played anyhow, completing their contest just in time. The next two games were cancelled. Mother Nature's mistreatment was commonplace for the river city; in the great flood of 1937 Crosley Field disappeared under 21 feet of water. A couple of Reds pitchers got creative and rowed a boat over the center field fence, a gag seen far and wide after a photographer captured it on film.

In late May, the 1939 pennant was raised on the center field flagpole during pre-game ceremonies. Joining the festivities were several elderly fans who'd seen the 1869 Reds play; Cincinnati was all about tradition. The Brooklyn Dodgers had some tradition of their own and planned to start a new one by capturing the 1940 flag. Winning their first nine games, they took a spot at the top, and the Reds joined them in the clouds by going 15–4. It was a two-horse race throughout the season, with both jockeying back and forth in the early months. Brooklyn clung to a one-game lead when the Nazis took Paris in mid–June, and it was a dead heat when the French surrendered a week later. In early July, the Reds owned a half-game lead while British pilots began their "Finest Hour" defense in the Battle of Britain.

Named manager of the National League all-star team, McKechnie finally got the job that eluded him twice before. As head of the defending NL champs, he couldn't be denied him this time. He brought along Walters and Derringer, who combined for four shutout innings in a 4–0 win at Sportsman's Park in St. Louis. Playing a hunch that paid off quickly, McKechnie started Boston's Max West in right field instead of all-star veteran Mel Ott, and the less-famous player clubbed a three-run homer in the first inning. Yes, McKechnie had the golden touch.

Brooklyn played poorly after the all-star break, going 9–14 the rest of the month, and Cincinnati took advantage by winning 15 of 21. Heading into August, the defending pennant winners held a fat lead of 7½ games. The Reds were built to go 15 rounds, and nobody else could match their pace. They had a quality four-man rotation that chewed up innings, and they hardly ever lost a lead when Beggs came in to close out games. The offense was nothing to brag about but Werber still scored lots of runs and McCormick still drove in a bunch. Besides, with strong defense and a shutdown pitching staff, they didn't need to score much.

On the last day of July the Reds lost a heartbreaker in New York, blowing a 4–1 lead with two outs in the ninth inning. Willard Hershberger was the starting catcher that day and he took the loss particularly hard, blaming himself for calling the wrong pitches. Two days later, he went 0-for-5 in the second game of a doubleheader loss at Boston. The last-place Braves had dropped nine straight before that sweep. Cincinnati still held a comfortable six-game lead in the pennant race, but Hershberger couldn't let it go. Pressed into regular duty because of an injury to Lombardi, he felt inadequate and couldn't stand the pressure.

Another doubleheader was scheduled for the following day, but Hershberger said he was sick and stayed at the hotel. At some point he went into the bathroom, slashed his neck open with a razor blade and bled to death over the bathtub. He didn't kill himself because of poor performances on the baseball field — real or imagined. Willard Hershberger was mentally ill, a victim of crippling, unrelenting depression. His father had killed himself, so it may have been hereditary, or maybe he never got over the trauma of finding the bloody corpse with a shotgun hole in the chest.

The son's suicide shocked everybody, but did not surprise everybody. Only recently, McKechnie saw the disturbing depths of how far his moody, 30-year-old catcher had sunk. In Hershberger's final game, he did not attempt to field a swinging bunt, letting the pitcher make a long run to grab it. McKechnie came out of the dugout and asked him if something was wrong. "Yes, Bill, there's plenty," he responded. "I'll tell you tonight." After the game, they sat in the empty grandstand and talked awhile, but Hershberger wouldn't open up. When they met again before dinner he finally unburdened himself.

McKechnie would never reveal exactly what was said. "He cried like a kid. Seemed he cried for an hour and then he told me he was worried about the club losing the games he had caught."[3] By the time they parted ways, Hershberger seemed in better spirits; it had to be a relief getting all that off his chest. When he didn't accompany the team to Braves Field the next day, McKechnie figured he just needed a little more time to compose himself. McKechnie wanted him at the field, though, even if he couldn't play. A team official called Hershberger's hotel room and he promised he'd come out later. It didn't happen, so someone went to check on him.

A gruesome discovery followed, and when word got back to the ballpark, McKechnie rushed to the hotel. All his soothing words of encouragement and reinforcement had gone for naught. Hershberger was too far gone. The team later assembled in their manager's hotel room, where stunned silence was the order of the day. Every now and then, somebody would share a memory about the departed. Some used to tease him about his insomnia or hypochondria, but everybody liked "Hershie." He was a home-owning, confirmed bachelor who liked radios, collected guns and provided for his mother. On the diamond, his energy won legions of fans, and he became especially popular with women, some of them inquiring if they could become Mrs. Hershberger.

Above all else, he was a talented player who hit for average, ran with speed and caught a good game behind the plate. Whenever lumbering Lombardi failed to track down a foul fly near the dugout, some fan would invariably yell, "Hershie would've got it." Good enough to be a starter on other teams, Hershie liked the role of back-up and never pushed for a career-enhancing trade. The Reds catchers came as an inseparable package and had nicknames that implied as much: "Big Slug" for Lombardi, "Little Slug" for Hershberger.

Well-liked, athletically gifted and financially secure, Hershberger seemed to have everything going for him, but in 1940 severe depression was a life sentence at best and fatal at worst. Decades later, McCormick remembered, "Most of the time, Willard was a nice, easygoing fellow, but he could be moody. Sometimes his spirits would be way up, other times way down. The night before it happened, he was way down."[4] Today, they call that bi-polar.

Refusing to look at the body, McKechnie had it sent to a mortuary where it stayed until claimed by the victim's mother. Hershberger had vowed to take care of her after his father's death and just recently bought her a house back in their home state of California. On August 8, the Reds held a brief memorial service at Crosley Field, where longtime groundskeeper Matty Schwab lowered the center field flag to half-mast. Fans and players stood for a moment of silence, then life and the season went on. The Reds' lead didn't seem so comfortable now; if they suffered an emotional letdown, there was plenty of time to blow a five-game edge. McKechnie urged his players to win it for Hershie.

They won it easily, finishing 12 games in front after going 38–21 post-suicide, and putting it away with an 11-game winning streak in mid–September. On the final day of the season, they secured win number 100—the first such triple-digit output in franchise history. Last year's team was great, but this one was sublime. Even the vaunted Yankees would be hard-pressed to beat Cincy in 1940, but they never got a chance to try. In a thrilling American League pennant race, Detroit took the crown by one game over Cleveland and two over New York. The Tigers won 90 games, a paltry figure compared to the 1939 Yankees' total of 106 and ten fewer than the current NL champs. Yet oddsmakers still favored them to win it all.

Some pundits speculated that the Reds wanted a different team to prevail in the AL race. Detroit owned a fearsome hitting attack, led by the league's best batter, Hank Greenberg. Scoring 178 fewer runs than the Tigers, Cleveland would've supposedly made a much easier opponent. McKechnie didn't buy that theory for a minute because the Indians had a dominant young pitcher named Bob Feller, who could shift the World Series balance all by himself. He'd take his chances with the Tigers. "We should win, I honestly believe we have a much better all-round club than the Tigers,"[5] he told reporters.

Detroit fans disagreed, pointing at their team's superior hitting attack and two excellent pitchers at the top of the rotation. That was more than enough to win a title. Maybe Cincinnati and its deeper pitching staff ranked better for the marathon of a regular season, but the World Series was a sprint. The Reds also had an injury problem that threatened to derail everything they'd worked for. Lombardi suffered a severe ankle sprain in mid–September and didn't heal in time for the Fall Classic. The backup catcher, of course, was deceased, and nobody else had enough experience to play on such an important stage. A gaping hole opened at the most important everyday position in baseball, and folks had to wonder if it would swallow Cincinnati's title hopes.

Enter Jimmie Wilson, longtime catcher for the Phillies and Cardinals before becoming a coach. Joining a makeshift three-man rotation, he'd played a few games behind the plate after Lombardi went down. Now he had the position all to himself for the World Series. At the age of 40, he donned the tools of ignorance and hoped for the best. Also sidelined by injury was smooth-fielding second baseman Lonny Frey, victim of a falling water cooler lid that gashed and smashed his foot. But at least they had a conventional backup infielder ready to step in. Cincinnati fans remained upbeat as their city prepared to host the first two games.

Just as he'd done the previous year, Derringer took the hill for Game 1. Coming off a 20–12 season, he matched up against Detroit ace Bobo Newsom, a big, barrel-chested southerner who'd gone 21–5. The pitchers' duel didn't last long, as Derringer couldn't even make it out of the second inning. Tigers batters went wild in that frame, scoring five times on five hits, and that was more than they needed. Scattering eight hits, Newsom held the home team to a pair of runs in a 7–2 victory. He giddily bounced around the clubhouse afterward, predicting another American League cakewalk. "Yes sir, if we hit as we did today we may win it in four straight. I don't think we'll come back to this ball park after we get through with the Reds in Detroit."[6] A gregarious good old boy who loved the sound of his own voice, Newsom enjoyed his first taste of the World Series spotlight. Manager Del Baker took it down a notch but still predicted happy days ahead: "No use to be quoted, but we're going to win just as quickly as we can. If we can win in four that will be just swell. It may take six, it may take seven, but we're going to win."[7]

Newsom's mood later changed to deep sorrow when word arrived that his father had died of a heart attack. In town to witness his son's arrival on the biggest stage in sports, he proudly watched it all but didn't live to see another game.

Walters put an end to the sweep talk in Game 2, tossing a three-hitter in a 5–3 Reds victory. After surrendering two runs in the first inning, he mixed pitches and showed the form that made him a 22-game winner in the National League. An unlikely hero emerged in the person of Jimmy Ripple, a late-season addition from the waiver wire, whose two-run homer provided the margin of victory. It was the Reds' first World Series triumph since 1919, and several members of that team, Edd Roush included, cheered it from the stands. Afterward, some hometown fans gathered near the Tigers dugout and chanted, "Hold that tiger."

Detroit got the bats going late in Game 3 and pulled away to a 7–4 home win at Navin Field, then Derringer redeemed himself by throwing a five-hitter in a Series-tying 5–2 success. Now the Reds were guaranteed of bringing the battle back to Crosley Field. Pitching in honor of his deceased dad, Newsom became a serious, sympathetic figure in Game 5. As a huge crowd of 55,000 cheered him along, he came through with the performance of a lifetime, shutting out the Reds on three hits and allowing only one runner to reach second base. With their ace blistering his side-armed fastball past overmatched batters, the Tigers would've felt safe with one run but scored a bunch anyhow. Their 8–0 victory gave them a 3–2 Series lead. Too emotional to accept congratulations, Newsom waved off approaching teammates in the clubhouse.

Greenberg highlighted the Tigers' 13-hit offensive with a tape-measure homer that landed some 20 rows deep in the upper deck of the left field seats. With the action shifting back to Cincinnati, it was up to Walters to get those bats under control again. By the end of Game 6, he'd done that and much more, outscoring the Tigers all by himself. In one of the finest performances in World Series history, Walters threw a five-hit shutout and hit a home run in a 4–0 Cincinnati triumph. Getting more worn down with each passing game, Wilson delivered a sixth-inning single and eventually came around to score the third run. It came at a high price, though, as he pulled two right-leg muscles during the journey. McKechnie urged his coach/catcher to call it a day and rest those weary bones, but Wilson wouldn't hear of it. "I'll tape the damned things up and finish, I'm gonna see this through," he said.[8]

With Derringer in line for the deciding Game 7, Reds confidence soared through the roof and into low-lying clouds. For two years, he'd been a money pitcher who performed better under pressure. Meanwhile, in the other dugout, manager Baker seemed uncomfortable with his options. Schoolboy Rowe was used up and he'd pitched terribly in two starts anyhow. Dizzy Trout bombed during his lone outing, and Newsom needed more rest after pitching two days earlier. The only logical choice was Tommy Bridges, the Tigers' No. 3 starter who went the distance in a Game 3 victory. He'd given up ten hits and four runs in that win, however, and was the oldest hurler on the staff.

Baker went with Newsom on two days' rest because he'd been so good in his first two outings. It was a huge gamble that somehow paid off, as Newsom held the Reds scoreless through six innings. Waiting nervously for its offense to show life, a smallish crowd of 26,769 was rewarded in the bottom of the seventh. McCormick led off with a double down the third base line, then hesitated when Ripple followed with a long drive to right. Unsure whether the catch would be made, he hovered between second and third until the ball bounded off the wall. A quick relay came to second base, with Dick Bartell having a chance to get McCormick at the plate, but he never looked that way. To him, it must've been unthinkable that a runner wouldn't score easily on a long double.

Wilson came up next and sacrificed Ripple to third, then light-hitting shortstop Billy Myers chased him home with a bouncing single. Given a 2–1 lead, Derringer cruised to the checkered flag without incident. For the first time in 21 years the Reds were World Series champions, and Bill McKechnie had taken them from worst to first in the space of three short years. Inheriting a team of weak hitters, poor defenders and average pitchers, he remolded it into one with great pitching and defense. The offense proved good enough and better than most. In the World Series, Werber hit .370, Ripple batted .333 with a team-best six RBI, and the surprising Jimmie Wilson posted a .353 average. Family legend says Wilson's wife came onto the field after Game 7 and grabbed second base as a memento. Some official told her she couldn't take it and she responded with something like, "Oh yes I can." Since her husband stole second at one point, she insisted on completing the theft. Visiting

The stoic Scot was all smiles after his Cincinnati Reds won the 1940 World Series. Joining the celebration were sons Bill Jr. (left) and Jim. Young Bill wore a batboy's uniform during his dad's tenure as Pittsburgh Pirates skipper, and Jim donned a Braves outfit during the Boston days. Now 17 years old, Jim had graduated to more advanced duties, such as bullpen catcher (courtesy Carol McKechnie Montgomery).

the winning clubhouse, Commissioner Kenesaw Landis approached the sore-legged 40-year-old and said, "You did our generation proud, Jim."[9] More than 30 years Wilson's senior, the commissioner was flattering himself with the "our generation" reference but his compliment stood unchallenged. McKechnie's sons were there, too, the adult Bill Jr. dressed in suit and tie, and Jim wearing a Reds uniform. Young Jim had graduated from batboy to bullpen catcher.

After the final out went into the books, bedlam quickly broke out downtown. From open office windows came torrents of confetti, falling on a growing mass of revelers that eventually included Mrs. McKechnie and daughter number two. Daughter number one was away at college. The 1919 championship inspired similarly raucous reactions, but folks said this party was way bigger. Both times, municipal pride swelled with the small city's triumph over big ones. In a front-page *Enquirer* article, Jack Cronin wrote, "Detroit can have its automobiles, its Joe Louis, and its Father Coughlin. Cincinnati has its World's Champion. And son, you can tell your grandchildren the old town really let down its coiffure to celebrate yesterday afternoon and last night."[10]

The spontaneous rejoicing of afternoon was later surpassed by a larger bash in the evening, as more and more residents worked their way downtown. A second torn-paper parade broke out, pleasing the masses but frustrating city employees who'd just finished cleaning up the first. Streetcars and automobiles were rerouted from areas where human traffic was densest. While Cincinnati celebrated, German bombs rained down on London in the biggest raid to date. The war would suck America into its vortex soon enough, but for now she could still enjoy her games, relatively stress-free. It was a good time to be a Reds fan and a great time to be the manager.

McKechnie's youngest child carried golden memories of those days into adulthood and still carries them today. Carol McKechnie was almost nine years old when her dad won his fourth pennant and second championship. She attended the World Series with her family, watching familiar faces turn into heroes. Throughout Cincinnati and beyond, so many star-struck fans would've given anything to touch the champions, but only a small percentage ever got the chance. Idols must keep a safe distance from the multitudes. To little Carol, however, the Reds were entirely approachable; she knew them and they knew her. Travelers on the same journey, they'd shared good times from the start at spring training in Tampa. Carol probably enjoyed the Florida trips a little more than the players, though, since she never had to run sprints or engage in endlessly monotonous practice drills. She remembers coach Hank Gowdy as a particularly affable adult, who liked to say he got his chin dimple from a German bullet in World War I. Those annual Florida sojourns had a family atmosphere, with warm feelings under a warm sun. "I loved

Tampa, I had a blast in Tampa when Dad was with the Reds," Carol remembers.

After spring training, she would return to school in Wilkinsburg while her father headed for Cincinnati. Six months later, he would return home, making it a two-parent household again. He always pulled off a smooth transition to stay-at-home dad. That 1940 title cemented McKechnie's nationwide reputation as the game's greatest leader, and *The Sporting News* made it semi-official by naming him "Manager of the Year." He wore no crown in Wilkinsburg, however. "Daddy was still Daddy," Carol said. "After the Series, he came home and went hunting.... It was a great scenario because I had Daddy home all winter."

When the next spring training rolled around, off the McKechnies went and the cycle repeated itself. In 1941, a team photographer asked Carol to sit down and pose for a picture. She was in a bad mood that day and refused, but the picture man kept after her and she eventually agreed to sit. The antsy young lady wasn't happy about it, though, and with cooperation in short supply, this modeling session seemed doomed to failure. A Reds cap was placed on her head and ended up askew, an amusing interlude that saved the day. A portrait of that picture hangs in Carol's home today, the sideways hat on top of curly, light-brown hair. Smiling and staring into the camera with piercing dark eyes, she looks like that's where she wanted to be all along. With her fresh-faced confidence capturing the spirit of spring training renewal, the photo supposedly took on a life of its own. One of Carol's brothers claimed it was chosen for a *Life* magazine cover but got bumped when Pearl Harbor was bombed. It never appeared anywhere but desks, walls and photo albums.

McKechnie was optimistic about the 1941 season and said so to the press. His boys went all the way while diminished by injury and the only in-season suicide in baseball history. Just think how good they could be after off-season healing of body and mind. Topping a 100-win season would be hard, but the team had improved every year under the Deacon so far and he had some surprises for the upcoming season. Johnny "Double No-Hit Vander Meer" was healthy again, though he couldn't shake the most cumbersome and unimaginative nickname in baseball. They never called the Bambino "60 home runs Ruth" or the Iron Horse "2,130 games Gehrig." After seeing little action the past two seasons and getting sent to the minors to work things out, Vander Meer looked like his old self again. His aching arm ached no more, and that was bad news for National League hitters.

The Reds were also anxious to unleash a young pitching prospect named Elmer Riddle, if they could find any room for him. With all the important pieces returning from the best staff in baseball and Vander Meer in the mix, this was an exceptionally tough rotation to crack and could go down as his-

At the age of 79, Carol McKechnie Montgomery posed next to a framed portrait of her younger self. Snapped by the team photographer in 1941, the picture shows her smiling face under a sideways Cincinnati Reds cap. According to family legend, the photo was going to run as a *Life* magazine cover until Pearl Harbor bumped it into oblivion (photograph by the author).

tory's greatest. Placing an airtight defense behind the pitching, Cincinnati might get by with an average offense. What nobody could foresee was that the hitters would be horrid, not average, and the rotation would just be very good, not supreme.

Cincinnati opened the season sluggishly, falling 12 games out of first place with a 19–23 record at the end of May. Derringer didn't have his good stuff and two other second-line starters struggled too. Suddenly, the tough-to-crack rotation needed help, and Riddle stepped in. McKechnie had brought him along slowly the past couple of years, and he learned much from the bench while listening to coaching advice, observing hitters and watching Walters and Derringer. When opportunity arose, the 26-year-old Georgian was ready. Armed with the full repertoire of pitches and a particularly nasty sinker, he won nine straight games heading into the all-star break. McKechnie managed the National Leaguers in Detroit that year and brought Wilson along to coach. Things went fabulously until the bottom of the ninth, when Ted

Williams launched a walk-off, three-run homer that gave the American League a 7–5 victory.

After the break, Cincinnati finally started playing like the defending champs, but it was too late. The Dodgers and Cardinals had pulled far ahead and surrendered little ground during the final months. In early September, McKechnie made an enormous error that never showed up in any box score. At the Chicago airport, he bought a ticket for Pittsburgh but boarded the wrong plane and wound up in Detroit. What's more, he didn't discover his mistake until trying to catch a taxi cab to Forbes Field. Newspapers had a lot of fun with that story, running a detailed recreation of the confused conversation between McKechnie and the cabbie.

Brooklyn ended up with 100 wins and a 2½ game edge on the Cardinals. The Reds were third at 86–66, which marked an impressive turnaround from the dark days of May and bland nights of June. Before 1939, it would've ranked as a great season in Cincinnati, but expectations ran much higher for the two-time defending NL champs. When McKechnie attended the World Series, as was his annual custom, he had a hard time enjoying himself. "We ought to be out there," he ruefully repeated on more than one occasion while sitting in a field box with his general manager and team owner.

There were significant silver linings, all in the pitching department. It looked like the Reds had a real prodigy in Riddle, who finished 19–4 and led the league in both winning percentage (.826) and ERA (2.24). Walters came within an eyelash of another 20-win season, while Vander Meer and his reborn fastball led the NL in strikeouts. In the category of team defense, Cincy led everybody in fielding percentage (.975).

With so many blessings, how could the Reds finish 12 games out of first? The answer became obvious with one look at the team's hitting statistics. Not one player hit over .290 and only one beat .270. Their power numbers ranked among the league's lowest. With 17 homers, 97 RBI and the most dependable glove among NL first basemen, only Frank McCormick could lay claim to anything resembling a productive season. Three years after winning the batting title and MVP award, Lombardi hit .262 with ten home runs.

In a year of transcendent milestones, the Reds faded from memory. Ted Williams and Joe DiMaggio owned 1941, the former hitting over .400 and the latter completing a 56-game hitting streak. They took the sport to a new level, with a nation investing itself in their pursuit of near-perfection. Williams and DiMaggio became superheroes that season, and nobody has duplicated their feats in the seven decades since.

Less than three months later, however, they were no longer the biggest news of 1941. On December 7, the Japanese Navy bombed Pearl Harbor and brought the United States into World War II as a full-fledged combatant.

Before that day, America had confronted aggressor nations through diplomatic channels and made huge material contributions to those who resisted them. Now flesh and blood would be committed to the cause. Thanks to entangled alliances, war with Japan also meant war with her Axis partners Germany and Italy — inevitable enemies who had bided time until spurred to make it official by that sneak attack in Hawaiian waters.

15

Old Wounds and
New Horizons

McKechnie was the best manager I played for. He was a great handler of pitchers, and he loved pitchers to give him nine innings. He would put you on a system of starting every so many days and we started regardless of who we were playing. He got you on that rotation, he got your system going, and he stayed with it.[1]— Johnny Vander Meer

Vander Meer flourished under McKechnie's direction, winning three straight strikeout crowns. With help from his coaching staff, the Deacon also molded an unlikely standout named Ray Starr in 1942. A longtime minor leaguer with little track record in the majors, the 36-year-old won 15 games and posted a 2.66 earned run average — just another feather in the cap of the pitcher's manager.

The Reds started selling off popular position players, sending Werber to the Giants and Lombardi to the Braves. Both were getting old by baseball standards and their productivity had dropped considerably. Lombardi was never much more than a slugger and when his offense disappeared, McKechnie gladly parted with him. The slow-footed catcher proceeded to make his former manager look bad when he won the NL batting crown in his first season with Boston. A 22-year-old rookie took over as Reds catcher and fit right in with a cast of mediocre hitters. Cincinnati went 76–76 that year.

The war hit baseball full force by 1943, with scores of players trading bats for rifles. Whether drafted or voluntarily enlisting, they left the easy life of professional sports for low pay and high risk. Most felt happy, if not honored, to do it. Joe DiMaggio and Ted Williams were gone, as were many lesser lights. McKechnie lost a coach when Hank Gowdy enlisted. Already a trench-warfare veteran of the first World War, the 53-year-old was turned down on his first application but eventually convinced Army officials to bring him back to the khaki family. He served stateside.

Repopulating the ranks of baseball was an army of 4F rejects, men physically unable to serve in the military. Under such conditions, it was tough to identify contenders and pretenders, but pundits saw enough at spring training to dismiss McKechnie's team. As one sportswriter put it, "Florida's itinerant correspondents are in complete accord that the Cincinnati Reds will finish so deep in the National League cellar they'll have to play the last half of the season wearing miners' lamps."[2] Not so long ago, they were the class of baseball.

Only a couple of position players remained from recent glory days, and the pitching staff had almost as few. Derringer and Goodman were sold to the Cubs during the previous winter, as Reds management continued unloading its fading veterans. Nobody broke out the miners' lamps, though, because the pitchers carried Cincinnati to a second-place finish. Clyde Shoun became the latest reclamation project, emerging from a mediocre career to go 14–5 and post a 3.06 ERA. With war-time attendance taking a nosedive, the figure 139 would prove a telling statistic too — that's the number of people that preteen Carol McKechnie counted while watching one Reds game.

Posting a monster win total for the second straight year, St. Louis went 105–49 in 1942 and finished 18 games ahead of the 87–67 Reds. The Cardinals prospered during wartime baseball, with a revolutionary farm system that churned out capable replacements for Service-bound players. They won the 1942 World Series when a lot of talent still remained in major league uniforms and kept rolling as the product became watered down. Twenty-two-year-old Stan Musial won his first batting crown in 1943.

Allied fighting men won major victories that year as the war began turning against Axis powers. It all started in spectacular fashion when 90,000 German soldiers surrendered to Soviet forces near Stalingrad. Allies took North Africa and Sicily, and invaded Italy while America fought solo in the Pacific, winning bloody victories at Guadalcanal and Tarawa. The Japanese Navy was already reeling from the previous year's defeats in two major sea battles. Overall, things looked promising but baseball soldiers would not return home any time soon.

When the massive D-Day invasion force stormed Normandy beaches on June 6 of 1944, the Reds owned a 24–18 record and trailed league-leading St. Louis by four games. It was a race, so far. A few days later, Cincinnati's player shortage became so acute that it temporarily rounded out the roster with a 15-year-old schoolboy from nearby Hamilton, Ohio. Pitching two-thirds of an inning in a blowout loss to St. Louis, southpaw Joe Nuxhall surrendered two hits, five walks and five runs. The 6-foot-2 man-child left town soon afterward, taking a 45.00 ERA with him. He would return as an adult and become very popular at Crosley Field, first as a longtime pitcher, then as a longtime broadcaster.

With Musial leading the charge in 1944, the Cardinals racked up another phenomenal win total (105) and blew away the field. Cincinnati went 24 games over .500 while placing second, though, and that qualified as another strong, first-division finish. Keeping with the annual tradition, McKechnie plucked yet another pitcher from obscurity and developed him into something special. This time it was Utah native Ed Heusser, owner of a career 22–24 record over four seasons. His win-loss mark was nothing special in 1944 but he won the league ERA title with a low mark of 2.38. Maybe war-time hitters weren't very good but nobody held them down as well as Heusser. Winning a league-high 23 games, Bucky Walters still had the stuff that baffled pre-war hitters, but he could only finish a very close second on earned run average. Also flying high across the big league radar was rookie southpaw Arnold Carter, who posted impressive debut stats of 11–7 and 2.60.

Was there no limit to how many rabbits McKechnie could pull out of a hat? "Bill knows pitchers probably better than anyone in the business and is a marvel at getting the best out of them," said his right-hand man, Jimmie Wilson. "But you can search me how he does it year in and year out. He's a wonder."[3] Before the season was through, McKechnie signed a two-year contract extension.

More players left for war in 1945, and the major leagues lost its last star when Musial joined them. As a result, unprecedented opportunities arose for men with any baseball experience. A small advertisement in *The Sporting News* announced: "FREE AGENT. Righthand Pitcher open to offers. Four years' experience in Classes A, B and C." There were no ads for the sale of miners' lamps, which was a shame because the Reds could've used some that year. They dropped to 61–93, 37 games out of first place, and not a single silver lining could be located. The Reds were still in the hunt at the time of Adolph Hitler's suicide in late April but stood 8½ back while Marines secured Okinawa during late June. When atomic bombs dropped on Hiroshima and Nagasaki in early August, the Deacon's boys were hopelessly out of it, and on the day of Japan's surrender, rested 25 games from first.

A victim of Cincy's slow-moving house-cleaning and liquidation sale, Frank McCormick was sold to the Phillies for $30,000 in December. His departure left back-up second baseman Lonny Frey as the lone position-player holdover from the championship years, and a couple of pitchers were still around. After a three-year hiatus brought on by war travel restrictions, the Reds returned to Tampa for Spring Training in 1946. Now 14 years old, Carol McKechnie looked a lot different walking on a beach than she had at 11. When one young prospect asked her to the movies, Deacon Bill issued a wide-ranging edict: His daughter could NOT date ball players — ever. He knew what they were like. Did Carol even *want* to date them, though? "Oh yeah, sure!" she answered in 2011.

Vander Meer returned from war, as did relief specialist Joe Beggs, and both pitched pretty well in 1946, but it made little difference. This time, Bill's boys finished 20 games under .500. The thrill of war victory did little to pacify the agony of baseball defeat in Cincinnati, where frustrated Reds fans wondered aloud if the game had passed up their 60-year-old manager. They didn't turn on him as quickly as folks had in Pittsburgh and St. Louis, but they did turn. It mattered little that he was the most successful manager in franchise history, producing two pennants, one World Series title and seven first-division finishes during his nine-year reign. Those two losing seasons were whoppers, though, and they came back-to-back in 1945 and 1946. They were the last thing on his resume and the first things fans remembered.

On September 23, newspapers reported that Bill McKechnie had resigned as manager of the Cincinnati Reds. In truth, he was forced out. It fell to general manager Warren Giles to pull the trigger, and he did so with great regret, still believing McKechnie was the best man for the job. "In baseball you are forced to bow to the will of your patrons and ... McKechnie, failing to win, had aroused their antagonism," Giles told the *New York World-Telegram* in 1950. "He became the symbol of the club's frustration and I was forced to make him the scapegoat. Actually I was more to blame because it is my job to bring in the players and no manager, not even the best, can win without players."[4]

The players sent McKechnie out with a win on September 25, rolling to a 6–0 road shutout of St. Louis. A season-ending series with Pittsburgh still awaited, but this would be his final game. After securing the final out at Sportsman's Park, the Reds milled around in a subdued clubhouse, waiting their turn to shake the boss's hand and wish him good luck. McKechnie loudly praised sore-armed Bucky Walters, who tossed a shutout on sheer guts: "Bucky was one of the men who helped make my nine years in Cincinnati happy ones."[5] As he left to shower, coach Gowdy whispered, "What a grand guy! Baseball certainly can't afford to let him stay out."[6]

He stayed out about a week before the Cleveland Indians signed him to coach under boy-manager Lou Boudreau, a 28-year-old star shortstop who'd been the "Tribe" chief since 1942. Boudreau was a hugely popular figure among home fans, but a bigger personality had recently arrived in the person of Bill Veeck, new owner and master promoter. Veeck thought Boudreau a nice boy but mediocre manager, who made important decisions by hunch. He wanted to replace him with Casey Stengel but didn't dare try — not yet, anyhow. First impressions were important, and it wouldn't make good business sense to alienate customers right off the bat. Deciding instead to search for an accomplished coach, he got excited when McKechnie became available. In his 1962 autobiography, Veeck wrote, "I had hired Bill McKechnie at the end of 1946,

Signed for big money by new owner Bill Veeck, McKechnie joined the Cleveland Indians as a coach. He didn't miss managing one bit and told at least one interviewer that the coaching position was the best job he'd ever had (courtesy Carol McKechnie Montgomery).

as soon as I read he had been fired as manager of the Reds. I got to Bill before anybody else by tracking him down at the Cincinnati railroad station as he was leaving town. McKechnie was a great handler of pitchers and a man I hoped Louie would lean on."[7]

To make sure he got his man, Veeck offered a big $20,000 salary plus bonus incentives on attendance for 1947 and beyond. It would've been a sweet deal for a manager, so it rated as phenomenal for a coach. A front-page story trumpeted the news in the *Cleveland Plain Dealer* when Deacon Bill agreed to join the fold, and a supportive Boudreau was quoted as saying, "I know Bill will be of great help to us." A longer story reported the death sentences handed down to 11 Nazis at the Nuremberg trials. Convicted of war crimes and crimes against humanity, they all earned dates with the hangman's noose. The most famous convict, Luftwaffe commander Hermann Göring, took his own life with poison before that day arrived.

Veeck fought in the war, though not against Nazis. He joined the Marines and got shipped out to kill Japanese in the Pacific theater. A wartime injury crippled his right leg, and complications eventually caused its amputation, but none of it ever slowed him down back home, where he brought investors together to purchase the Indians. In Cleveland he found a huge market to tantalize with his giveaways, fireworks, circus acts and other assorted stunts. Veeck believed the ballpark should be a fun place to visit and that fun was good for business, but he also believed in building winners. Winning, of course, was *great* for business. Cleveland hadn't captured a pennant in 26 years, though, and contended only three times during that span. A strong candidate for the American League's worst offensive team, the 1946 Indians finished 68–84, 36 games out of first place. Bob Feller didn't miss a beat in his return from the Navy but, beyond him, the pitching staff was mediocre. Veeck had his work cut out for him and he took his first big step by getting the coach of his choice.

McKechnie made it clear very quickly that he was not a manager-in-waiting. He had no ambitions beyond coaching, and his current job was the best of his career. It came with all the money of a managing position but very little of the heat. All this coach had to do was handle pitchers and follow Boudreau's directions. Sportswriter Dan Daniel wrote, "There is every reason to believe that the Boudreau-McKechnie arrangement will prove most successful. But there are obvious handicaps in such setups. McKechnie is 60, Lou is not yet 30. Here we have a man giving orders to a veteran more than twice his age, who has been in baseball longer than Boudreau has been in this world. Lou's experience as a pilot is confined to his brief term of leadership in Cleveland. He still has much to learn. Especially in the handling of pitchers. And that's where McKechnie comes in."[8]

The Indians made big strides in 1947, posting a winning record of 80–74 and, whether it was McKechnie's doing or not, an inexperienced pitcher emerged from the pack to go 11–5. If he kept that up, Bob Lemon might just become a solid No. 2 man to complement Feller. Across both leagues, the season saw its heroes and crowned champions but it all paled in comparison to what took place on opening day in Brooklyn, when Jackie Robinson broke the major league color line. Eleven weeks later, Cleveland got in on the barrier breaking, when Larry Doby became the first black player in the American League. Doby had much in common with Robinson beyond the obvious: both attended college, served in the military and played professional baseball among their own kind. Doby was a key member of the Newark Eagles team that won the Negro World Series in 1946. Always looking for ways to improve his team and create a buzz, Veeck made Cleveland the second franchise to showcase a black man at its ball diamond.

While Robinson enjoyed immediate success and led his team to the World Series, Doby saw limited action and hit poorly when he did play. He got the cold shoulder from most teammates, and that bothered him as much as his .156 batting average. Jackie Robinson's trail blazing hadn't made things any easier for the next guy; Doby heard acid-tongued taunts in certain cities and was often banned by local custom from joining teammates in restaurants or hotels. He didn't expect a segregation mentality in his own clubhouse, though. Boudreau assured him that the boys would come around, eventually. A few were friendly from the start, and the silver-haired coach became his mentor. "There was one person on the ball club that I could go to and that was a fellow by the name of Bill McKechnie, who was the coach at the time," Doby reflected, decades later.[9] It was the Deacon, in fact, who prevented the rookie from self-destruction during a game in St. Louis. When a fan came down the aisle and made a nasty comment about the wife of Doby, Doby dropped his bat and started for the stands. Still somewhat athletic for an old guy, McKechnie grabbed Doby's belt, pulled him back and admonished, "You can't go up in those stands."[10]

Robinson couldn't do something like that and he was Rookie of the Year, so the punishment would've been especially severe for an ineffective black ballplayer if his only multiple-hit performance came in a fistfight with a white customer. Doby remembered McKechnie telling him, "You're going to have to go through a lot, but you're going to have to grit your teeth. If you don't stick it out, it might take a long time before another Negro gets a chance."[11]

Doby always felt comfortable at the Indians ballpark, where fans reserved judgment at first but eventually became enthusiastic supporters. He also liked the city because its residents were used to black athletes; the Cleveland Browns football team was integrated before the Indians, and Jesse Owens had exploded into national track and field prominence as a Cleveland high schooler, before heading south to Ohio State University.

A southern sojourn awaited McKechnie, too, but his involved a permanent move to Bradenton, Florida. His other three children were adults with lives of their own, but the youngest was forced to leave her friends and suburban Pittsburgh behind to attend high school with strangers in a sleepy, foreign town. She didn't like the idea then and still doesn't today. "I hated it! I hated it!" says Carol McKechnie Montgomery. "It was the worst time. Don't ever move a child in high school. That's a cruel thing to do." She used to take down the "For Sale" sign from her Wilkinsburg yard, but the passive protests had no effect. Greeted down south with all the warmth due a Yankee carpetbagger, Carol did eventually find a comfort zone. For her father, it wasn't just the attraction of sun, sand and spring training; he bought into a large-scale, produce growing and shipping business down there and needed to be near it. He liked to walk among the tomatoes with a salt shaker in his pocket and reduce inventory. A fellow investor in West Coast Marketing was Jimmie Wilson, his former assistant coach and World Series secret weapon.

The Florida move didn't make spring training any easier, as the Indians had just switched to an Arizona site when McKechnie came on board. Before that, the team held camp in Clearwater, a town not far from Bradenton. With one black player on the roster and another to arrive in mid-season, it was just as well that they headed west instead of south. The McKechnies brought their black maid down from Pennsylvania, and she was treated so poorly that they sent her back.

Doby joined the pantheon of famous black Clevelanders after making a position switch in 1948. Leaving second base behind, he took his commanding athleticism to center field, a move that seemed to jump-start his talent-battery and justify Veeck's faith. Doby said McKechnie was "very instrumental" in converting him. He became the pet project of McKechnie and hitting coach Tris Speaker, the greatest center fielder of all time.

Veeck added two more expensive hires to the coaching staff, one of them the recently deposed manager of the St. Louis Browns (Muddy Ruel) and the other a past-his-prime Indians hurler who got bumped up to pitching coach (Mel Harder). He even procured a commitment from Hank Greenberg, the recently retired Detroit Tigers star and current Indians executive. With so little belief in his manager, Veeck compensated, or perhaps overcompensated, by surrounding him with knowledgeable baseball men. The pitching coach addition had an extra benefit of lightening McKechnie's load so he could focus on higher duty as assistant manager. The pieces were in place at the top, but only players can win a pennant, and it turned out that Cleveland had a lot of good ones.

Best of them all was Boudreau, who put together a career year that ended with his selection as American League MVP. With a .355 average, 116 runs and 106 RBI, his stat line told much of the story but not all. Sweet Lou also brought a less tangible quality as baseball's best money player — he made the clutch plays at bat and in the field when his team needed them most. The Indians also had two good power-hitting infielders, an outfielder who racked up 204 hits, and that aforementioned converted second baseman who hit .301 as a center fielder. Two years after displaying a terrible offense, Cleveland led the league in team batting average.

Pitching was their greatest strength, though, with a 3.23 staff ERA that was light years better than everybody else's. Feller won 19 games and led the league in strikeouts but wasn't the best, or even second-best, starter on the roster. Bob Lemon had one more win and a much lower earned run average, while rookie southpaw Gene Bearden bested both of them with a 20–7 record and league-low ERA of 2.43. For all their many assets, however, the Indians could not pull away from the field.

Looking to reinforce a tiring staff and sell even more tickets, Veeck made a midseason acquisition of living legend Satchel Paige, the longtime Negro Leaguer and barnstormer. Known for a blazing fastball, pinpoint control and quirky personality, "Satch" was supposedly 42 years old but lied so often about his age that nobody knew for sure. Veeck believed him to be at least 48 and didn't care a whit, because he knew the old dog could still hunt. Boudreau didn't want him but agreed to a tryout, with himself at the plate and Paige on the mound. Unable to make solid contact during their session, the young player-manager changed his tune and welcomed Cleveland's newest pitcher. They planned to use him as a spot starter and reliever. A *Sporting News* editorial criticized the move as a naked publicity stunt that damaged baseball's integrity, but Paige made detractors eat their words, going 6–1 with two shutouts and a 2.47 ERA.

Tied at 96–58 when the regular season concluded, the Indians and Red Sox moved on to a one-game playoff at Fenway Park. After much soul-searching and consultation, Boudreau decided to pitch the rookie Bearden on one day's rest. He had three future Hall of Famers on the staff but went with the hot hand. Bearden had beaten worse odds than these; it seemed certain he'd never pitch again after suffering grisly injuries from a torpedo attack in the Pacific. With a plate in his head and a hinge in his knee, he made it all the way to the majors on the strength of a mystifying knuckleball.

Red Sox manager Joe McCarthy pored over all the permutations of past performance, days of rest, youth and experience, lefty vs. righty and short left field fence. When finished, he made the surprise choice of 36-year-old Denny Galehouse for starter. A lesser light in the Boston sky, Galehouse had a pretty good track record against Cleveland, and McCarthy wanted a righty in a park that was hard on southpaws. His decision would go down as one of the worst in Red Sox history.

Showing no ill effects from Paige's late-night craps game, the Indians scored four early runs and coasted to a pennant-clinching 8–3 victory. At game's end, teammates lifted Bearden on their shoulders, while Boudreau sprinted to a box seat to embrace his wife. Veeck ran as fast as an artificial leg would carry him and joined the on-field back-slapping. Taking in the scene, sportswriter Red Smith later wrote, "It was, really, a considerably bigger game than a World Series game, for they play a World Series every year but this was the only post-season play-off in the American League's forty-eight summers. And in a World Series there's always a fat consolation prize for the loser, but this was a case of life or death."[12]

Receiving radio-relayed updates from classmates at her Florida high school, Carol McKechnie exploded with joy at game's end. She marched into her principal's office and announced, "I'm going to the World Series!"

"No, you're not," he answered.

"Oh yes, I am," Carol insisted.

It wasn't long before she boarded a north-bound airplane, accompanied by West Coast Marketing magnate Max Cohen. Like the rest of the Indians, her father celebrated late into the night at the team hotel. "It never gets old, it never gets old," he repeated, referring to the latest of his five career pennants.[13] Nobody worried about packing bags because they weren't leaving the city any time soon; a World Series awaited them at Braves Field. Coaches' thoughts soon drifted to the next battle, and McKechnie blurted, "Let's get out of here. Let's go over and take a look at that other ballpark."[14] He'd spent some of the best and worst years of his career there in the 1930s. They'd long since abandoned the "Bees" nickname and no longer referred to the stadium as the "Beehive." Led by a devastating pitching combo of Warren Spahn and Johnny Sain, the Boston Braves rolled to their first pennant since 1914. They'd certainly never come close to such success when Deacon Bill ran the show, but he never had a Spahn and Sain, or any reasonable facsimile.

After breaking Beantown hearts in the AL drama, Cleveland finished the job by knocking off the Braves, four games to two. Bearden tossed a shutout in Game 3 and wrapped up the clinching contest in a relief appearance. It was a Hollywood ending to an unlikely story of survival and triumph. He never pitched another great game, and rarely had any good ones.

What a whirlwind for Bill McKechnie. At an age when most men dreamed of retirement, he left a small-market franchise that once loved him, signed with a one-legged carnival barker, worked under someone half his age, made a ton of money and helped mold a loser into a champion. He witnessed unimaginably huge home crowds of 70,000-plus — figures they couldn't reach in Cincinnati if two people sat on every seat and each standing-room patron carried another on his shoulders. One World Series game saw over 80,000 pack into Municipal Stadium.

These were special times in pastime history, times McKechnie only could've read about if he'd retired after the Reds rejection. Instead, he stood with legends named Paige and Feller, and with the growing legend of Veeck. Life began at 60 for Wilkinsburg Bill, or at least his second life did. According to back-up infielder John Beradino, he deserved more credit for Cleveland's turnaround: "[Boudreau] always consulted Bill McKechnie.... McKechnie didn't get the credit, but he was always huddling and discussing strategy with Boudreau."[15]

The Indians set a new attendance record in 1948, with over two and a half million fans turning out for fun and winning baseball. Pulling in over $42,000, McKechnie made more from accruing gate bonuses than from his salary. Money, however, was not the motivating factor for the highest-paid coach in baseball history. He said his presence in Cleveland came down to one thing: Boudreau needed him. If Boudreau ever resented McKechnie's appointment, he got over it quickly. The two men became fast friends and often referred to each other by pet nicknames: "Louie" for one, "Pops" for the other.

They'd been through a lot in the last year and so had the baseball world. Babe Ruth died in mid-summer, a feeble shell of his former self by the time throat cancer was through with him. He never got that much-desired shot at managing, though it's doubtful McKechnie felt any guilt over his role in preventing it at Boston. Joe Tinker died, too, and his passing marked the end of something special to Chicago Cubs fans. He was the last surviving member of the famous Tinker-to-Evers-to-Chance double play combination, immortalized in poem.

Outside sports, the year saw a series of historic happenings and milestones. Israel was born, an assassin killed Mahatma Gandhi, the Berlin Airlift began, and Harry Truman upset Thomas Dewey in the presidential election. America stood at the edge of enormous change, with the old guard slowly fading away, a new one taking the wheel, and children soaking it all in as fuel for future disenchantment. The counter-culture generation wore short pants at this stage, but its time would arrive. Coming within a couple of weeks of each other in July, a famous death and obscure birth demonstrated the dizzying levels of transformation that lay ahead. Departing the earth was that old Indian fighter and World War I hero, General John "Black Jack" Pershing; arriving in a small town outside Cleveland was Jerry Casale, future co-founder of DEVO, a post-punk, geek-sheik, new-wave rock band that set the off-beat standard for music videos in the 1980s.[16]

Yes, the times were a-changin'.

16

Golden Years

I never could enjoy a drink. I saw what drink did to ballplayers who were ten times more talented than I was. I hung on, while they flashed briefly and were gone. What a tragedy. That's why I never touched the stuff.
— Bill McKechnie[1]

Nobody questions the sincerity of a man who was witness to the sad self-destruction of Grover Cleveland Alexander and many others. But the Deacon took a drink now and then. "He was Scottish, come on!" confirmed Carol McKechnie Montgomery. She used to see her dad imbibe after mowing grass in the hot noonday sun. "When Dad drank a beer you couldn't see him swallow ... just pour it down. He'd have two beers until he cooled off." Carol put another misconception to rest when told that newspapers reported her father a wealthy man from oil investments. "Oh God, you gotta be kidding. Never! He never hit the big one. He was a very good baseball man but he was a terrible investor and businessman." What about that "Deacon" nickname? Was he really a church deacon, as was sometimes reported? "No. In fact, we never got to church on time — ever." Don't get her wrong; Carol adored her father and confirms his reputation as a wonderful man of high morals and unique achievement. When asked an honest question, however, she'll separate the myth from the man.

The Indians did not repeat as American League champions in 1949, though they still had a pretty good year. Led by the league's top pitching staff, they won 24 more games than they lost and placed third, eight games behind the pennant-winning Yankees. McKechnie coached another All-Star Game, doing it for the American League this time. As manager of the squad, Lou Boudreau chose to bring two Cleveland coaches with him — Deacon Bill and Muddy Ruel.

Once again, McKechnie found himself on the front lines for another major milestone. Black players joined the all-star cast for the first time —

three on the NL team and one (Larry Doby) representing the AL. It looked like the senior circuit had an edge with Jackie Robinson, Roy Campanella and Don Newcombe supplementing white stars like Stan Musial, Johnny Mize and Ralph Kiner. Boudreau didn't have that kind of firepower but he did have Ted Williams and a couple of DiMaggios — Dom and Joe. The more famous brother was actually a controversial choice for all-star honor because he'd been sitting on the Yankees bench with an injury. Fans chose the starting lineup but managers selected the reserves, and Boudreau added DiMaggio's name to his list. When an AL starter was sidelined by injury, he moved right into the starting lineup and had a big game, delivering two hits and three RBI in an 11–7 win over the National Leaguers. His brother scored twice on a couple of hits, making it a great day for the DiMaggios.

McKechnie announced his resignation in December, saying he was through with baseball. Forty-two years after breaking into the majors, he planned to embrace a second career as farmer. Now he could devote himself full-time to the truck crop business. Carol remembered it being a "worrisome thing." A lot can go wrong with such an enterprise, and when frost came in, they had to fight it with helicopter wind and heat from lit burners. According to one acquaintance, McKechnie said he almost lost his shirt in that venture before a wealthy investor came in and saved the day.

While McKechnie occupied himself outside baseball, Lou Boudreau's Cleveland run came to an end after the 1950 season. Veeck was long gone by then and new ownership wanted a different manager too. "Louie" went to the Red Sox as a player and was named manager shortly after the 1951 campaign ended. Taking over a strong but underachieving squad, he promised that anybody was subject to trade for the right price — even Ted Williams. As it turned out, Uncle Sam had first dibs on the Splendid Splinter and offered nothing in return. Pilots were in big demand during the Korean War, and Williams had Marine Corps flying experience from World War II. Aviation technology changed in the interim, but old pilots were expected to be quick studies.

Boudreau wanted to hire a pitching coach for the coming year and knew where to find a great one with loads of experience. McKechnie soon agreed to come out of retirement to help the Sox at spring training in nearby Sarasota. He was too busy to commit to anything more. "I don't know if I can get away," he told one reporter. "We have 500 acres of tomatoes and plant the only tomatoes in the country. But I don't see how I can let my boy down."[2]

He did not let him down. The team struggled without Williams and finished two games under .500, but the pitching staff's ERA improved greatly over 1951's figures. McKechnie coached again the following year, with the numbers dropping again and the team's record rising to 84–69. He wasn't all about pitching, though; there were other lessons offered from the man who had learned hitting and defense from Honus Wagner. McKechnie also had some experience dealing with the mentally ill and put that to use with young Jimmy Piersall. He'd never seen a right fielder with more explosive talent but, at times, the kid acted positively insane. Not the amusing, prankster kind of crazy that Rabbit Maranville mastered but a disturbing version that went way too far. It had to make the Deacon think of Willard Hershberger, the Reds backup catcher who committed suicide. Piersall was far more manic, but the two shared a tendency to cry.

Imagine a disruptive child, desperate for attention, and multiply it by 100. That was Piersall. He mimicked and mocked opposing pitchers, brought water guns to the playing field, started fistfights and occasionally crawled around on hands and knees while imitating a dog. Nothing changed when the Sox demoted him to the minors. Institutionalized toward the end of the 1952 season and prescribed shock treatment, Piersall returned to Boston the following year, toning down his behavior from sheer lunacy to tolerably zany. With his well-documented nervous breakdown behind him, he went on to a long career. Piersall credited McKechnie for using a stern hand to guide him through some rough patches: "He'd get me even madder than some umpires. But then I'd realize what he was trying to do — that he was trying to help me and keep me out of trouble — and I'd get a hold on myself. I have an idea now, looking back, that he was a coach on the Red Sox with one purpose, and I was that purpose."[3]

Purpose and caretaker soon headed separate ways. At the end of the 1953 season, Boudreau fired McKechnie and 54-year-old fellow coach Oscar Melillo. Boudreau told McKechnie that he wanted young men now. The 67-year-old Scot never saw it coming and remained mystified by the logic for a long time to come. When Boudreau first courted him for the Boston coaching job, he publicly opined about how nice it would be if McKechnie became a 50-year man in baseball. With his earliest minor league debut as a starting point, McKechnie was getting close to a golden anniversary. "He's already in 47 and he's certainly able enough to work at it for three more seasons," Boudreau told a reporter. With the number at 49, McKechnie had the gold rug pulled out from under his feet. A *Boston Globe* account told of Boudreau getting pressured from above to release the coaches. Two years after arriving at Fenway Park, his own job already stood in jeopardy and he no longer had the power to save his friends. The team wasn't contending, so somebody had to be sacrificed at the altar of impatience. Old-timers were an easy target; they ranked as wise sages when their teams won big and out-of-touch relics when they didn't. Things didn't get any better after they left, and a couple years later, Boudreau got the boot too. He never got along with his superstar, though Ted Williams later insisted he liked Boudreau just fine and was treated well by him. He did *not* think the man was a good manager, though.

McKechnie left baseball for good, stuck on 49. If he didn't lose any sleep over missing the 50-year milestone, maybe it was because he hadn't really served 49 full seasons in the game. Two years had passed between the latest jobs in Cleveland and Boston, and he worked outside the game in 1919. Still, 46 years was nothing to sneeze at.

Though disappointed by how things ended with Boudreau, McKechnie had lots to look forward to as he returned to his scenic river home. It was his second house since moving to Florida — the first being a rental — and baseball gave him the means to build it. Uncomfortable partings were part of the game, but for McKechnie, the good times far outweighed the bad. Reaching every boy's dream by becoming a major leaguer, he took it to another level as one of history's greatest managers. He stood on equal footing with legendary magnates and formed fatherly relationships with countless players.

He certainly wouldn't crow about it, but he met at least one president (Calvin Coolidge) and knew several famous entertainers such as Al Jolson, Eddie Cantor, Harry Lauder and Red Skelton. Show biz folk often mingled with baseball notables back in those days. There's a group picture with McKechnie posing near Mary Pickford and Douglas Fairbanks, and family lore says he tried to visit the deathbed of his friend George M. Cohan in 1942. Arriving at the New York City home of the world-famous composer/entertainer, he was told by the man's wife that Cohan "would love to see you but doesn't want you to see him." Better to send Bill home and have him remember the old song-and-dance man as he used to be.

So many special memories and special people had passed through his life, and now he could spend every day with the most special one of all — Beryl Bien McKechnie. After 42 years of marriage, the sight of her could still make him swallow tobacco if he wasn't careful. She'd never had a job or needed one; Beryl only served the most important function of all, raising four children while chasing her husband across the country. She was a hardy woman who would've done well in pioneer times. Talk about tough? When ice formed on the car windshield, Beryl sometimes melted it with body heat from her hands. Before interstate highways existed she used to pack up the family, strap chains on car tires and embark on three-day journeys to spring training. McKechnie usually departed about a month before the rest of them. Beryl had maids but wouldn't hesitate to scrub floors on hands and knees. She'd certainly earned a restful retirement, watching the Manatee River flow by.

In 1952 Edd Roush built a house nearby, as he and his wife joined a growing subculture of "snowbirds" who owned winter homes in the Sunshine State. They'd spent winters in that same area before, pulling a small trailer down from Indiana and camping next to a relative's house, but Essie tired of life on wheels. Edd's twin brother arrived to help him construct a modest residence, made of sap cypress wood and situated near a bayou, just a few blocks from McKechnie. Fate had brought the two men together yet again. It started in Federal League Indianapolis, then continued to Newark and the Polo Grounds and twice in Cincinnati, first as players and next as manager/coach. Now they reunited as old men and neighbors.

Their wives were well-acquainted, too, so all four socialized together. Sometimes they went to a yacht club on Anna Maria Island, where their arrival inspired the organ player to serenade them with "Take Me Out to the Ball Game." Sometimes the men hunted together and turned the kill into dinner for all; they knew how to cook too.[4] When seasons changed, the Roushes began planning their annual pilgrimage back home to the Southern Indiana town of Oakland City, place of their births. It was as special to them as Wilkinsburg was to the McKechnies, or perhaps even more special. After all, Bill and Beryl *did* leave their hometown and relocate to Bradenton, year-round. Wilkinsburg never felt slighted, though, and still considers McKechnie a native son.

In one of life's great ironies, Roush had become a fixture at spring training — ironic because he hated it as a player and did everything he could to avoid those annual southern sojourns. His frequent holdouts were sometimes just ploys to avoid camp. Taking an entirely different view in retirement, he developed into a semi-official, in-uniform greeter of returning players and served supporting roles on the practice field too. Ballparks attract old ballplayers.

As a longtime spring training site of major league teams, Bradenton had the pastime in its blood and baseball retirees in its phonebook. Dizzy Dean owned a gas station there in the 1930s, sometimes operating the pump if newspaper cameras were present to provide publicity. Hank Johnson may not have been a household name outside Florida but he won local fame as Bradenton's lone home-grown major leaguer. He didn't just get a cup of coffee, either; he was good enough to stick around for a decade. Armed with a swift fastball and sharp-breaking curve, Johnson became a front-line starter for the Yankees team that swept McKechnie's Cardinals in the 1928 World Series. He didn't pitch in the post-season but helped his teammates get there during a close AL pennant race.

In the final season of his career, Johnson threw 31 innings for McKechnie and the pennant-winning Reds of 1939. His signature moment arrived during September of 1928 when he became the last pitcher to face Ty Cobb. The Georgia Peach made an out and retired soon afterward, leaving the unavoidable joke that Cobb knew it was time to quit when he couldn't hit a guy like Hank Johnson. Over the years, Johnson made that joke himself. Son of a pioneer Manatee County couple, he would eventually leave his birthplace behind to chase the baseball dream in big cities. At New York , the small-town boy would work alongside household names such as Babe Ruth, Tony Lazzeri, Waite Hoyt and Herb Pennock. He roomed with famous players through the years and returned to Bradenton with entertaining anecdotes about his experiences. Regarding Lou Gehrig, he said, "Lou was a real fine guy but kind of a loner. I remember once during a lightning storm, Lou crawled under the bed he was so frightened."[5] Everything was community property when young Leo Durocher became his roomie. "He'd take anything you had. He'd wear your new clothes even before you had a chance to wear them."[6]

Home to the Boston Braves for eight years, Bradenton retained its position when the franchise shifted to Milwaukee in 1953. One year later, a skinny 20-year-old named Hank Aaron arrived at camp and quickly caught Roush's attention. The old batting champ knew a great hitter when he saw one and told manager Charlie Grimm that the guy was special. Scheduled for shipment to the minors at the end of camp, Aaron caught another break when a starting outfielder injured his ankle. He won the vacant roster spot and never took another swing at minor league pitching. Twenty-three years later, Hammerin' Hank retired with a record 755 home runs and a career .305 batting average.

There was no telling what or who somebody might see at spring training. The state could offer more than baseball, however. Florida had become a major tourist destination by mid-century, leading to a boom in travel and recreation industries. With so many visitors driving down for the mild climate and endless beaches, state officials averted gridlock and further deterioration by investing big bucks in improving the inadequate road system. Workers had recently finished construction of the Sunshine Skyway Bridge, an expansive passageway over Tampa Bay that chopped 40 miles off the previous route between St. Petersburg and Bradenton. At sunset, it's a gateway to the exquisite panoramic beauty of sea and sky.

Ranking a close second to tourism on Florida's industry chart was agriculture, and that's where McKechnie sank a lot of his savings. He got it back in 1956 when a new moneyman bought everyone out. Jimmie Wilson did not live to see that day and barely survived long enough to witness *any* developments from his investment. Only 46 years old, he suffered a fatal heart attack at a Palmetto restaurant on May 31, 1947. Some believed he died of a broken heart, caused by the death of his son in World War II. He was never the same after that.

McKechnie moved into the 1950s with hopes of a comfortable, low-stress lifestyle. He still dabbled in baseball but didn't travel far to do it. In addition to his visits to the Braves' camp, he helped organize a star-studded clinic for youngsters in Sarasota and played a large role in the March of Dimes old-timers game that drew an impressive array of former legends to Al Lang

Field in St. Petersburg. He stuck to managing and left playing to younger old men, like Roush. Next to induction day at Cooperstown, that charity game provided the nation's greatest opportunity for autograph-hunters. Behind closed doors, Bill and Beryl enjoyed the simple things. Both were good cooks and prolific bakers. Their children probably didn't taste store-bought bread until they moved out or ate at a friend's house. Bill had his specialties — doughnuts and pound cake, as two examples. He cooked a stew for the dogs that was so good, humans ate the leftovers. That house always smelled like meal time.

McKechnie watched sports on the television that Beryl bought for him, and he sat glued to the set when Don Larsen tossed a perfect game in Game 5 of the 1956 World Series. "Don't you hit that ball, don't you hit that ball!" he yelled at Brooklyn batter Dale Mitchell, one of his former players from the Cleveland days. Needless to say, McKechnie rooted for a history-making outcome. Perhaps the McKechnies watched the flowering of commercial television with pioneers such as Milton Berle, Ed Sullivan, Jackie Gleason and Lucille Ball. McKechnie's daughter said he was more of a "Gunsmoke" man, though. Those mega-watt stars actually hurt the national pastime by providing a cheap and convenient alternative form of entertainment. Many of the variety shows simply brought vaudeville to a new medium, but real change was happening across the country and the world.

The 1950s saw the revolutionary explosion of rock-n-roll music and a hip-swiveling sensation named Elvis Presley. Soviet dictator Joseph Stalin died after 29 tyrannical years of power, the United States got into and out of the Korean War, a new vaccine was throwing no-hitters against polio, and Edmund Hillary conquered Mount Everest. Hitting closer to Mr. McKechnie's world, the Brooklyn Dodgers and New York Giants relocated to west coast cities after the 1957 season. In 1959 two more stars arrived on the scene — Alaska and Hawaii, the 49th and 50th twinkles on Old Glory.

Sadly, McKechnie's bride did not make it to the end of the decade; Beryl Bien McKechnie died of congestive heart failure on October 26, 1957. Her husband had already made grim phone calls to family, explaining that death could come at any time. He'd taken care of her while health slipped away and was bedside when her suffering finally ended. Beryl had been sick a long time, both physically and mentally. In her autobiography, Carol McKechnie Montgomery was very straightforward about her mother's psychological condition, calling it "postpartum psychosis." It overwhelmed Beryl after the births of her last three children, and then she suffered a vicarious version when her daughters had babies in 1954. Reclusive, anti-social and vulnerable to nervous breakdown — Carol could read the symptoms in her mother's voice when they spoke by telephone.

Beryl had hit rock bottom in 1944, after a serious car wreck put her in a Georgia hospital for a week or so. Returning to Wilkinsburg didn't improve her mood any, and she remained stuck in a somber, sobbing place for well over a year. It seemed tragic that she spent her final years in that place, but Carol won't let the final act define her mother. For a big majority of her life, Beryl was that happy, loving mother who sang in the kitchen while cooking for her family. Gregarious and outgoing, she provided a counterbalance to her reserved husband. That's the person her daughter remembers best.

Also shuffling off their mortal coils that year were Humphrey Bogart, Laura Ingalls Wilder and Louie B. Mayer. Life went on for those left behind and, even with a hole in his heart where Beryl used to be, Bill McKechnie remained a kind, approachable gentleman. He stayed active among the baseball retirement community and kept baking at home. A local newspaper reporter dropped by periodically to talk baseball with the man who knew more about it than just about anybody on earth. On Sundays, Kent Chetlain used to ride his bike to the *Bradenton Herald* office to turn on the sports wire, and his route took him by the Deacon's house. "I went by and Bill McKechnie would usually be raking or doing something in the yard. Or sometimes if I had a question to ask him or wanted to see him, I would ride my bike into his driveway, get off and ring the bell and he'd invite me in.... We would sit and talk baseball in his living room and look out and see the river and the boats and everything, and it was really very pleasant."[7]

Chetlain talked baseball with a lot of famous people over the years, some of whom he met through McKechnie. McKechnie used to give him a call when playing host to well-known cronies, and they'd set up a picture session with a *Herald* photographer. It became a comfortable acquaintance between legend and newspaperman. Chetlain hadn't always been a journalist, though; a former sports editor of the *Sanford Herald* and *Orlando Evening Star,* he made a drastic career change when Tropicana offered him more money to install and service orange juice vending machines. Transferred to the company's home office in Bradenton, he served as a truck dispatcher next.

Chetlain returned to journalism around the same time that Beryl McKechnie died, joining the *Herald* as a news reporter. He covered baseball, too, keeping busy with spring games and the new Winter Instructional League for rookies. He eventually became sports editor, which brought him even closer to pastime notables who passed through Bradenton.

McKechnie did a lot off traveling after Beryl's death, visiting his children and grandchildren, and they'd come down to Bradenton for get-togethers. In 1960 the family took a World Series vacation together, attending the classic battle between the Pirates and Yankees. It also gave them a chance to visit the old Wilkinsburg stamping grounds. They went crazy with the rest of Pitts-

burgh when Bill Mazeroski smashed his famous Series-winning home run in
Game 7. A year later, the Reds made the World Series for the first time since
1940 and officials invited McKechnie to Crosley Field to throw out the first
pitch for Game 4.

Hall of Fame voting would take place a few months later, and that always
caught the attention of Baseball America. Meeting the five-year retirement
requirement, Jackie Robinson was eligible now, and so was Bob Feller.
McKechnie had appeared on the ballot twice in the mid–1940s and twice
more in the early 1950s but received very few votes. In 1962, he wasn't even
a consideration to the all-powerful Baseball Writers' Association of America
(BBWAA), which makes up the entire electorate. Edd Roush led all candidates
in 1960 but didn't get the mandatory 75 percent required for election. Younger,
less-qualified candidates had leapfrogged past him for a couple of decades,
and when he finally stood at the top, it still wasn't enough. Now out of the
game for more than 30 years, he fell under the purview of the Committee on
Veterans and so did McKechnie.

The results came out in February: Robinson and Feller were selected by
the BBWAA, Edd Roush finally made it to baseball Valhalla and, in the biggest
upset since little Mickey Rooney married gorgeous Ava Gardner, McKechnie
got in too. Speaking to press afterward, a giddy Bill Jr. said, "We had sort of
expected that Eddie Roush would be named this year. That, of course, pleased
us, but when Dad was named it made it all the more of a thrill because it was
unexpected."[8] From his perch at the *Bradenton Herald*, Kent Chetlain saw
things unfolding for his two favorite candidates. In 2010, he spoke about why
they made it: "I think that several things conspired there. The veterans committee was just a recent thing and they were subject to a lot of lobbying. At
the time Roush was trying to get in, he'd come in and talk to the sports editor
of the *Bradenton Herald* and be complaining about the fact that he didn't get
any recognition.... Those campaigns took effect."

Both winners were unanimous choices by the 12-man committee of
experts on old-time baseball. Some thought the latest selections weren't old
enough, though. In an article that ran in *The Sporting News*, Dan Daniel
wrote,

> With the backlog of deceased stars of the long ago so heavy, it was quite a
> surprise to see the veterans' group pick Roush and McKechnie. It had been
> regarded as fairly certain that John Clarkson and John Montgomery Ward
> would be chosen this time. Miller Huggins ... fell out of favor in one short
> year and McKechnie came virtually out of nowhere. The election of Roush
> and McKechnie played up the danger that outstanding heroes of the long
> ago, no longer around to plead their causes through living appeal, might
> fall farther and farther in the background with the passing years.[9]

Roush brought a different brand of logic to the argument: put guys like him and McKechnie in while they're still alive to enjoy it. McKechnie got the call while visiting his son, James, in Syracuse. Grandson Jamie answered the phone and heard Branch Rickey at the other end, asking for Bill. The two icons spoke briefly, then "Grandpa" passed along the news in hushed tones that indicated his awe over the honor. Roush acted nonchalant when contacted by media, emphasizing that his selection was long overdue and others might die of old age before they reach that 30-year retirement cutoff for Veterans Committee consideration. By snubbing Roush over and over, the BBWAA whipper-snappers had proven themselves ignorant on players from before their time. Deep down, though, Roush was happy and he didn't hide it from his wife.

Already well-known throughout west-central Florida, McKechnie and Roush became even bigger celebrities in baseball country. The following summer, Roush's Hoosier hometown threw a huge, two-day celebration in his honor, and Wilkinsburg had something planned for its own native son. Better yet, the Baseball Hall of Fame was sending out invitations to a Cooperstown induction party that would surpass everything that came before it.

If only McKechnie had just handed over his valuables to those armed robbers.

17

Tributes

*In a sentence I'd say he was the greatest manager I ever played for, the greatest manager I ever played against, and the greatest man I ever knew....
I don't know what more I can say.* — Paul Derringer[1]

Derringer spoke those words after learning about the death of his beloved former boss. A powerfully built man who knew how to use his fists, he probably wished he had been there when those punks broke into McKechnie's house. The 75-year-old was all alone, however, trying to stall the armed intruders with conversational quips. It worked for a while but when words failed, the old Deacon stood tall, grabbed a five-foot long floor lamp and started swinging. One account had him connecting with the top of a head. The taller assailant swung back with his iron pipe, landing blows on his aged adversary and damaging the lamp's long, metal leg. Bruised but unbowed, McKechnie held his own in this bizarre variation of sword fighting, deflecting the full force of most pipe poundings and counterattacking when he could.

What about the second man with the gun? As an experienced hunter and gunman, McKechnie immediately identified it as a fake — a starter's pistol, probably. The little guy holding it was not a factor. McKechnie made a strategic retreat to the bedroom, grabbed a shotgun from under his bed and rushed back out to show them how a real firearm worked. They were gone, having fled in such haste that one left his paper-bag mask on the floor.

Needless to say, Bill McKechnie did not die that night. After law enforcement had been notified, a newspaper photographer arrived some time later and McKechnie posed with the bent floor lamp, missing its light bulb and shade. A chair was overturned in the foreground. The next day, he told a news reporter, "I had no intention of letting them get any money — it didn't come that easy for me."[2]

Nearly five decades later, his youngest daughter seemed only mildly entertained by the retelling of that story. To her, the end result had been entirely predictable. "Dad was a natural, all-around good athlete, so it wasn't surprising to me that he could take care of those two guys." Even with the wrinkles and silver hair, he could still handle himself in a scrap. John McGraw would've been proud.

On the morning of July 23, four new members took their place among the legends of the National Baseball Hall of Fame in upstate New York. Induction day was always a royal event for the village of Cooperstown, with its small population swelled by visiting fans and baseball's society sect. Taking their places atop a wooden platform on Main Street, the inductees gazed out at the large crowd that paid them tribute. Attendance estimates vary wildly depending on the source, with a current Hall of Fame website putting the number at 10,000-plus. Other contemporary accounts estimated in the 4,000–5,000 range. Regardless of what the actual number was, we know that 28 of them arrived in a convoy from Wilkinsburg, and McKechnie's birth town was missing a mayor that day.

Honus Wagner's daughters were there, representing McKechnie's first major-league mentor, who died in 1955. Also sitting in the crowd were the grandson of Home Run Baker, whose failing health prevented him from attending, and the widows of McGraw, Christy Mathewson and Eddie Collins. Serving as master of ceremonies, Commissioner Ford Frick introduced Roush first. Sounding nothing but polite and appreciative, the straight-talking Hoosier did not repeat his complaints about the election process. He'd already made his point. Jackie Robinson spoke next and, in all honesty, he was the guy most came to see. Fifteen years after breaking baseball's color barrier, he became unofficial valedictorian of the class of 1962. Other inductees only made baseball history, but Robinson made *American* history as an agent of social change. A grandson of slaves had risen to the pinnacle of white society's favorite sport, and nobody else could match that story. Robinson felt honored to get selected in his first year of eligibility and happily thanked his mother, wife, Branch Rickey, and the sportswriters who elected him. He also expressed gratitude to all the supportive Americans who helped him through the tough times of integration.

After Robinson finished, it was McKechnie's turn. Introducing him to the crowd, Commissioner Frick stuck his foot in his mouth when he implied that McKechnie's managing made up for a mediocre playing career. Quickly extricating it, he explained, "I don't say that belittlingly because he was a good ball player. But his forte in baseball has been one of guidance and leadership and direction. He's been around a long time. Everybody knows him. To my knowledge he has never done a wrong thing and that's a pretty high recommendation."[3] McKechnie stepped to the microphone and started with a small joke, something about the unfamiliarity of being third on the induction lineup card. In his minor league days he was more likely to hit leadoff, and in his weak-hitting major league tenure, he usually occupied a slot much closer to the bottom than top. Completing the shortest speech of the day, he fought back tears to say, "Mister Commissioner, ladies and gentlemen, anything that I have contributed to baseball I have been repaid today seventy times seven. Thank you very much."[4]

He never could've finished a longer address. In her entire life, Carol McKechnie had seen her father cry only four times: when she told him she was getting married, at her wedding, at her mother's funeral, and when he spanked her once as a child.[5] Now a mother of four sons, Mrs. Don Matchett almost saw him cry a fifth time on induction day. Across that entire stage, nobody felt more humbly grateful than Bill McKechnie. All of his offspring were there, proud to see their old man get his due. The old man was proud of them too; each went to college and carved out separate identities in life.

The class of 1962 stands for a picture after induction ceremonies at the National Baseball Hall of Fame. Pictured, from left, are Edd Roush, Jackie Robinson, Bob Feller and William Boyd McKechnie (National Baseball Hall of Fame Library, Cooperstown, New York).

Beatrice attended Penn State University where she met and later married a football player, who joined his family's chicken hatchery business in New Jersey. "Bea" was good with her hands, smart and tough-minded, all qualities that came in handy while she and her husband raised five daughters.

A chip off the old block, Bill Jr. followed his father into baseball and became a successful executive. He was captain of the Penn State team and handled first base so well that there was talk he would ask for a tryout with his dad's Boston Braves. Dad was known to say that son's hands were too small for the major leagues. Bill Jr. became a general manager of multiple minor league teams, moved on to minor league farm director of the Cincinnati Reds, then climbed the corporate ladder to the presidency of the Florida State League and the Pacific Coast League. In some ways, Bill Jr. was more successful than Bill Sr.

Jim McKechnie had a stuffed resume, too, though he wasn't much like his dad or big brother. A hockey goalie at Penn State and a pilot in World War II, he became a well-known radio sports broadcaster in Syracuse, New York. Jim could, and did, handle just about any sport but won local fame for his work in professional basketball, delivering rapid-fire, play-by-play accounts for the Syracuse Nationals. On and off the job, this McKechnie had a whole lot of personality. As one columnist put it, "To Jim McKechnie, the best life had to offer was always a good ballgame, an enticing woman, a stiff drink between puffs on a cigarette. And not necessarily in that order." [6]

Then there was Carol, the apple of her father's eye for so long. Despite a somewhat sickly childhood, she grew into a vibrant young lady who could sing, play piano and fill out a scorecard. She got married the same day she graduated from her Florida college, became a Navy wife and started a family. All the Deacon's children were leaving their mark on the world and all were there to share his special moment in Cooperstown. Bob Feller spoke last at the induction ceremony, giddily rambling from one topic tangent to the next. When he finished, the diverse foursome posed for pictures, with Roush and McKechnie serving as bow-tied bookends.

A couple of months later, McKechnie returned to Pennsylvania for Wilkinsburg's 75th anniversary celebration. He became "Wilkinsburg Bill" all over again and officials made him honorary mayor during the week-long event. His primary duty was touring the borough in a paddy wagon and arresting residents who weren't dressed in vintage clothing.

Bradenton officials paid homage to their hometown Hall of Famers by renaming city ballparks after them. Braves Field became McKechnie Field, and a lesser facility wore Roush's name. The Milwaukee Braves were relocating anyhow, so they might as well take the name with them. Other franchises took their place and generations of major leaguers would pass through spring training in Bradenton with the name of "McKechnie" on their lips.

McKechnie stands next to his Hall of Fame plaque, displayed amongst festive decorations at the 1962 induction ceremony in Cooperstown. He was so overwhelmed by the honor that he nearly cried during his brief acceptance speech (National Baseball Hall of Fame Library, Cooperstown, New York).

Life returned to normal for McKechnie and that was fortunate, since his modesty would only allow so much adulation. Moving into his late 70s, he still managed for the March of Dimes old-timers game in St. Petersburg. Spearheading a similar venture in his own town, he became chairman of the Hall of Fame Dinner, an annual event that brought famous old-time players to Bradenton for a banquet during spring training season. They usually procured a well-known guest speaker too.

Back on Riverview Boulevard, McKechnie lived a quiet widower's life among familiar neighbors. He visited the Roushes and interacted with Jimmie Wilson's family, who'd built a house nearby. Months before her own untimely death at the age of 53, Wilson's granddaughter Pamela Wilson reminisced on those special days of her youth: "In this whole neighborhood, we never locked our doors back then. We just walked in and out of their houses. Everybody was family."[7] She was quite young at the time, so it certainly made a strong and lasting impression on her. What were Pam's strongest memories? "Just of Dizzy Dean coming here for dinner [and] us sitting on his lap," she answered. Next door neighbor Bob Darsey also remembers bringing his son over to her house to meet Diz and sit on his lap.

Pointing down the street, Pamela continued, "Edd Roush was over there, Mr. McKechnie was around the other corner. Nobody ever thought to get their autographs because they were people that were here all the time. We would go to Mr. McKechnie's house and he would make bread.... Mr. Roush used to sit over there and smoke his cigar and yell [to] people when we'd ride by on our bikes."

A bungled armed robbery attempt did little to change their outlook. It might've even enhanced that sense of security, since shotgun Bill sent the punks running. Those idyllic times couldn't last forever, though. McKechnie's health began to deteriorate in the mid–1960s, and disease was one intruder he couldn't scare away. He developed adult onset leukemia.

McKechnie wasn't done yet, though. Receiving widespread attention for a speech he made at a Pittsburgh banquet in 1964, he offered solutions to fix modern baseball. Bring back the spitball and the quick pitch, he said. Batters would stop swinging for the fences all the time if facing a hard-to-time, fluttering spitter; they'd shorten their stroke, make contact more often and become better hitters. Meanwhile, the quick pitch would prevent batters from taking so long to get ready in the batter's box and speed up a slow, dull game. "I'd like to see baseball return to the game it was 40 years ago," he said. "I'd like to see the days of the bunt, the hit and run, a return to fundamentals."[8]

On February 13, 1965, McKechnie managed the National League old-timers to a 2–1 victory over the AL in the 10th annual March of Dimes game. He would not manage another. Cancelling a Texas trip for another old-timers contest, the 79-year-old was hospitalized on August 28 and diagnosed with "virus pneumonia." He stayed a week and was unable to attend the funeral of his friend, Paul Waner, who died in Sarasota during the interim. Waner served as one of those cautionary tales about the evils of drink, though he *did* compile over 3,000 hits and make the Hall of Fame while under its grip. Maybe sobriety could've sparked even greater achievement, or maybe stronger demons would've stepped in. Pundits preferred the "what if" scenario of unrealized potential. A longtime Pirates star, Waner played his rookie season under McKechnie in 1926. McKechnie left the following year but the brief partnership had lasting effects. "I was with him for just a few months but it was the best break I ever got in baseball because he was a great manager, in every way," Waner told Ed Rumill of the *Christian Science Monitor*. "I mean, he

Standing with relatives in his hometown, Bill McKechnie wears an honorary mayor's hat and decorative tie during Wilkinsburg's 75th anniversary celebration in 1962. The former "village" officially became a borough in 1887, a year after Bill was born there. Shown, from left, are nieces Mary McKechnie Monson and Blanche McKechnie Shontz, Bill, and sister-in-law Blanche Kane McKechnie (courtesy Tom Shontz, McKechnie's great-nephew).

In his old age Bill McKechnie (center) was a regular at various baseball functions. This one was probably a hometown tribute in Wilkinsburg, Pennsylvania (courtesy Tom Shontz, McKechnie's great-nephew).

knew people. He was sympathetic to your problems on the field and off. He could be a father to you when he felt he had to be and a taskmaster when that was needed. And, of course, he knew baseball — the complete book." [9]

The two men became further acquainted as retirees of neighboring cities (Sarasota and Bradenton) and attended some of the same baseball functions. Now both had stared the Grim Reaper in the eye and one blinked. Though her father was quite sick at the time, Carol believed he knew when Waner passed away at the age of 62. Over time, McKechnie's condition improved enough to allow him to come home, but it wasn't long before he returned to the hospital in worse shape than ever. He couldn't eat or drink because of a bad bronchial condition, but intravenous feeding seemed to improve his strength and, over time, he became healthy enough for another discharge.

Somewhere along the line, sports editor Chetlain called McKechnie on the phone and asked if he would come out to his namesake field and pose for a picture with a hotshot St. Louis Cardinals prospect named Ted Simmons.

Bill McKechnie is immortalized as a bronze-tinged statue at the Cincinnati Reds Hall of Fame and Museum. He played baseball for that franchise but did his greatest work from this position (photograph by the author).

The ballyhooed rookie had just signed a contract with the Cards, who sent him south to join Sarasota's entry in the Winter Instructional League. The first game would take place in Bradenton. McKechnie had a bad cold and didn't feel well but he soldiered on for the dual causes of promotion and a friend in need. He looked gaunt in the picture that followed, while Simmons radiated youth and unlimited possibilities.

Not long afterward, McKechnie left his home for the final time; he had pneumonia, and the leukemia had ravaged his weakened system. On October 29, 1965, William Boyd McKechnie made his final out at Manatee Memorial Hospital. He was 79 years old.

A long roster of baseball men attended the funeral, some of them quite famous but most of whom would not sound familiar in 2012. McKechnie treated them all the same — with respect. Nevertheless, a starting lineup card would mention National League president Warren Giles, Cleveland Indians manager Birdie Tebbets, Johnny Vander Meer, Paul Derringer, Heinie Groh and Heinie Manush. Branch Rickey wanted to come but was critically ill himself. The list of local friends and fans read like a who's who of Bradenton and Manatee County.

After the simple, dignified service was complete, Derringer and some other retired baseball folk gathered in the parking lot and passed around a bottle of booze. Chetlain joined the group and they all took one last shot in honor of the dearly departed. Though he was something of a teetotaler himself, McKechnie surely would've appreciated the gesture. He was Scottish, come on.

McKechnie's managing record speaks for itself: 25 years, 3,647 games, 1,896 victories, four pennants, two World Series titles. Then there was that off-the-record triumph with the Cleveland Indians champions of 1948. For so many who knew him, however, his character trumped anything accomplished on the ball diamond.

"He was a wonderful Christian man, I think of that more than I think of the ball player," said his former neighbor, Anne Darsey.[10]

Going further back, an 89-year-old retired physician remembered the time McKechnie reached out to his family in a time of crisis. Fred Bode's parents were good friends with the McKechnies in Wilkinsburg, and he used to run around with Jim when they were teenagers. Sometimes they attended hockey games together with tickets provided by the Deacon. When Bode's physician father was scammed out of a bunch of money, the family finances took a crippling hit.

"Fred, I know of your problems and my checkbook is at your disposal," McKechnie told Bode's dad, who was also named Fred. The junior Bode also recalls eating the meat of freshly hunted kill at the McKechnie house and being careful not to bite into a lead pellet. So many of his pleasant memories have nothing to do with the sport that made McKechnie famous. Bode loved to hear war stories from the national pastime, though. "He was a fantastic story teller and don't you know I can hear him still," he said wistfully. "The stories were just unreal."

They don't make them like Bill McKechnie anymore.

Chapter Notes

Chapter 1

1. "Life Story Shows McKechnie's Skill Not Due to Miracles," *The Sporting News*, December 16, 1937, 5.
2. Wilkinsburgpa.gov.
3. Wikipedia.org, and brooklineconnection.com.
4. 1900 Federal Census.
5. Author's interview with Carol McKechnie Montgomery.
6. "Life Story Shows McKechnie's Skill Not Due to Miracles," *The Sporting News*, December 16, 1937, 5.
7. *Washington Reporter*, March 13, 1906.
8. "Life Story Shows McKechnie's Skill Not Due to Miracles," *The Sporting News,* December 16, 1937, 5.
9. "A Twenty-Five Thousand Club," *Washington Reporter*, June 10, 1907, 1.
10. "Senators Close the Season at East Liverpool Tomorrow," *Reporter*, September 15, 1906.
11. "Were the Final Contests Sold?" *Reporter*, September 20, 1906, 8.
12. "Past Season Doings of P.O. & M. League Players," *Reporter*, September 22, 1906, 8.
13. "Local Players Are Leaving," *Reporter*, September 18, 1906, 8.
14. Usgwarchives.net, allumgeneology.com, rootsweb.ancestry.com, and watsonfiles.info.

Chapter 2

1. "Lost Life Preservers," *Canton Repository*, July 6, 1908, 6.
2. *Washington Reporter*, March 1, 1907, 8.
3. "Directors Put It Up to the Fans," *Reporter*, June 17, 1907, 1.
4. "Star Eastern Pitcher Signed; Potters Say Farewell Today," *Reporter*, July 18, 1907, 8.
5. "Greater Washington a Reality," *Reporter*, December 10, 1907, 1.
6. "Wahoo Placed Under Arrest," *Canton Repository*, May 19, 1908.
7. "Quality of Major League Baseball Lower Than in Years Past," *Repository*, July 12, 1908.
8. "2,000 Hear Carrie Nation," *Repository*, October 11, 1908, 1.
9. "Anson Talks of Old Players," *Wheeling Register*, April 4, 1909.
10. "Base Ball," *Register*, April 29, 1909, 9.
11. "Bright (?) Feature of the Game Umpiring of Gosney," *Register*, June 2, 1909, 8.
12. "Baseball at Night," *Oakland City* (Indiana) *Journal*, June 25, 1909.

Chapter 3

1. "In Pittsburgh," *Sporting Life*, January 29, 1910, 12.
2. "Pirate Points," *Sporting Life*, April 2, 1910, 9.

3. "McKechnie, Flag-Winner in 3 Cities, Dead," *The Sporting News*, November 13, 1965, 25.

4. From McKechnie file at Baseball Hall of Fame.

5. "Browns' Boss," *Sporting Life*, March 12, 1910, 15.

6. "Clarke Quits!" *Sporting Life*, September 10, 1910, 3.

7. "Pittsburgh Pencillings," *Sporting Life*, August 17, 1912, 25.

8. Frederick G. Lieb, "McKechnie Stretches Hits by Picking Spots for Pitchers," *The Sporting News*, September 23, 1937, 3.

9. "Battle of Brains in World's Series Will Find Managers of Pittsburgh and Washington Equally Matched," *Port Arthur News*, October 2, 1925.

10. Bill James, *The Bill James Guide to Baseball Managers from 1870 to Today* (New York: Scribner, 1997), 70.

Chapter 4

1. *Indianapolis Star*, March 24, 1914.

2. "Big Leagues Ordered to 'Play Fair,'" *Star*, March 4, 1914, 10.

3. *Star*, March 24, 1914.

4. Robert Peyton Wiggins, *The Federal League of Baseball Clubs* (Jefferson, NC: McFarland, 2010), 43; Susan E. Dellinger, "Getting Along Famously," 108; *Celebrating Baseball*, Summer, 2006, 77.

5. Susan E. Dellinger, "Getting Along Famously," 108; *Celebrating Baseball*, Summer, 2006, 77.

6. "Indianapolis Federals Capture 15th Straight," *Indianapolis Star*, June 25, 1914.

7. "Team of Macks May Play Hoofeds," *Star*, October 9, 1914, 7.

8. "Braves Decline Offer to Meet Hoosier Fed Champs," *Star*, October 15, 1914.

9. "Hoosiers Happy," *Sporting Life*, December 12, 1914, 10.

Chapter 5

1. "Federal Judge Landis Advises Baseball Peace," *New York Times*, April 27, 1915.

2. "Newark News Nuggets," *Sporting Life*, May 8, 1915, 11.

3. "Federal League Given Enthusiastic Reception By 900 Fans At Banquet," *Newark Evening News*, April 16, 1915.

4. "Sinclair, Thoroughly Angry, Ready to Fight Organized Baseballdom with Its Own Contract Weapons," *Evening News*, April 30, 1915.

5. *Evening News*, May 3, 1915.

6. Susan E. Dellinger, "Getting Along Famously," 108; *Celebrating Baseball*, Summer, 2006, 78–9.

7. "Suffrage Talk Chases the Jinx from Peps' Park," *Newark Evening News*, June 26, 1915.

Chapter 6

1. "McGraw Not Surprised at Giants Winning Thirteen Straight Games," *The Syracuse Herald*, May 25, 1916, 17.

2. Frank Graham, *The New York Giants: An Informal History of a Great Baseball Club* (New York: Putnam's, 1952), 84–5.

3. "Sisler's Showing Wins Praise from Taciturn Leader," *St. Louis Post-Dispatch*, March 3, 1916, 18.

4. "McGraw Not Surprised at Giants Winning Thirteen Straight Games," *The Syracuse Herald*, May 25, 1916, 17.

5. "National League Notes," *Sporting Life*, July 15, 1916, 7.

6. "Comment on Current Events in Sports," *New York Times*, July 17, 1916, 8.

7. Author's interview with Edd Roush.

8. "Reds Show New Spirit as Matty Takes Hold of Team," *Cincinnati Post*, July 22, 1916, 2.

9. "Baseball Men Exonerated," *New York Times*, August 22, 1917, 13.
10. "Giants Set Record for Straight Victories with Twenty-One," *New York Times*, September 26, 1916, 12.

Chapter 7

1. "Pep Displayed by Recruits," *Cincinnati Enquirer*, March 6, 1917.
2. "Bill McKechnie Real Baseball Philosopher," *New York Tribune*, March 25, 1917, 3.
3. "War Will Not Hurt Baseball," *Enquirer*, April 11, 1917.
4. Frank Graham, *The New York Giants: An Informal History of a Great Baseball Club* (New York: Putnam's, 1952), 99.

Chapter 8

1. "Matty Quits Reds for New Army Job," *Evansville Courier*, August 29, 1918, 8.
2. 1920 Federal Census.
3. Author's interview with Edd Roush.
4. H.L. Mencken, *A Mencken Chrestomathy: His Own Selection Of His Choicest Writings* (New York: Vintage, 1982), 573.
5. "Fan at Joliet Stabs Herzog of Cubs' Team," *Chicago Tribune*, October 1, 1920, 1.
6. "Yell 'Bill,' 'Wally' or 'George' at Pongo's Training Camp and You Start a Riot," *Minneapolis Tribune*, March 20, 1921, C8.
7. "Notes of the Millers," *Minneapolis Tribune*, April 18, 1921, 10.

Chapter 9

1. Frederick G. Lieb, *The Sporting News*, September 23, 1937, 3.
2. Ralph Berger, Bioproj.sabr.org.
3. Frederick G. Lieb, *The Pittsburgh Pirates* (Carbondale: Southern Illinois University Press, 2003), 195.
4. " 'Characters' Fooled McKechnie," *Pittsburgh Press*, May 13, 1962, sec. 3, p 5.
5. "Western Teams in Prime Fettle for Eastern Invasion," *Philadelphia Evening Public Ledger*, Night Extra, July 6, 1922, 18.
6. Frederick G. Lieb, *The Pittsburgh Pirates* (Carbondale: Southern Illinois University Press, 2003), 201; *The Sporting News*, October 16, 1924, 1.
7. Frederick G. Lieb, *The Pittsburgh Pirates* (Carbondale: Southern Illinois University Press, 2003), 202.
8. Gene Schoor, *The History of the World Series: The Complete Chronology of America's Greatest Sports Tradition* (New York: William Murrow, 1990), 103.
9. "Honoring McKechnie," *Wilkinsburg Progress*, September 25, 1925.
10. "Pittsburgh Wins National League Flag," *Chicago Tribune*, September 24, 1925, 19.

Chapter 10

1. "Bucky Harris Confident as Team Holds Drill," *Washington Post*, October 7, 1925, 17.
2. Frederick J. Lieb, *The Pittsburgh Pirates* (Carbondale: Southern Illinois University Press, 2003), 196.
3. Ibid., 207.
4. "Round One!" *Washington Post*, October 8, 1925, 6.
5. *Post*, October 10, 1925, 15.
6. Frederick J. Lieb, *The Pittsburgh Pirates* (Carbondale: Southern Illinois University Press, 2003), 211. In a letter dated July 26, 1965, made public after his death, Rice insisted that he had in fact made the catch, holding on to the ball despite having been momentarily "knocked out" following his head-first fall into the stands. "At no time did I lose possession of the ball,"

he wrote. A copy of Rice's letter can be found in his clippings file at the National Baseball Hall of Fame.

7. "Goslin Sets Home Run Record," *Washington Post*, October 12, 1925, 13.

8. "Covey Named for Today by Harris," *Washington Post*, October 12, 1925, 13.

9. Frederick J. Lieb, *The Pittsburgh Pirates* (Carbondale: Southern Illinois University Press, 2003), 213.

10. Ibid., 215.

11. "Corsairs Hit Stride, Says McInnis," *Washington Post*, October 14, 1925.

12. "Pirate Quarters Turn Madhouse with Title Won," *Chicago Tribune*, October 16, 1925, 27.

13. "Buc Manager Overjoyed at Result," *Washington Post*, October 16, 1925.

14. "Pirates Seize World Baseball Crown as They Make Nats Walk Plank, 9 To 7," *Washington Post*, October 16, 1925, 1.

15. Frederick J. Lieb, *The Pittsburgh Pirates* (Carbondale: Southern Illinois University Press, 2003), 219.

16. "Pirate Quarters Turn Madhouse with Title Won," *Chicago Tribune*, October 16, 1925, 27.

Chapter 11

1. "Battle of Brains in World's Series Will Find Managers of Pittsburgh and Washington Equally Matched," *Port Arthur* (Texas) *News*, October 2, 1925.

2. Frederick J. Lieb, *The Pittsburgh Pirates* (Carbondale: Southern Illinois University Press, 2003), 222.

3. "Carey Wages Fight in Rebellion Ouster," *The Sporting News*, August 19, 1926, 1.

4. Frederick J. Lieb, *The Pittsburgh Pirates* (Carbondale: Southern Illinois University Press, 2003), 223.

5. "The Lesson," *The Sporting News*, August 26, 1926, 4.

6. "Back of the Home Plate, Observations of a Veteran Scribe," *The Sporting News*, August 26, 1926, 4.

7. "Bill McKechnie Is Fired as Pilot of Pirate Club; Fans Demanded It, Reason," *The Daily Courier* (Pennsylvania), October 19, 1926.

8. "St. Louis Cardinals Name O'Farrell Manager," *Chicago Tribune*, December 28, 1926, 17.

9. Peter Golenbock, *The Spirit of St. Louis: A History of the St. Louis Cardinals and Browns* (New York: Avon, 2000), 103.

10. "Off-Season Baseball Notes," *St. Louis Post-Dispatch*, November 3, 1927, 29.

11. Westbrook Pegler, "No Espionage for Yanks and Cards Yet They Win," *Chicago Tribune*, October 3, 1928, 25.

12. "Huggins to Use Zachary, 'Slow' Pitcher, Next," *St. Louis Post-Dispatch*, October 6, 1928, 13.

13. "We Presented Yanks with 6 of 7 Runs, Says M'Kechnie," *Post-Dispatch*, October 8, 1928, 13.

14. "Altrock Wonders Why Huggins Pays Seven Other Men," *Post-Dispatch*, October 10, 1928.

15. Gene Schoor, *The History of the World Series: The Complete Chronology of America's Greatest Sports Tradition* (New York: William Morrow, 1990), 127.

16. "Breadon, Anxious to Take Rest, Refuses to Divulge His Plans," *St. Louis Post-Dispatch*, October 11, 1928.

17. "Deacon Bill Close Follower of Game Via TV Networks," *The Sporting News*, October 4, 1961, 4.

18. "McKechnie Recalled by Breadon to Take Over Managing Cardinals," *Post-Dispatch*, July 23, 1929, 13.

19. "McKechnie Fate Being Decided by Wilkinsburg Ballots Today," *Post-Dispatch*, September 17, 1929, 19.

20. "McKechnie Still Regrets Ban He Slapped on Old Alex in '29," *The Sporting News*, October 4, 1961, 4.

21. "Wray's Column," *St. Louis Post-Dispatch*, October 12, 1929, 5S.

Chapter 12

1. "Dizzy Dean Has His Little Say," *Boston Globe*, February 27, 1935, 20.

2. *Globe*, March 4, 1935, 7.

3. Babe Ruth, with Bob Considine, *The Babe Ruth Story* (New York: Scholastic Book Services, 1948), 210.

4. "Braves Accept Babe as Matter of Course," *Boston Globe*, February 27, 1935, 19.

5. "Babe Ruth to Manage Braves in 1936 — He Arrives at Back Bay at 5:40 P.M. Today," *Globe*, February 28, 1935, 20.

6. Ibid.

7. From McKechnie file at Baseball Hall of Fame.

8. Ibid.

9. "Ruth Proves Inspiration for Braves' Squad," *Boston Globe*, March 6, 1935, 20.

10. "Babe Ruth Hero of Braves' Opening Victory Accounting for All Four Runs Made by Boston," *Globe*, April 17, 1935, 28.

11. "Eddie Shore Thaws Out at the Stoves in Braves' Clubhouse," *Globe*, April 17, 1935, 29.

12. "Braves Drop First One to the Reds," *Globe*, May 14, 1935.

13. "Babe Ruth Is Given His Unconditional Release by the Braves — Leaves for New York Today," *Globe*, June 3, 1935, 8.

14. Babe Ruth, with Bob Considine, *The Babe Ruth Story* (New York: Scholastic Book Services, 1948), 213.

15. "McKechnie---" *Globe*, June 14, 1935, 22.

16. "McKechnie Statement 'Forced,' Ruth's View," *Globe*, June 4, 1935, 22.

17. "Ruth Leaves for New York," *Boston Evening Globe*, June 3, 1935, 1.

18. "The Sportlight, by Grantland Rice," *Boston Globe*, April 12, 1937.

19. "The Sportlight, by Grantland Rice," *Globe*, April 15, 1937, 23.

20. "Daniel's Dope," *New York World-Telegram*, July 27, 1937.

21. "McKechnie's Daughter Soon Will Face Crisis," *Boston Globe*, October 4, 1937, 9.

Chapter 13

1. Donald Honig, *Baseball When the Grass Was Real* (New York: Coward, McCann & Geoghegan, 1975), 243.

2. "Reds Pick McKechnie as Leader for Two Years," *Cincinnati Enquirer*, October 19, 1937, 1.

3. Ibid.

4. Casey Stengel and Harry T. Paxton, *Casey at the Bat: The Story of My Life in Baseball* (New York: Random House, 1962), 158.

5. Author's interview with Edd Roush.

6. "Today's Players Poorly Trained, Says Hall of Famer," *Evansville Sunday Courier and Press*, April 15, 1973, 2-C.

7. Lee Allen, *The Cincinnati Reds* (Kent, OH: Kent State University Press, 2006), 260.

8. From the Hall of Fame collection of Lawrence Ritter's tape-recorded interviews.

9. C. Paul Rogers III, Bioproj.sabr.org.

10. "Short Rest Would Help Gehrig," *Cincinnati Enquirer*, April 16, 1939, 35.

11. "Yanks Long Way from Super Team, *Enquirer*, October 1, 1939.

12. "Yanks Go Wild and McCarthy Sheds a Tear," *Chicago Tribune*, October 9, 1939, 19.

13. "Reds Beaten Team," *Enquirer*, October 9, 1939, 11.

Chapter 14

1. "Gets More Out of Less Than Any Other Pilot," *Charleston Daily Mail*, August 27, 1939.
2. Leo Durocher, *Nice Guys Finish Last* (New York: Simon and Schuster, 1975), 150.
3. Frank E. Carey, Associated Press, "Cincy's Little Slug Was Just Too Serious," *Evansville Courier*, August 4, 1940, B2.
4. Donald Honig, *Baseball, When the Grass Was Real* (New York: Coward, McCann & Geoghegan, 1975), 245.
5. "Honestly, Redlegs Are Best, Says Tight-Lipped Deacon," *Cincinnati Enquirer*, October 1, 1940, 14.
6. "Baker Exults Over Hitting of His 'Old Men,'" *Chicago Tribune*, October 3, 1940, 23.
7. Ibid.
8. "Spirit of Reds Flames Anew After Victory," *Tribune*, October 8, 1940, 19.
9. "After 21 Years Cincinnati Has Its Big Night," *Tribune*, October 9, 1940, 23.
10. "Paul Defeats Bo-Bo, 2–1, in Sensational Game; 26,769 Present," *Cincinnati Enquirer*, October 9, 1940.

Chapter 15

1. William M. Langford, *Legends of Baseball: An Oral History of the Game's Golden Age* (South Bend, IN: Diamond Communications, 1987), 192.
2. "Season of Blues Seen for Reds," *The Sporting News*, April 4, 1943, 10.
3. "McKechnie's Mastery Remains a Mystery," *The Sporting News*, May 25, 1944, 10.
4. Joe Williams, "Cincy Fans Forced Giles to Can McKechnie," *New York World-Telegram*, April 1, 1950.
5. "'Not Ready to Quit Game'—McKechnie," *The Sporting News*, October 2, 1946, 15.
6. Ibid.
7. Bill Veeck with Ed Linn, *Veeck as in Wreck: The Chaotic Career of Baseball's Incorrigible Maverick* (New York: G.P. Putnam's Sons, 1962), 155.
8. Dan Daniel, "The Mentor Behind the Field Manager," *The Sporting News*, December 18, 1946, 3.
9. Fay Vincent, *The Only Game in Town: Baseball Stars of the 1930s and 1940s Talk About the Game They Loved* (New York: Simon & Schuster, 2006), 182.
10. Ibid., 184–5.
11. Dave Anderson, *Pennant Races: Baseball at Its Best* (New York: Doubleday, 1994), 169.
12. "The Man Who Hates Ties," *Red Smith on Baseball: The Game's Greatest Writer on the Game's Greatest Years* (Chicago: Ivan R. Dee, 2000), 67.
13. Dave Anderson, *Pennant Races: Baseball at Its Best* (New York: Doubleday, 1994), 183.
14. Ibid.
15. *We Played the Game: 65 Players Remember Baseball's Greatest Era, 1947–1964* (New York: Hyperion, 1994), 75.
16. Jade Dellinger and David Giffels, *We Are DEVO!* (London: SAF, 2004).

Chapter 16

1. Chris Anderson, "Two Paths to Glory," *Sarasota Herald-Tribune*, August 20, 1995, 15A.
2. "McKechnie Agrees to Coach Red Sox Hurlers in Spring," *The Sporting News*, October 31, 1951, 3.
3. Ed Rumill, "McKechnie: Knew Plays, When to Use Them," *Christian Science Monitor*, November 4, 1972.
4. Susan E. Dellinger, "Getting Along Famously," 108; *Celebrating Baseball*, Summer, 2006, 81.
5. Kent Chetlain, "Bradenton's Johnson Was a World Champion in 1928," *Sarasota Herald-Tribune*, August 29, 1982, 3B.

6. Ibid.

7. Author's interview with Kent Chetlain.

8. Frederick Lieb, "Neighbors McKechnie and Roush Taking Bows," *The Sporting News*, February 7, 1962, 2.

9. Dan Daniel, "Deacon Bill, Roush Voted into Shrine," *The Sporting News*, February 7, 1962, 2.

Chapter 17

1. Kent Chetlain, "McKechnie Best Manager for, and Best Against — Derringer," *Bradenton Herald*, November 2, 1965.

2. "Bill McKechnie Wields Lamp on Boy Robbers," *Bradenton Herald*, July 12, 1962, 1-B.

3. Induction transcript from Baseball Hall of Fame.

4. Most sources, including the HOF transcript, quote McKechnie as saying "*seven* times seven" and not "seventy times seven." The latter comes from a passage about forgiveness in the Book of Matthew and is surely what he meant to say. His daughter's autobiography quoted the "seventy times seven" version.

5. Carol McKechnie Montgomery, with Jerry Hanks, *The Deacon's Daughter* (Infinity Publishing, 2011), 72.

6. Bob Snyder, "'Snyde' Remarks," *Syracuse Herald-Journal*, August 10, 1984.

7. Author's interview with Pamela Wilson.

8. "McKechnie Wants Spitter Back; Raps Slow Pace of Games on TV," *The Sporting News*, February 15, 1964, 15.

9. "McKechnie: Knew Plays, When to Use Them," *Christian Science Monitor*, November 4, 1972.

10. Author's phone interview with Bob and Anne Darsey.

Bibliography

Alexander, Charles C. *Breaking the Slump: Baseball in the Depression Era.* New York: Columbia University Press, 2002.

Allen, Lee. *The Cincinnati Reds.* Kent, OH: Kent State University Press, 2006.

_____. *The National League.* New York: A.S. Barnes, 1952.

_____, and Tom Meany. *Kings of the Diamond: The Immortals in Baseball's Hall of Fame.* New York: Putnam, 1965.

Anderson, Dave. *Pennant Races: Baseball at its Best.* New York: Doubleday, 1994.

Bradley, Leo. *Underrated Reds: The Story of the 1939–40 Cincinnati Reds, the Team's First Undisputed Championship.* Owensville, OH: Fried, 2009.

Broeg, Bob. *Superstars of Baseball.* St. Louis: Sporting News, 1971.

Bucek, Jeanine, editor. *The Baseball Encyclopedia,* 10th edition. New York: Macmillan, 1996.

Burnett, Gene. M. *Florida's Past: People and Events That Shaped the State.* Sarasota: Pineapple Press, 1991.

Cobb, Ty, with Al Stump. *My Life in Baseball—The True Record.* Garden City, NY: Doubleday, 1961.

De Chambrun, Clara Longworth. *Cincinnati: Story of the Queen City.* New York: Scribner's, 1939.

Dellinger, Jade, and David Giffels. *We are DEVO!* London: SAF, 2008.

Dewey, Donald, and Nicholas Acocella. *The New Biographical History of Baseball.* Chicago: Triumph, 2002.

Durocher, Leo. *Nice Guys Finish Last.* New York: Simon and Schuster, 1975.

ESPN Sports. *ESPN Sports Century: 1900–1929, 1930–1959, 1960s.* Chicago: Rare Air Media, 1999.

Field Enterprises Educational Corporation. *The World Book Encyclopedia.* Chicago: Field Enterprises, 1975.

Fitzgerald, Ed. *The Book of Major League Baseball Clubs: The National League.* New York: A.S. Barnes, 1952.

Gannon, Michael. *Florida: A Short History.* Tallahassee: University of Florida Press, 1993.

Goldenbock, Peter. *The Spirit of St. Louis: A History of the St. Louis Cardinals and Browns.* New York: Avon, 2000.

Graham, Frank. *The New York Giants: An Informal History of a Great Baseball Club.* New York: Putnam, 1952.

Honig, Donald. *Baseball America: The Heroes of the Game and the Times of Their Glory.* New York: Macmillan, 1985.

_____. *Baseball When the Grass Was Real: Baseball from the Twenties to the Forties, Told by the Men Who Played It.* New York: Coward, McCann & Geoghegan, 1975.

James, Bill. *Whatever Happened to the Hall of Fame? Baseball, Cooperstown and the Politics of Glory.* New York: Simon & Schuster, 1995.

Knepper, George W. *Ohio and Its People.* Kent, OH: Kent State University Press, 1989.

Langford, William M. *Legends of Baseball: An Oral History of the Game's Golden Age.* South Bend, IN: Diamond Communications, 1987.

Leary, Edward A. *Indianapolis: The Story of a City.* Indianapolis: Bobbs-Merrill, 1971.

Lieb, Frederick. *The Pittsburgh Pirates.* Carbondale: Southern Illinois University Press, 2003.

Madden, W.C. *Baseball in Indianapolis.* Charleston, SC: Arcadia, 2003.

Martin, James Kirby, et al. *America and Its People: Volume Two from 1865.* Glenview, IL: Scott, Foresman, 1989.

McCarthy, Kevin. *Baseball in Florida.* Sarasota: Pineapple Press, 1996.

McGraw, John. *John J. McGraw: My Thirty Years in Baseball.* Lincoln: Bison, University of Nebraska Press, 1995.

Mencken, H.L. *A Mencken Chrestomathy: His Own Selection of His Choicest Writings.* New York: Vintage Books, 1982.

Montgomery, Carol McKechnie, and Jerry Hanks. *The Deacon's Daughter.* Infinity Publishing, 2011.

Neft, David, et al. *The Sports Encyclopedia: Baseball.* New York: Grosset & Dunlap, 1974.

Reidenbach, Lowell, and Joe Hoppel. *Baseball's Hall of Fame: Cooperstown, Where the Legends Live Forever.* New York: Grammercy, 1999.

Rhodes, Greg, and John Snyder. *Redleg Journal: Year by Year and Day by Day with the Cincinnati Reds Since 1866.* Cincinnati: Road West, 2000.

Ritter, Lawrence. *East Side, West Side: Tales of New York Sporting Life, 1910–1960.* New York: Total Sports, 1998.

_____. *The Glory of Their Times: The Story of the Early Days of Baseball, Told by the Men Who Played It.* New York: William Morrow, 1984.

Robinson, Ray. *Matty: An American Hero.* New York: Oxford University Press, 1993.

Roseboom, Eugene Holloway, and Francis Phelps Weisenburger. *A History of Ohio.* New York: Prentice-Hall, 1934.

Ruth, Babe, with Bob Considine. *The Babe Ruth Story.* New York: E.P. Dutton, 1948.

Schoor, Gene. *The History of the World Series: The Complete Chronology of America's Greatest Sports Tradition.* New York: William Murrow, 1990.

Smith, Red. *Red Smith on Baseball: The Game's Greatest Writer on the Game's Greatest Years.* Chicago: Ivan R. Dee, 2000.

Sports Illustrated. *Sports Illustrated 2005 Almanac.* New York: Sports Illustrated Books, 2004.

Stengel, Casey, and Harry T. Paxton. *Casey at the Bat: The Story of My Life in Baseball.* New York: Random House, 1962.

Vincent, Faye. *The Only Game in Town: Baseball Stars of the 1930s and 1940s Talk About the Game They Loved.* New York: Simon & Schuster, 2006.

Veeck, Bill, and Edd Linn. *Veeck as in Wreck: The Chaotic Career of Baseball's Incorrigible Maverick.* New York: G.P. Putnam's Sons, 1962.

We Played the Game: 65 Players Remember Baseball Greatest Era. 1947–1964. New York: Hyperion, 1994.

Wolf, Dave. *Amazing Baseball Teams.* New York: Random House, 1970.

Works Progress Administration. *Stories of New Jersey.* New York: M. Barrows, 1938.

_____. *They Built a City: 150 Years of Industrial Cincinnati.* Cincinnati: Cincinnati Post, 1938.

Index

233